EARTHQUAKE

How America's Ever-changing
Healthcare System Victimizes Americans

*Welcome to America's Game of Baseball
Played on Tectonic Plates*

By Brian H. Casull, MD, MPA
COL (R) United States Army Medical Corps

EARTHQUAKE: HOW AMERICA'S EVER-CHANGING HEALTHCARE SYSTEM VICTIMIZES AMERICANS

Copyright © 2019 Brian Casull

1405 SW 6th Avenue • Ocala, Florida 34471 • Phone 352-622-1825 • Fax 352-622-1875
Website: www.atlantic-pub.com • Email: sales@atlantic-pub.com
SAN Number: 268-1250

No part of this publication may be reproduced, stored in a retrieval system, or transmitted in any form or by any means, electronic, mechanical, photocopying, recording, scanning, or otherwise, except as permitted under Section 107 or 108 of the 1976 United States Copyright Act, without the prior written permission of the Publisher. Requests to the Publisher for permission should be sent to Atlantic Publishing Group, Inc., 1405 SW 6th Avenue, Ocala, Florida 34471.

Library of Congress Cataloging-in-Publication Data

Names: Casull, Brian, author.
Title: Earthquake : how America's ever-changing healthcare system victimizes Americans / by Brian Casull.
Description: Ocala, Florida : Atlantic Publishing Group, Inc., [2019]
Identifiers: LCCN 2018043368| ISBN 9781620236406 (paperback) | ISBN 1620236400 (paperback)
Subjects: LCSH: Medical care—United States. | Medical policy—United States. | Health services accessibility—United States. | Accountable care organizations (Medical care) | Health care reform—United States.
Classification: LCC RA395.A3 C393 2019 | DDC 362.10973—dc23
LC record available at https://lccn.loc.gov/2018043368

LIMIT OF LIABILITY/DISCLAIMER OF WARRANTY: The publisher and the author make no representations or warranties with respect to the accuracy or completeness of the contents of this work and specifically disclaim all warranties, including without limitation warranties of fitness for a particular purpose. No warranty may be created or extended by sales or promotional materials. The advice and strategies contained herein may not be suitable for every situation. This work is sold with the understanding that the publisher is not engaged in rendering legal, accounting, or other professional services. If professional assistance is required, the services of a competent professional should be sought. Neither the publisher nor the author shall be liable for damages arising herefrom. The fact that an organization or Web site is referred to in this work as a citation and/or a potential source of further information does not mean that the author or the publisher endorses the information the organization or Web site may provide or recommendations it may make. Further, readers should be aware that Internet Web sites listed in this work may have changed or disappeared between when this work was written and when it is read.

TRADEMARK DISCLAIMER: All trademarks, trade names, or logos mentioned or used are the property of their respective owners and are used only to directly describe the products being provided. Every effort has been made to properly capitalize, punctuate, identify, and attribute trademarks and trade names to their respective owners, including the use of ® and ™ wherever possible and practical. Atlantic Publishing Group, Inc. is not a partner, affiliate, or licensee with the holders of said trademarks.

Printed in the United States

INTERIOR LAYOUT AND JACKET DESIGN: Nicole Sturk

Over the years, we have adopted a number of dogs from rescues and shelters. First there was Bear and after he passed, Ginger and Scout. Now, we have Kira, another rescue. They have brought immense joy and love not just into our lives, but into the lives of all who met them.

We want you to know a portion of the profits of this book will be donated in Bear, Ginger and Scout's memory to local animal shelters, parks, conservation organizations, and other individuals and nonprofit organizations in need of assistance.

*– **Douglas & Sherri Brown**,*
President & Vice-President of Atlantic Publishing

Rebecca, this endeavor would not have been possible without the love and support of my wife for going on 53 years. We raised each other. I love you.

Table of Contents

FOREWORD 1

PREFACE, FOR AMERICANS WHO WISH TO BECOME INFORMED CONSUMERS OF HEALTHCARE 5

    Big Picture 6

    The Ballpark, or "Healthcare Park" 8

    A Call To Arms 8

INTRODUCTION 11

    What Will You See Along the Way? 12

    The Ballpark 13

        Where is your seat at the ballpark? 14

PART A: YOUR TOP HEALTHCARE CONCERNS

CHAPTER ONE: LOSING THE BENEFITS OF MEDICARE AND MEDICAID 21

    Medicare 22

        Traditional Medicare 22

        How do physicians charge? 23

    Medicare Advantage 25

        Prescription Drug Coverage 26

Medigap Plans 27
Medicaid 27
Other Government Health plans 30
    The Veteran's Administration 31
    The Tricare Program 31
    Indian Health Service 32

CHAPTER TWO: SEEING THE DOCTOR OF YOUR CHOICE 33

Understanding ACCESS to Healthcare 33
    The Three Steps 34
Gaining Entry into the Healthcare system 35
    Geographic Availability 37
    Personal Relationship 37

CHAPTER THREE: HEALTHCARE COSTS 41

What Drives Healthcare Cost? 42
An Introduction To Healthcare Cost And Variability 43
What Is The Return on Investment (ROI)? 47
Non-Medical Drivers Of Healthcare 48
Non-coverage of a relatively large portion of the population 50
    A snapshot in time 50
    Uninsured 50
    Underinsured 51

CHAPTER FOUR: HEALTHCARE COSTS AND PROVIDER VARIABILITY 53

How Providers Code 53
Payment Models 55
Physician Fees 58

CHAPTER FIVE: HEALTHCARE COSTS AND PROCEDURES 61

The Cost Of Procedures 61
Variability 63
Medical Devices 64
A CASE STUDY: The Call To Arms 68

CHAPTER SIX: HEALTHCARE COST AND PRESCRIPTION DRUGS 75

Prescription Cost Drivers 76
    Monopoly rights 76
    Medicare drug benefit 77
    Availability of generic drugs 78
    Physician prescribing practices 78
How It's Done: Marketing and Direct-to-consumer Advertising (DTCA) 78
    Direct-to-consumer advertising 79
    Indirect marketing 79
    Research and development 79
CASE FILE: Pharmacy Cost 80
    The "market value" of a drug 81
The Tectonic Plate 82
Lowering Drug Prices 83

CHAPTER SEVEN: HEALTHCARE COST AND PATIENT COMPLIANCE 89

Patient Compliance 89
Compliance Along the Healthcare Continuum 89
CASE STUDY in Compliance 90
Compliance Along The Healthcare Continuum 93
Are You An Informed Consumer? 95

PART B: THE LAW OF THE LAND

CHAPTER EIGHT: WHAT IS HEALTHCARE INSURANCE? 99

Setting the Stage: The Affordable Care Act 99
The Affordable Care Act 99

A Summary Of The Pros And Cons 102

The Bumpy Ride: How The ACA Repeal Might Impact You 105
Coverage for people with preexisting conditions 105
Mandates to buy insurance 107
Other insurance market reforms 108
Cost-free preventive services for patients 110
Medicaid expansion 111
Subsidies in the market place 112
Innovation Center and value-based payments 113
Closing the Medicare prescription drug 'donut hole' 113
Taxes funding the ACA 114
Independent Payment Advisory Board 115

The Challenge Continued 115

CHAPTER NINE: TECTONIC PLATES 119

Healthcare Consumer's Concerns About The ACA 119

The Tectonic Plates 120

Tectonic Plate Impact on the Affordable Care Act (ACA) 120
ACA revamp must include conservative values 120
Preexisting conditions 121
Coverage mandates 122
Other insurance market reforms including cost-free preventive services 124
Medicaid expansion 125
Subsides in the marketplace 126

Addressing Your Concern About Stabilizing the ACA marketplace 130

Changes in the Individual marketplace Premium and
Out-Of-Pocket Costs 131
    ACA exchange plans 131
    Premiums 133

Impact of the Tectonic Plates on the ACA Individual marketplace 133
    Premiums 133
    Out-of-pocket costs under the ACA 135
    Tectonic Plate Alert! 136
    Tax provisions 137

"Nobody Dies because they don't have access to healthcare." 138
    Literature Review: 139
    My Research 140

PART C: THE TECTONIC PLATES YOU MAY NOT HAVE KNOWN ABOUT

CHAPTER TEN: HOSPITALIZATION 147

When to Hospitalize? When to Observe? 147
    The "two-midnight rule" 148

The Issue of Readmission 151

Impact on the Second Party? 152
    Hold harmless 153

CHAPTER ELEVEN: QUOTES ON MENTAL ILLNESS & ADDICTION 155

Mental Health 155

CASE STUDY: Suicide Attempt by Any Other Name 156

How Prevalent is Alcoholism? 158

The Issue Of Drug Addiction 160
    The issue of overdose and death 161
    Decline in U.S. life expectancy 161
    Relapse 162

CHAPTER TWELVE: THE VIEW FROM THE PARKING LOT 163

The Uninsured 163
    Relationship between cost and access 164
Underinsured 165
    For the individual marketplace 167

CHAPTER THIRTEEN: MEDICAL ERRORS AND TORTS: DEATH FROM MEDICAL CARE ITSELF 169

Medical Errors 169
Quality Assurance 170
CASE NUMBER: Space, The Final Frontier 174
CASE STUDY: Medication Error Resulting in Death 178
Medical Malpractice Cases, Or Torts 180
A CASE STUDY In (Alleged) Malpractice 182

CHAPTER FOURTEEN

WHEN THERE IS NO CONSENSUS 185

Grading the Medical Literature 186
CASE STUDY: The Case In Point 190

PART D: FOOD FOR THOUGHT

CHAPTER FIFTEEN: THE BASICS OF HEALTHCARE COVERAGE 201

Healthcare 101..201
The Third-Party Payor...201
Premiums 203
Deductibles 204
Copayment 205
Coinsurance...205
Summary of Benefits and Coverage..206

Benefit Coverage 210
The Cost...210
Medical Necessity..212
Experimental 213

Utilization Review...215

CHAPTER SIXTEEN: PROTECTION AGAINST TECTONIC PLATES 219

The Appeal Process..219
Appealing Health Plan Decisions 220

The Appeal Process..223
The scorecard..223

Accreditation...225
The Joint Commission...225
NCQA..226
URAC..226

CHAPTER SEVENTEEN: ACCOUNTABLE CARE ORGANIZATIONS 229

Accountable Care Organizations..229
Return On Investment 231

Tectonic Plate Alerts 233
    Alert #1 233
    Alert #2 233

CHAPTER EIGHTEEN: A CASE STUDY IN HEALTH PLAN ENGINEERING 237

    A Case Study In Health plan Engineering: Abu Dhabi 238

    A Case Study In Health Plan Engineering: United States 238

POSTSCRIPT: ARE YOU LISTENING? 249

    Consumers Of Healthcare 250

    Providers Of Healthcare 251

    Decision-Makers 252

    Moving Forward 255
        Find the return on investment 255

    How I Would Approach Healthcare 256

    Three Things Are Clear 262

ABOUT THE AUTHOR 265

ACKNOWLEDGMENTS 267

ENDNOTES 269

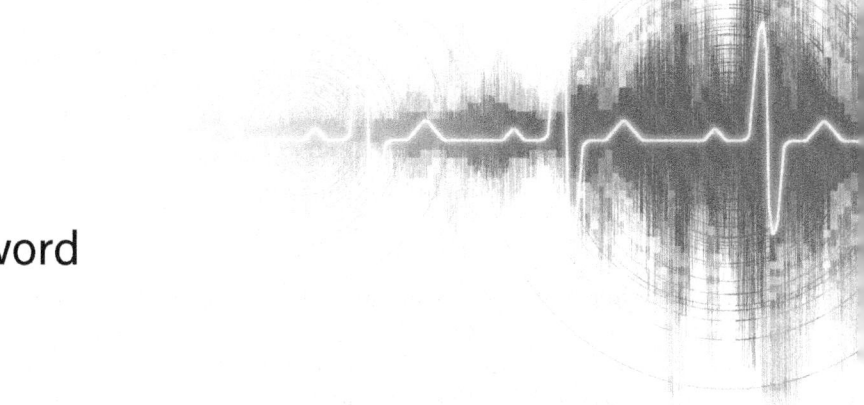

Foreword

American healthcare is uniquely complicated. And there are some real devils hiding out in these details. The book you're holding in your hand is an attempt to help you understand how the American healthcare system works. If you don't need to understand it today, you may well need to tomorrow when you get sick. It could literally save your life.

It's hard to understand the system here. People in other modern nations are baffled at why we put up with it; they are incredulous when we try to explain things like networks and quickly give up trying to understand us. After all, their lives don't depend on it. They all have some sort of single national solution, something easy to understand that gives them peace of mind, better healthcare, and economic security. But we do not.

Instead, we're confused. And in our confusion, we blindly leap (or are pushed!) into the gaps and cracks. The better we understand the system we have today, the better we'll be able to safely navigate through it when it may really matter for our lives.

Case in point.

Shortly before Dr. Casull asked me to write this foreword, a patient called me and wanted to know which drug plan would cover Rytary. His neurologist had prescribed this for his Parkinson's Disease. He was unable to find any drug plan that covered it. Someone told him that I used to work at a large national pharmacy benefit manager and thought I could help.

This was really important to him. He used to work in sales, but due to the way Parkinson's was making his hands shake, he had to stop. "They can't see you sweat in sales," he said. He lost that job and has been uninsured for more than a year. Rytary is imperfect, but it's made him able to function reasonably well. He even drives for Uber on good days. But the drug is expensive, costing hundreds of dollars per month that he doesn't have. So he's gratified and fortunate that the drug manufacturer has been willing to send him a three-month supply if he applies for "patient assistance."

This is humbling, humiliating, and unreliable. There are typically gaps of a week or more in between these three-month supplies while he waits for his renewed application to get re-approved. During these gaps, his Parkinson's takes over his life, and he can barely function, certainly not drive. And the manufacturer could simply stop providing this at all, if they so choose. Even though we have his permission, we're not using his name in this book.

I found no drug plans he could purchase that would include this "wonder" drug. Then I wondered, what was this drug? I had never heard of it, and neither had any of my colleagues in primary care, neurology, or geriatrics. None of us. Why not, if it was such a miraculous innovation?

It turns out that the "miracle" here is a pharmaceutical manufacturer taking advantage of patent laws to produce a drug that offers an exclusive place on the market. Rytary is a new branded version of an old drug, Sinemet CR. Rytary has a 3 percent difference from the chemical makeup of Sinemet CR, a difference without any apparent clinical impact. Sinemet CR's patent has long since lapsed, so there is a generic version readily available at a small fraction of the cost of Rytary. But Rytary's tiny difference in the milligram content means that a pharmacist can't just automatically substitute the generic without contacting the physician. And nobody, including busy pharmacists, wants to call a physician's office.

Call me a cynic, but I suspect this is precisely why the manufacturer tweaked the dosage when they released Rytary to the market. Patent law gives them a niche without any competition, but they are providing no new clinical value that I can identify. I suspect that the reason drug plans don't cover this expensive drug is because it's not clinically important enough to justify its high price.

Exactly how was this patient supposed to figure this out? As far as he knew, this drug was working, helping him with a disabling condition, and he didn't want to take a chance on anything different. It took my digging as far as I could into the medical literature and FDA database to be confident that there is no reason to prefer Rytary over the generic. To the best of my knowledge, Rytary has only been compared with short-acting versions of Sinemet, not the comparable long-acting versions. How was he supposed to have the skills to do this work? And why should we expect him to spend his time doing that? No other modern country would ask this of its citizens.

That's why Dr. Casull has written this book. Unlike what some have said, most of us already know that healthcare is complicated. Most of us watch some version of the news, have seen descriptions and explanations, and may have tried to read our insurance policies. But it's like a foreign language, unfamiliar and difficult to embrace.

That's where metaphors can help: cue a discussion of baseball, tectonic plates, and medicine.

Each has transformed over the past century. Each has gotten stronger, and each can shed light on the other, but it took Brian Casull, MD to point it out.

Healthcare is one of the world's oldest professions, with origins that date back thousands of years. There are entire libraries devoted to medicine. Never has the science of medicine been as powerful as it is today, with genetically designed pharmaceuticals and non-invasive surgery.

Baseball isn't as old as medicine, but it is older than the United States of America. Baseball was imported here from England before we revolted. It evolved from an informal activity in backyards and playgrounds and gradually grew in popularity. Players became stronger, the game faster, and the growth of popular appeal led to a wealth of rules, codes, and regulations.

Tectonic plate theory is not quite 100 years old but has quickly become the accepted explanation of why the world's continents seem to be floating and could fit together. Looked at from this perspective, it seems that we could still see continents moving if we had enough time.

What you see at a baseball game depends on where you're sitting. Those in the premium box seats may get the best angle on the pitcher and batter, but those out in the bleachers get to see the way the batter is squinting into the sun, the subtle hand signals from the catcher, have a chance at catching that home run ball, and they might even have access to the ballpark's best beer and hot dog vendors. Where we sit, often determined by what we're able to pay, determines what part of the game we have access to and what parts are not available to us.

Add in tectonic plate theory, have the seating and bases and outfields in constant motion, and you've got one complicated ball game.

That's healthcare, in a nutshell, and Dr. Casull is taking it straight on. He seems to embrace the rapidly shifting landscape and offers us guidance on how to hold on for the ride.

In his hands, these metaphors aren't nearly as strained as you might imagine. Instead, they help us understand how things work. He walks us through access to care, the cost of healthcare, the current and potential future role of insurance, and what individuals can do today when thrust into the tectonic cracks rampant throughout the system.

Watching a baseball game that's being played on shifting tectonic plates: vintage Brian Casull, MD. Read on, learn, and enjoy.

Ed Weisbart, MD, CPE, FAAFP
Chair, MO Chapter of Physicians for a National Health Program

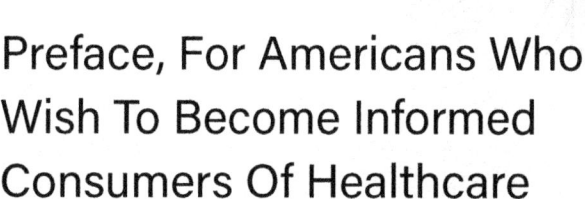

Preface, For Americans Who Wish To Become Informed Consumers Of Healthcare

This book is designed to address American healthcare in transition and assist those who have to navigate its perilous topography. Whether you are a healthcare provider, a healthcare decision maker, or the person actually wondering how you can get to that needed healthcare, we all need advocates.

In my professional lifetime of almost 50 years in healthcare, I have learned how to facilitate healthcare for my patients and clients. My goal is simple: help you become an informed consumer of healthcare.

In the for-profit health insurance model that drives American Healthcare in transition, the consumer (you — the patient) is left out of the decision-making process. This current model is broken!

The chapters that follow are the means of providing regular content to support the mission of becoming informed consumers of healthcare no matter what your particular emphasis might be. Furthermore, I would invite you to link to my website www.americanhealthcareintransition.com for additional discussion or to ask me a question. I would like to be of assistance by knowing how best to reach your stakeholders or what your particular hot healthcare topic of concern might be.

BIG PICTURE

Today, the for-profit health insurance model drives American healthcare in transition (non-profits make money, they just don't share it with stockholders). This model is broken! What does the model look like? It is a four-party system:

1. The PROVIDER of healthcare

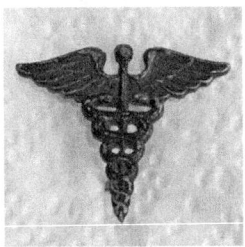

2. The CONSUMER of healthcare

3. The PAYOR of healthcare

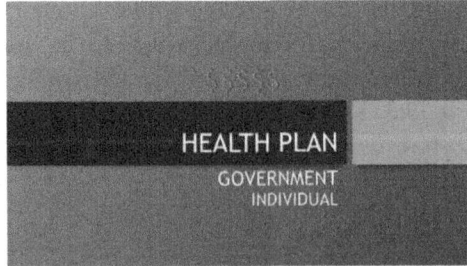

4. And lurking behind the scenes are the Decision-makers. Depending upon the model, they can be physicians, physician executives or non-medical administrators, and other functionaries of the for-profit healthcare insurance model. They can even be congressman and senators.

DECISION MAKERS

This model is much like a baseball park — where you sit is dependent upon the seats you can afford to purchase (or have been purchased for you, as the case might be). Where you sit is determined by the type of healthcare insurance you have (or do not have). The amount of actual healthcare coverage you enjoy (or lack) and the amount of money you pay for healthcare is related to where you sit in that ballpark.

Where do you, the patient (consumer of healthcare), currently sit in the Healthcare Ballpark?

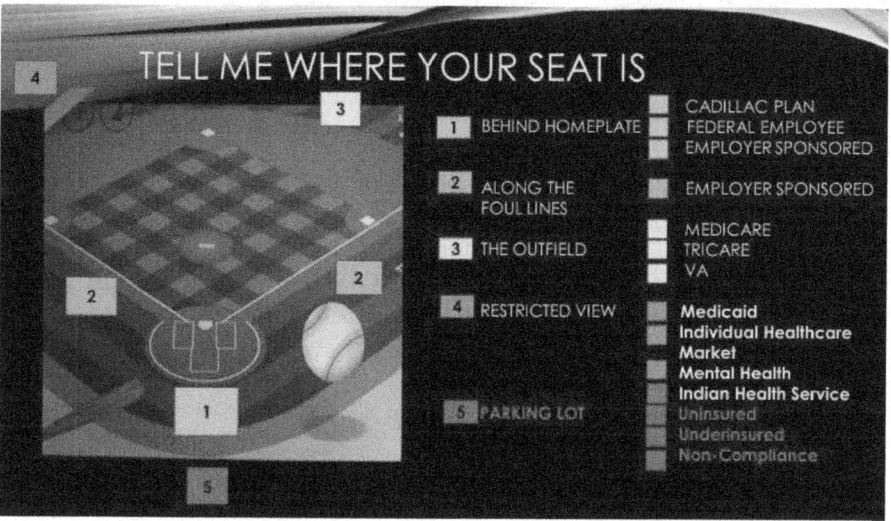

THE BALLPARK, OR "HEALTHCARE PARK"

Added to the preferred hierarchy of seating arrangements is the X-factor. These are the often out-of-your-control occurrences. In the American Healthcare "system", these are the **tectonic plates** with **caprice ebbing and flowing (the ground moving under our feet)** that lead to **earthquakes. These are the movements that disrupt American Healthcare in transition and keep it in 'transition.'** And make no mistake about it, there be earthquakes here.

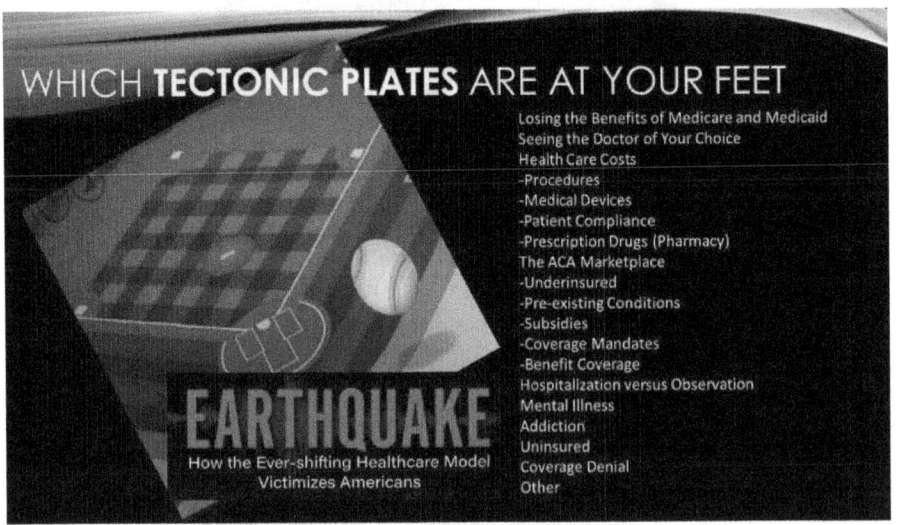

Which tectonic plates are at your feet?

A CALL TO ARMS

I would share with you one tectonic plate — and there are many — that tore apart a middle-aged man's life. His story illustrates that tectonic plates can be disruptive of the best laid plans, even if they are made from the premier seating section in our American healthcare game of baseball. So, this is a 'call to arms.'

Preface, For Americans Who Wish To Become Informed Consumers Of Healthcare

Why a call to arms? Our gentleman indicated the following:

> You work for a 'monopoly company' with one of the best healthcare packages around, so you don't really look behind the facade to see what is really covered. No one is looking to have a catastrophic event. You trust the company. The health-plan. The dental plan. Routine things. The basic fundamentals. Emergency room. Common cold. Basic dental work. You don't think about the long-term consequences of a major catastrophic event that may lead to a need for long-term care.
>
> I went to work one morning. When I arrived, I realized it was daylight savings, and I had arrived one hour early. I didn't realize it at home. I got a bite to eat and then laid back in the driver's seat until it was time to go to work.

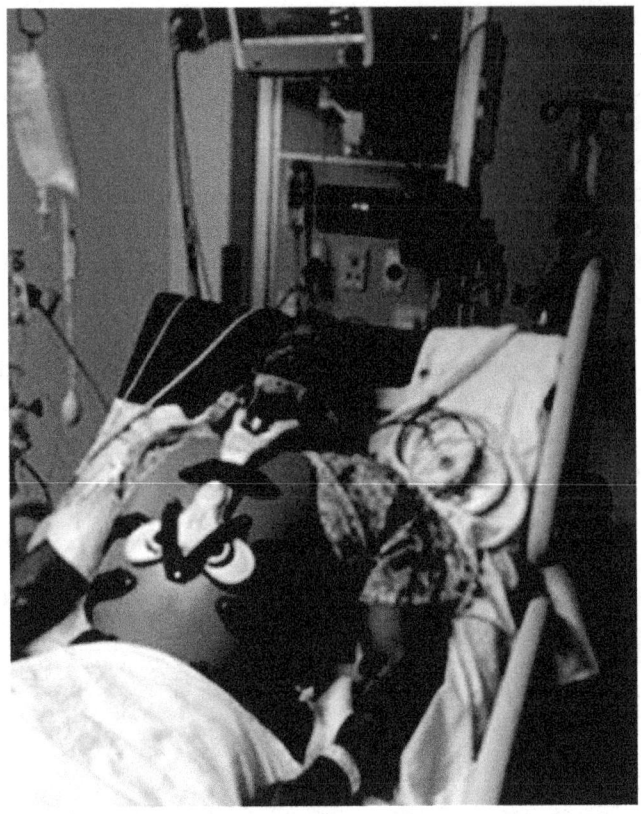

I woke up to them (the fire department) pulling me out. They asked me if I could move my legs. I think I told them I couldn't. I asked them what happened, and they said I was in an accident. I was wondering how that could happen because I was parked. They said I was hit from behind. To be honest with you, I don't really remember how I felt. I don't remember the ride to the hospital. The next thing I remembered was that I was in the ICU.

We will visit this patient again.

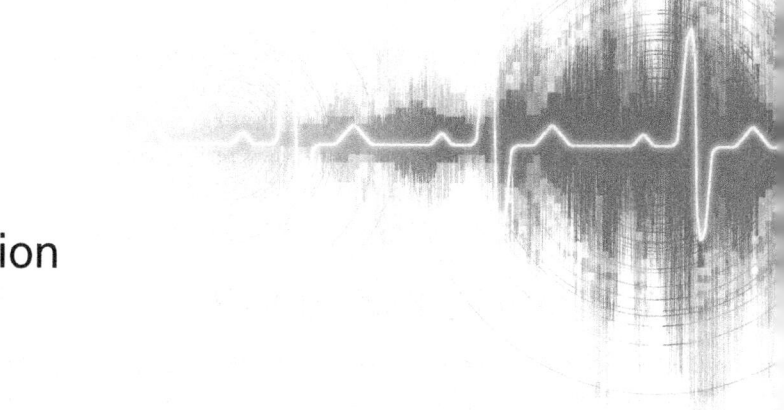

Introduction

Healthcare is not a "system" in the United States. Rather it is like a game of baseball where your perceived and actual coverage is determined in large part by where you sit in the ballpark of healthcare. The privileged (so-called "Cadillac Plans") get to sit behind home plate in plush box seats. Those with employer-provided healthcare enter the turnstiles along the foul lines from the dugouts to the outfield. Good box seats. Good view. The outfield may not be as desirable, but Medicare, Veterans Health Administration (VHA), and Tricare are not healthcare plans to be insulted and taken for granted.

However, when we get to the bleachers and their partially obstructed view of the old healthcare American pastime, our vantage point begins to suffer somewhat with significant limitations. What fans sit here? Some might say those with Medicaid or those on a limited income (with or without insurance subsidies). Those who sit in these seats might obtain their insurance through insurance exchanges (or whatever the present administration decides to replace them with) are the 'lucky' fans here. The Indian Health Service offers bleacher seats, but, more often than not, this fan base finds itself outside of the ballpark altogether. But even these obstructed seats are better than not being admitted to the ballpark at all, like the uninsured!

And what about the underinsured? Those without employer/government-sponsored healthcare who don't qualify for federal aid? In essence, they shoulder the full burden of their healthcare insurance costs. They enter the ballpark rarely, dependent on the fluctuating price of the ticket — the individual marketplace is not their friend — and that ticket price is about to get steeper for the everyday American. Then there are those who have good affordable healthcare with incomes to match but choose not to visit the doctor for whatever reason; the non-compliant. Where do they sit when not occupying their assigned seat at the game?

And just what are the basic tectonic plates upon which we each play the healthcare game of baseball? The never-ending relationship between **COST of care, ACCESS to care, and the QUALITY of that care.** Are you a "victim" of American healthcare in transition? Can you become an Informed Consumer? It is my hope that this discussion, written from a Physician Executive's perspective, will help you come to understand the American healthcare "system."

WHAT WILL YOU SEE ALONG THE WAY?

Let me begin by previewing just what it is that we will do together during our journey. And let me emphasize, we will journey together, hand-in-hand. We will discuss how the seat an individual has in Healthcare Park impacts the care they receive.

I will set the stage by introducing what we, the people, are worried about. And people are worried about healthcare. PART A does just that, as we talk about the potential of losing Medicare or Medicaid, and the access to your doctors. We will discuss the all-important worry of how your pocketbook will be impacted by the current state of American healthcare in transition; the cost of healthcare, especially prescription drugs.

This discussion will include the introduction of the concept of return-on-investment. It will highlight the importance of getting the most bang for our healthcare buck (cost). We will again visit access and quality while introducing a new player, the non-medical drivers of healthcare.

For the remainder of PART A, we will address some additional concerns you might have. In essence, they are issues about the cost of healthcare, access to healthcare, and quality of healthcare you are currently receiving.

PART B begins with the current law of the land, the Affordable Care Act (ACA). This will lead us to another set of concerns you may have about American healthcare in transition. This will lead us to the tectonic plates that impact the ACA as we speak and potentially affect your healthcare coverage. I will also discuss the ACA Individual marketplace in some detail.

In PART C, I will discuss other tectonic plates that you may not be aware of but need to know about in your journey to become an informed consumer. Here come the aftershocks!

The issues discussed include hospitalization; the neglected subject of mental health, including the major tremor of the current health epidemic of addiction; and medical errors, all the things that go "bump" in the night.

We will end our journey together with PART D. Here we will discuss the fundamentals of healthcare coverage that remain constant even if the ground beneath them does not. This discussion will point out the other potential impacts on your wallet. Things that you might not realize are out there or that they have the power to become tectonic plates and disrupt your healthcare.

But we will not remain on the tectonic mine field forever. We will discuss what you can do about your healthcare and explore how to use the appeals process when other pathways fail. There will be other helpful hints as well. Along the journey I will make suggestions about how to deal with making our American healthcare in transition more efficient and user-friendly for you, the reader — be you consumer, provider, decision-maker, or advocate. However, because our current system in broken, it may require major surgery. So, buckle up and join me as we travel through our national neighborhood healthcare diamond, but mind the shifting ground beneath your feet.

THE BALLPARK

> "Baseball is 90 percent mental and the other half is physical."
> — Lawrence Peter "Yogi" Berra (1925-2015)[1]

In this section, I will establish our metaphor of the healthcare game of baseball set on tectonic plates. This will be our invitation to begin addressing the basic question: just what is health insurance? Depending upon which side of the aisle (Democrat or Republican), your socioeconomic status, which way you lean (right/left/centrist), whether you are an employee or employer, whether you are a veteran or active duty/retiree, American Indian or Alaskan Native, a senior citizen, a millennial, Gen X, baby boomer, or none of the above; your bias will come into play.

That being said, let me try to establish some basic principles upon which you may hang your proverbial hat as we move forward. There are some principals which are basic and probably apply regardless of where you sit in Healthcare Park or what happens to the current healthcare law of the land: the Affordable Care Act, or ACA.

Think of this discussion as a shortcut guide to healthcare, a basic premise to build upon. In its pages, you will find definition and discussion about healthcare products funded by employers/employees or the taxpayers. We will visit those who elect not to carry healthcare insurance and those who go without for other reasons, such the uninsured and non-compliant. Americans have their appointed seats in the Baseball Stadium of Healthcare. How we view our seats is as subjective as it is dependent upon the summary of benefits and coverage.

How will I do this?

Picture this: a baseball stadium. "Baseball and healthcare?" you might be asking. Bear with me for a second while I expand upon this concept. I will establish the analogy that healthcare is a baseball game that has excellent seats at the ballpark, great seats at the ballpark, and good seats at the ballpark. There are also those with something left to be desired, those with an impeded line of sight as far as healthcare coverage is concerned. We will discuss those who sneak in during the seventh inning stretch and how much access to the game (coverage) they actually have. We won't forget those souls who stand out on the street, looking up longingly to the stadium and the cherished game being played on the hallowed diamond inside. Waveland Avenue is behind the left field bleachers. For many who yearn for baseball tickets (insurance coverage), it will be the closest they ever come to entering the ballpark proper.

Some might say that if the healthcare insurance game is played in the same ballpark, all the seats are worth sitting in, depending upon your viewpoint as an observer and utilizer of healthcare. The quality of the seats, the view of the game, and the nearness to the action will all change as you move around the ballpark from one location to another.

And who said that the game is always played in the same park? Just like in baseball, there are many leagues from the Independent League to AAA-level that play at different geographical locations. Each location evolved their baseball (read healthcare) differently. From the "Friendly Confines" of Wrigley Field to the "House that Ruth Built" in New York, from staid, old Fenway Park to the era of "cookie cutter" stadiums, each structure has different architects, designs, infrastructure, amenities, etc. With that come unique construction issues and pitfalls in design. So, just as the seat location in the ballpark is a major variable in our game of tectonic plates and American Healthcare, I would suggest that where and when the venue was built may be just as important. And that is only one of our variables.

Where is your seat at the ballpark?

At the end of the day, the myriad "home parks" where our game of Healthcare Baseball is played adds to the instability of our American healthcare in transition, not to mention the tectonic plates upon which each of those storied diamonds were, are, and will be constructed.

How you view healthcare and how your perceptions impact your healthcare reality depend upon where you are sitting — what you see right in front of you, so to speak.

Let us say that you have purchased really good seats right **behind home plate**.

Your view is the home plate umpire, the catcher, and the batter. The pitcher has a somewhat prominent position in your field of view, but for the most part, the rest of the playing field is less clear and left up to your experience and interpretation — not to mention the Jumbotron that flashes giant pictures of the action on the screen. Perhaps the press could be likened to that ballpark phenomenon. Depending on the ballpark, this function may be highly variable as an asset to your understanding of the game (or healthcare). Some might surmise that the healthcare available to some federal workers and very good employer provided health plans would put you in the catbird location of home-plate box seats. These might be the so-called "Cadillac Plans," or Concierge Medicine.

Then there are those of you have purchased box seats along the **foul lines**, from the dugouts on out toward the foul poles. Your primary emphasis, as well as interpretation of the game, comes from the first and third base umpires and the fielders manning the hot corner and the first base bag. The coaches in the first and third base coaches' boxes also have a major role to play in your perception of the game. The other infielders may have some importance in your peripheral vision. Perhaps those sitting in the stands around you are the folks lucky enough to get their healthcare through their employers.

Then there is the **outfield**. Naturally the outfielders are the components of the game viewed most vividly from these seats. Perhaps those folks with TRICARE and VA Healthcare form the majority of folks in the choice outfield seats. Perhaps Medicare would also fall into this category of seating arrangement. The view is good but can come with some limitations, but generally, you can enjoy the game.

But what about the **bleacher seats?** There is an old expression in baseball called the "Bleacher Bums" in the "cheap seats." You sort of see the outfielders but don't expect to see anything else with any degree of clarity. Perhaps this distorted view of healthcare is what is available to the less fortunate. Perhaps this includes Medicaid or the ACA, if you can afford the healthcare insurance available on the Individual Exchanges. It also includes The Indian Health Service as it is currently performing, although most of their group perceive themselves as on the outside looking in.

The view from the **parking lot** — and where is that group of folks with healthcare they do not use, typically for a variety of reasons but most frequently economic? This group of fans is really not homogenized. Rather, there are those who have good seats at the ballgame but elect not to use them for fear or inconvenience or not being

macho (compliance). A second group includes the underinsured whose insurance coverage is problematical. They rarely enter the ballpark, and when they do, their choice to enter is driven by the price of admission. But even that coverage is better than the view of those who cannot afford a ticket to the game: the uninsured. They might get lucky and sneak in after the seventh inning (emergency room), but for the most part they put off going into the ballpark for as many reasons as there are those who find themselves on the outside looking in. But the cost of the ticket is usually too steep.

And what type of healthcare does Congress have? I always assumed that Congress had the same largess as other Federal Employees with the deluxe seats behind the plate. At the end of the day, it is a Healthcare Exchange.

What is different for Congress from most of the rest of the country is the plethora of plans available. The DC Health Link offers HMOs, PPOs, and the "Precious Metal" exchange plans, as well as a 'catastrophic' plan for those who qualify. "They choose a gold-level Obamacare policy and receive federal subsidies that cover 72 percent of the cost of the premiums."[2] And unlike our underinsured and uninsured friends, this patient population can afford the cost.

PART A

Your Top Healthcare Concerns

Nationally, voters ranked healthcare as the top issue going into the mid-term elections of 2018.[3] If we break down the components of that concern, the focus becomes losing Medicare/Medicaid, not having access to your physician, and the cost of healthcare (especially prescription drugs).[4] We will look at all of these specific concerns in PART A (and more).

CHAPTER ONE

Losing the Benefits of Medicare and Medicaid

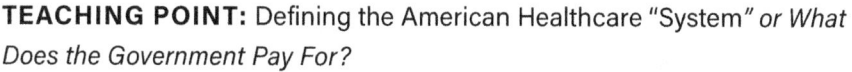

TEACHING POINT: Defining the American Healthcare "System" *or What Does the Government Pay For?*

At the heart of our discussion is an understanding of what the American healthcare "system" is — or isn't! As we speak, it is essentially a four-party system based on the for-profit health insurance model. I will discuss all of this in due time. This chapter focuses on that portion paid for by the government.

In the days of American healthcare prior to the ACA, there was a disjointed array of disconnected, yet interconnected and interfacing, healthcare pieces with different philosophies, sources of income, ability to document care, etc. The list goes on and on. Some were government-sponsored. Others were employer-provided. Then came the Affordable Care Act, whose purpose was to improve affordability and accessibility of healthcare and to oversee, coordinate, and govern the many pieces in play.

This discussion is brought to you in part by Medicare's official website, CMS.gov. Medicare and Medicaid are two of the healthcare pieces that are paid for by the government. The Centers for Medicare and Medicaid Services (CMS), previously known as the Healthcare Financing Administration (HCFA), is a federal agency within the United States Department of Health and Human Services that is charged with overseeing these two programs.

MEDICARE

Health Spending by Major Sources of Funds: Medicare was 20 percent of all national healthcare expenditures in 2016. Medicare spending in 2016 was lower than in the previous two years when spending increased 4.8 percent in 2015 and 4.9 percent in 2014. The slower growth in 2016 was due to slower growth in spending for both the Medicare fee-for-service (2.2 percent in 2015 to 1.8 percent in 2016) and Medicare Advantage (11.1 percent in 2015 to 7.4 percent in 2016) portions of Medicare.[5]

Altogether, Medicare cost the federal government $684 billion in 2017.[6] For those of you worried about cuts to Medicare — which you should be — as a candidate, Trump promised not to cut Medicare if he became president. However, President Trump is doing exactly that in his proposed budget for 2019. Does $554 billion in cuts to Medicare over time sound like it might impact you, the 55 million Americans who are over age 65 or living with disabilities? This is a 7.1 percent cut to Medicare by 2028.[7]

Traditional Medicare

To better understand where your pocket book is at risk, let us first discuss the component parts of Medicare. Medicare is essentially designed to cover people who are 65 years or older or are disabled (SSDI, the Social Security Disability Insurance*), or those with **end-stage renal disease** (ESRD).[8] The original Medicare has always been administered directly by the federal government. I get my Medicare this way; most people do, and it has two parts[9]:

- Part A (Hospital Insurance): includes medically necessary hospital, skilled nursing facility, home health, and hospice care; free if you paid Social Security.
  - Both you and your employer pay 6.2 percent for Social Security and 1.45 percent for Medicare (and if you are a high earner, you pay another 0.9 percent for Medicare.) That makes the Medicare coverage something that you do pay for.
  - However, if you paid in through social security, there is no additional cost for Medicare Part A.

---

*Supplemental Security Income (SSI) and Social Security Disability Insurance (SSDI) are both federal programs that provide cash payments to people who meet the federal definition of "disabled." But the similarities between the two programs end there.

CHAPTER ONE: Losing the Benefits of Medicare and Medicaid

- Hospital spending was 32 percent for all National Health Expenditures in 2016 and grew 4.7 percent.[10] Twenty-five percent of Medicare spending was for hospital care.[11]

- Part B (Medical Insurance): medically necessary doctor services, preventive care, durable medical equipment, hospital outpatient services, laboratory tests, x-rays, mental healthcare, and some home health and ambulance services; requires a monthly premium for this coverage.

- You pay a premium for Part B, essentially based on your previous income.

- The standard Medicare Part B monthly premium for 2019 will be $135.50, a modest increase of just $1.50 per month over the standard premium in 2018. In addition, the annual Medicare Part B deductible will increase, but by just $2, to $185.

- Physician and Clinical Services was 20 percent of all National Health Expenditures in 2016 and grew 5.4 percent.[12] Twenty-three percent of Medicare spending was for physician services.[13]

How do physicians charge?

I will now take a minute to talk about how physicians code. Why? Because you need to understand the coding process in order to understand the next tectonic plate I will describe below.

Physicians code their encounters with you **based on intensity of service**. Visit types are generally divided into 'new patient visit' and 'established patient visit'. CPT (Current Procedural Terminology) coding is used to standardize medical communication across the board, which identifies the services provided and are used by insurance companies to determine how much physicians will be paid for their services.[14] They are considered 'evaluation and management' (E&M) codes.

New patient visit CPT CODE 99201 is the least intensive service and is straightforward and problem-focused. The severity is usually considered self-limited or minor. Typical face-to-face time between the patient and doctor is 10 minutes. The CPT codes go up from there from 99202 through 99205. The **history and examination** go from expanded problem focused through detailed to comprehensive. The **medical decision-making** goes from straightforward to low/medium/ and high complexity. The **presenting problem severity** is described in stages of low to moderate/moderate/and moderate to high. Face times increase on a graduated scale from 20 minutes to an hour.

There is a similar intensity scale for **established patient visits** under CPT codes 99211 through 99215. They have the same graduated set of 'history and exam', 'medical decision-making complexity,' and 'problem-solving complexity'. Face-to-face time is shorter, ranging from five to 40 minutes.

There is plenty of advice on how physicians can maximize their coding. For example, the Journal of Family Practice featured an article entitled "10 Billing and Coding Tips to Boost Your Reimbursement."[15] All specialties and their literature do it, so I am not just picking on Family Practitioners, but I will use this article as an example.

The article begins by indicating that virtually every family practice is missing opportunities to maximize reimbursement. And what is the standard reimbursement? At the current Medicare reimbursement rate of $96.01 for a 99214 visit and $63.73 for a 99213 visit, if a physician does not code at least one level 99214 visit per day, the yearly income loss could be $8,393.

So where does the tectonic plate come in, other than the search for upcoding? Here is where the first tectonic plate lurks, the one that might impact you. And what of these proposed changes to Medicare? What would you lose? Some of the proposed changes to Medicare would **target reimbursements for doctors.** What does that tectonic plate look like?

Proposed changes for paying physicians under Medicare:

- Offering physicians basically the same amount, regardless of the patient's condition or complexity of services provided
- One rate for new patients
- One rate for established patients

For established patients, the proposal calls for a payment rate of about $93 in place of the average ranges of $45 to $148 as you move up the ladder of office visit intensity.[16]

By removing the "paperwork" to document complexity for patient Level 2-Level 5 office visits, the Administration believes they will save 51 hours of clinic time per doctor per year. Does less than an hour per week seem significant to you?

But what is the net impact on you? Critics are saying this could lead to short-changing doctors who care for the sickest, most complicated patients. Ultimately, if you are a sick or complicated patient, this might discourage your physician from accepting your Medicare coverage. What it might do is compound the issue of "upcoding" the intensity of service being provided during an office visit. How? The proposal could increase the risk of "erroneous and fraudulent payments because doctors would submit less information to document the services provided[17]."

Nearly 300 patient and provider groups and other health organizations sent two separate letters to CMS administrator Seema Verma to protest proposed evaluation and management (E/M) service changes in the 2019 Physician Payment Rule.[18] In a letter that included the American Medical Association, about 150 other groups praised the rule's effort to cut back on physician paperwork.[19]

Another coalition headed by the American College of Rheumatology also commented:

> A broad coalition of 126 patient and provider groups — led by leading national organizations including the American College of Rheumatology — today sent a letter to the Centers for Medicare and Medicaid Services (CMS) urging the agency not to move forward with a proposal that would significantly reduce Medicare reimbursements for evaluation and management (E/M) services provided by specialists, citing concerns that these time-intensive services — which include examinations, disease diagnosis and risk assessments, and care coordination — are already grossly under-compensated and that additional payment cuts would worsen workforce shortages in already strained specialties like rheumatology.[20]

The final outcome? "CMS has finalized the Physician Fee Schedule for 2019, pushing back a controversial flattening of E/M codes to 2021 after a backlash from providers and physicians. The rule also cuts some E/M documentation requirements and removes duplicative notation requirements."[21]

MEDICARE ADVANTAGE

There is also Medicare Part C, which is actually a euphemism for Medicare Advantage Plans, or private Medicare. Medicare Part D is for outpatient prescription drug insurance and provided only through private insurance companies that have contracts with the government, never through the government itself. As you would imagine, Part C and Part D vary by plan as far as premiums are concerned.

Prescription Drug Coverage

The other tectonic plate is the change to the program's prescription drug coverage.[22] I will discuss the cost of prescription drugs, including Medicare prescription issues, later in this section. For now, here is a sneak preview since we are talking about impacting Medicare coverage.

Prescription drugs were 10 percent of all National Health Expenditures in 2016,[23] but 29 percent of all Medicare spending is on retail sales of prescription drugs.[24] Growth in National Health Expenditure retail prescription drug spending slowed in 2016, increasing 1.3 percent to $328.6 billion. This followed strong growth in 2014 and 2015, 12.4 percent and 8.9 percent, respectively. The growth reflected increased spending on new medicines as well as price growth for existing brand-name drug (especially drugs to treat hepatitis C).

Growth slowed in 2016 due to fewer new drug approvals, slower growth in brand-name drug spending (spending for hepatitis C drugs declined) as well as a decline in spending for generic drugs as price growth slowed.

The Trump administration wants to make it easier for **Medicare Part D** prescription drug plans to negotiate prices with manufacturers. This does not allow Medicare to negotiate drug prices, only the Medicare Advantage Plans to which you might be enrolled.

- According to the Kaiser Family Foundation[25]: the 10 top "stand-alone" drug plans have average premiums ranging from $20.21 to $83.68 per month. ($243 to $1,004 annually);
- The average monthly premium is $43.48, a 9 percent increase from 2017 and a 68 percent increase since 2006 ($526.56 annually);
- The premium is higher, the higher your income.

Officials also want to require plans to pass on a portion of any drug-maker rebates they get to their enrollees. If this results in reduced revenue for the Plan, there might be cost-shifting to you, the patient, through:

- higher premiums;
- higher deductibles;
- shifting drugs to higher cost tiers, explained further below.

Medicare Part D median out-of-pocket cost was $117 in 2015, an increase from $79 in 2011, but that was not the whole cost risk for Medicare beneficiaries such as you with Part D coverage. There were 220 Part D drugs with annual 2015 out-of-pocket cost of $1,000 or more, an 83 percent increase from the 118 such drugs in 2011.[26]

How does Medicare drug spending compare with costs across other types of healthcare insurance? Based on one Pharmacy Benefit Managers (PBM) findings:[27]

1. 2013 through 2014 for the 31.5 million insured Americans covered by this PBM — the annual prescription drug cost per capita was $1,370.

2. Due to insurance covering some (or all) of the cost of prescription drugs, the average out-of-pocket expenses for these insured members ended up being only $185.

3. Their average insured American had to cover 14 percent of the cost of their prescription medicines from 2013 through 2014.

MEDIGAP PLANS

Then there is a whole plethora of Medicare Supplement or Medigap plans. There are nine such plans and are known as Medigap Plans A, B, C, D, F, G ,K, L, and M. These plans are provided through private insurance companies, but plan types with the same letter must offer the same set of basic benefits regardless of location.

TEACHING POINT

MEDICAID

What about the Medicaid seats? Both individual state governments and the federal government are involved with this seat at the ballpark. The Medicaid program is jointly funded by the federal government and states. The federal government pays states for a specified percentage of program expenditures, called the Federal Medical Assistance Percentage (FMAP).[28] Federal percentage can range from 50 percent to 100 percent depending on the state.[29] Enhanced FMAPs provide ratios for states to follow in funding their State Children's Health Insurance Program, or SCHIP.[30]

Who's in the Program?

Its target population is the poor and disabled. While the government funds both Medicaid and Medicare, Medicaid's coverage differs from Medicare. Medicaid is the only game on the block where those at or below poverty level and/or have significant disabilities may have access to healthcare. Nearly 73.8 million individuals are enrolled in Medicaid and CHIP in the 50 states and District of Columbia reporting data for April 2018. More than 52 million were low-income individuals. There are certain requirements that may vary from state to state.

Children make up 41 percent of the enrollment but only 19 percent of the cost. While non-newly eligible adults are 22 percent of the enrollment but likewise represent only 15 percent of the cost. Newly eligible adults are fairly equally represented as far as enrollment and cost (13 percent versus 11 percent). Cost outstrips enrollment where you would expect it to, that being the disabled (15 percent of the enrollment but 40 percent of the cost) and the aged who make up 8 percent of the enrollment but 16 percent of the cost.

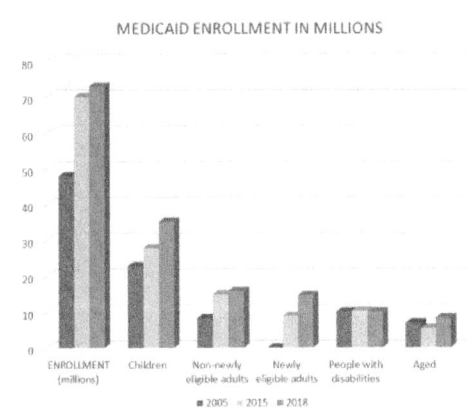

Adapted from multiple sources to include CMS.gov, Kaiser Family Foundation and others

Medicaid accounted for 17 percent share of all national healthcare spending in 2016. Total Medicaid spending decelerated in 2016, increasing 3.9 percent to $565.5 billion. The previous two years spending grew 11.5 percent in 2014 and 9.5 percent in 2015 respectively. The reason for the previous growth spurt was stronger growth in 2014 and 2015 was partially due to the initial impacts of the ACA's expansion of Medicaid enrollment during that period. The Federal Government bore the heaviest burden as federal Medicaid expenditures increased 4.4

percent. State and local Medicaid expenditures grew 3.2 percent.[31] The total 2017 cost of Medicaid was $600 billion, of which the federal government spent 61.5 percent ($368 billion) and the states 38.5 percent ($228 billion).[32]

The value of Medicaid is that "(a)dults and children enrolled in a Medicaid health plan had significantly better access to care and preventive services than people with no health coverage." In fact, the study indicated that "(a)dults and children enrolled in Medicaid health plans appeared to have access to care and preventive services at levels similar to people who have commercial health coverage.[33]"

There is another value to Medicaid, one that will become important when we discuss the Return on Investment for the money spent on healthcare in Chapter Three. "Medicaid programs have increasingly explored ways to address social issues to improve care and outcomes and reduce long-range costs."[34] These are the Non Medical Cost Drivers of healthcare. In some states, Medicaid payers are required to screen members for social needs (socio-economic status) and connect at-risk people with necessary community resources. These are the Social Determinants of Health (SDOH).[35]

The biggest issue that needs to be addressed as America's healthcare transitions is how the state and federal governments pay for Medicaid. This is where you may be impacted regarding loss of Medicaid coverage; it's the tectonic plate affecting this seat at the ballpark. Medicaid's current funding is a guaranteed federal matching rate based on what each state spends, except for an adjustment that allows a greater funding for the less affluent.

And this funding debate will only continue to grow. According to the Kaiser Family Foundation Tracking Poll, half of those living in states that had not previously expanded Medicaid want that expansion to include their state[36].

State and federal governments pay much more to provide medical care to the country's poor and disabled in 2018 than it did in 1966 when Medicaid was introduced; $554 billion was spent in 2015 as compared to $1 billion in 1966. "If all states implement the ACA Medicaid expansion, the federal government will fund the vast majority of increased Medicaid costs. The Medicaid expansion and other provisions of the ACA would lead state Medicaid spending to increase by $76 billion over 2013-2022 (an increase of less than 3 percent), while federal Medicaid spending would increase by $952 billion (a 26 percent increase)."[37]

As you can see, over one-quarter of the federal government increase could be driven not by rising healthcare costs but by the dramatic raise in Medicaid participants through the ACA, especially if all states implemented the Medicaid expansion. Republicans in Congress insist that Medicaid and other federal programs have become unsustainable. Medicaid's current funding, which is a guaranteed federal matching rate based on what each state spends, give or take a boost to less affluent states, should be replaced with a lump sum of money in order to reduce the federal share of Medicaid costs. This sum would be called a block grant, or funding based on the number of people enrolled in their program.[38]

Those in favor of the change to block grants say that it would cut costs and provide better care for the needy; the program has become unsustainable. Those on the other side believe that states would be forced to cut eligibility and benefits. The debate is another tectonic plate of which you should be aware.

TEACHING POINT

OTHER GOVERNMENT HEALTH PLANS

Before we leave this issue, I would like to remind you that there are three other government-sponsored forms of healthcare. I have not seen them discussed in terms of defining American healthcare in transition, but I will take a minute to mention them briefly. Each has a significant contribution to make in our understanding of the current "for-profit health insurance model" we are currently dealing with.

The Veteran's Administration

There is a far-reaching geographical impact of the Veterans Integrated Service Networks (VISN). The Veterans Health Administration (VHA), the healthcare entity of the VA, began as Old Soldier's Homes established after the Civil War. The road has been long from 'Old Soldier's Homes' established for Union Civil War veterans to what is now the "template for succeeding generations of federal Veterans' hospitals." After World War I the eligible population was increased to include veterans of all wars. Today's VA healthcare system now includes 152 hospitals, 800 community-based outpatient clinics, 126 nursing home care units, and 35 domiciliary.[39] Like other pieces of the healthcare "system" there are faults in the VA system.

And what are the faults? According to a 2014 interview with GAO healthcare team director Debra Draper, "As accusations of mismanagement, falsified records, and preventable patient deaths rock the Veterans Affairs healthcare system, some who are familiar with the VA say the failures are consistent with a pattern of well-documented problems." These are system wide and may be related not only to the outdated systems in place but also a "lack of accountability." This dysfunction in the VA "extends from the top to the bottom, at the highest headquarters down to local levels in some medical facilities[40]." Controversy continues at the time of this writing.

The U.S. Government Accountability Office (GAO) is an independent, nonpartisan agency that works for Congress. Often called the "congressional watchdog," GAO investigates how the federal government spends taxpayer dollars[41].

The Tricare Program

Tricare is under the auspices of the Department of Defense (DOD) and "provides healthcare for 9.5 million military service members, retirees, and family members."[42] Tricare includes the brick and mortar on-post military treatment facilities (MTFs) as well as the insurance arm which is self-funded and self-administered (TRICARE).[43] Having served 21 years in the military and then becoming the Corporate Medical Director for the West Region Tricare Contractor for 13 years, I must admit to a fondness for this program.

Indian Health Service

This is an agency within the Department of Health and Human Services (HHS). Those eligible for federal health services include American Indians and Alaska Natives. There is a long historical interaction between the federal government and the Indian Nations that goes all the way back to 1787 — and it wasn't always a positive one.

Over 2 million American Indians and Alaska Natives are members of one of the 567 federally recognized tribes. This has become a large and complicated task, as this population is exposed to all of the non-healthcare related determinants that impact health status. Would it surprise you that this group of healthcare beneficiaries has lower health status when compared with other Americans?[44]

CHAPTER ONE *What Have We Learned?*

$554 billion in cuts to Medicare sounds like it might impact you, the 55 million Americans who are over age 65 or living with disabilities. This impact may be felt through access to healthcare providers, but the greatest impact would appear to be on the cost of prescription drugs.

The value of Medicaid is that adults and children enrolled in Medicaid health plans appear to have access to care and preventive services at levels similar to people who have commercial health coverage. That is the good news. The bad news is in the political battle on how Medicaid should be paid for and the cost of the ACA expansion of Medicaid coverage.

There are three other government funded healthcare programs: The Veterans Health Administration (VHA), The Tricare Program, and the Indian Health Service. These are relatively small 'plans' compared to the number of covered beneficiaries under employer-sponsored and other government coverage or uninsured. Other public plans including those covered under the military or Veterans Administration are roughly 2 percent of the total covered beneficiaries. However, there will be future lessons to be learned from these government-provided healthcare plans.

CHAPTER TWO

Seeing The Doctor of Your Choice

Nationally, voters ranked healthcare as the top issue.[45] If we break down the components of that concern, one of the issues is losing access to the doctor of your choice.

UNDERSTANDING ACCESS TO HEALTHCARE

TEACHING POINT

The ability to see the doctor of your choice is called 'access'. According to the Kaiser Family Foundation*, you obtain **access to the doctor of your choice** from one of the following[46]:

Employer: Includes those covered by employer-sponsored coverage, either through their own job or as a dependent in the same household. Health insurance provided to employees by an employer or by an association to its members is called group coverage.

49 percent of health insurance coverage throughout the 2017 calendar year

Medicaid: Includes those covered by Medicaid, the Children's Health Insurance Program (CHIP), and those who have both Medicaid and another type of coverage, such as "dual eligible" who are also covered by Medicare.

21 percent of health insurance coverage throughout the 2017 calendar year

---

*Data is based on analysis of the Census Bureau's American Community Survey (ACS) by the Kaiser Family Foundation. The ACS asks respondents about their health insurance coverage at the time of the survey. Respondents may report having more than one type of coverage; however, individuals are sorted into only one category of insurance coverage.

Medicare: Includes those covered by Medicare, Medicare Advantage, and those who have Medicare and another type of non-Medicaid coverage where Medicare is the primary payer. Excludes those with Medicare Part A coverage only and those covered by Medicare and Medicaid ("dual eligible").

14 percent of health insurance coverage throughout the 2017 calendar year

Uninsured: Includes those without health insurance and those who have coverage under the Indian Health Service only.

9 percent of the population has no healthcare access, or the access they have is not standard and consistent.

Non-group: Includes individuals and families that purchased or are covered as a dependent by non-group insurance. This would include the ACA marketplace. Health insurance you buy on your own — not through an employer or association — is called individual or non-group coverage.

7 percent of health insurance coverage throughout the 2017 calendar year

Other Public: Includes those covered under the military or Veterans Administration.

1 percent of health insurance coverage throughout the 2017 calendar year

The Three Steps

As a simple overview, this may be defined as access to comprehensive, quality healthcare services because it is the means for promoting and maintaining health, preventing and managing disease, reducing unnecessary disability and premature death, and achieving health equity for all Americans.

Our ability to understand access to American healthcare encompasses three components: *coverage, services*, and *timeliness*. Health insurance *coverage* helps patients gain entry into the healthcare system. Lack of adequate coverage makes it difficult for people to get the healthcare they need and, when they do get care, burdens them with large medical bills.

The second component is *services*. Improving access to healthcare services depends in part on ensuring that people have a usual and ongoing source of care — that is, a provider or facility where one regularly receives care. Having a primary care provider (PCP) who serves as the usual source of care is especially important. Improving healthcare services includes increasing access to and use of evidence-based preventive services.

The third key feature is *timeliness*. Timeliness is the healthcare system's ability to provide healthcare quickly after a need is recognized. Measures of timeliness include three pieces: 1) the availability of appointments and care for illness or injury when it is needed, which leads to the second piece of the puzzle; 2) the delay in time between identifying a need for a specific test or treatment and actually receiving those services can negatively impact health and costs of care; and 3) actual and perceived difficulties or delays in getting care when patients are ill or injured likely reflect significant barriers to care.

There are three distinct steps to obtaining **access**:

1. Gaining entry into the healthcare system, which usually requires insurance coverage.

2. Accessing a location where "needed healthcare services are provided (geographic availability)."[47]

3. Finding a healthcare provider "whom the patient trusts and can communicate with (personal relationship)."[48]

GAINING ENTRY INTO THE HEALTHCARE SYSTEM

Gaining **access** usually requires insurance coverage. As I said before (and it is worth repeating): Health insurance coverage helps patients gain entry into the healthcare system. Lack of adequate coverage makes it difficult for people to get the healthcare they need and, when they do get care, burdens them with large medical bills. What proportion of Americans have no usual source of care?[49]

Let's look at a snapshot of uninsured figures. Due to the tectonic plates currently in motion, this data will give us a foundation:

Uninsured in 2016:

- Number of persons under age 65 uninsured at the time of interview: 28.2 million

- Percent of persons under age 65 uninsured at the time of interview: 10.4 percent

- Percent of children under age 18 uninsured at the time of interview: 5.1 percent

- Percent of adults aged 18-64 uninsured at the time of interview: 12.4 percent[50]

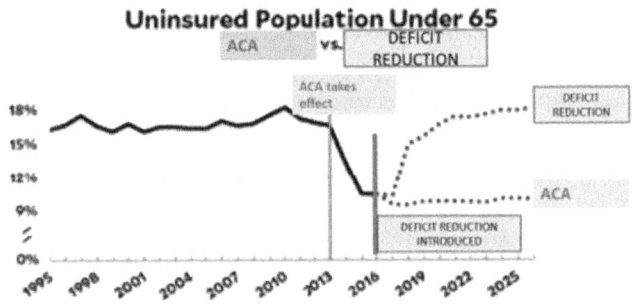

Adapted from www.motherjones.com/politics/2017/07/heres-exactly-how-many-people-will-be-uninsured-under-each-republican-health-care-bill/ and CDC historical as well as CBO projected data.

Deficit Reduction Masquerading as Healthcare Reform

And what are your chances of being impacted by healthcare reform? That is a misnomer: the healthcare debate has really been about **deficit reduction**. And the biggest targets remain Medicare, Medicaid, and the Affordable Care Act.

So, the correct question would be: Will our Congress' focus on debt reduction masquerading as healthcare reform impact you? The answer is yes, if the Congressional Budget Office is to be believed. Deficit reduction will lead to loss of healthcare coverage. According to a Gallup Poll at the end of January 2019 that is based on self-reported responses from tens of thousands of adults, we have already seen an increase in the number of uninsured from the 10.6 percent reported at the end of 2016 and the 12.4 percent reported in 2017. The poll found that the percentage of adults without insurance climbed to 13.75 percent for the fourth quarter of 2018. Without healthcare coverage, your access to the doctor of your choice is curtailed. So, the answer is definitely YES! Deficit reduction will impact your **access** to healthcare and the ability to see the doctor of your choice.[51]

Here is a snapshot of the potential impact of other Administration proposed/enacted reforms.[52] Under the ACA, 252 million people were insured in 2018.

If "Deficit Reduction" results in repeal of the ACA, an additional 19.2 million beneficiaries who are currently covered would become uninsured. The impact of the 2017 Tax Reduction Bill that removed the Individual Mandate will lead to an additional 15.6 million Americans choosing to go without healthcare insurance (I discuss that more fully in Chapters Eight and Nine). The impact of the Medicare Block Grants that were touched upon in Chapter One could result in an additional 25.1 million uninsured. The introduction of Short-Term Insurance and Association Health plans could potentially impact coverage for 17.5 million.

Geographic Availability

Improving access to healthcare services depends in part on ensuring that people have a **usual and ongoing source of care**[53] — that is, a provider or facility where one regularly receives care. Having a primary care provider (PCP) who serves as the usual source of care is especially important. Fifty percent of the uninsured, 12 percent of those with government sponsored healthcare, and a like percentage of those with employer sponsored healthcare have no usual source of care.[54]

Personal Relationship

It's important to find a healthcare provider whom the patient trusts and can communicate with.

Having a primary care provider (PCP) who serves as the usual source of care is especially important. PCPs can develop meaningful and sustained relationships with patients and provide integrated services while practicing in the context of family and community.

Having a usual PCP is associated with:

- Greater patient trust in the provider
- Better patient-provider communication
- Increased likelihood that patients will receive appropriate care
- Lower mortality from all causes

You've Got Medicaid — Why Can't You See the Doctor?

There are 70.5 million Americans utilizing Medicaid (Centers for Medicare and Medicaid Services, or CMS), patients who are primarily low-income healthcare consumers. There may be an access issue. Medicaid patients have difficulty finding physicians to treat them in a reasonable amount of time. Based on the data below by the Federal Centers for Disease Control and Prevention's National Center for Health Statistics, it would appear that there is some truth to decreased access.

Percentage of physicians accepting:

- New Medicaid patients has remained around 70 percent (participation rate varies by state/largely tied to reimbursement rates)
- New privately insured patients close to 85 percent
- New Medicare patients 83.7 percent (based on a national survey of more than 4,000 office-based physicians)[55]

As I said previously, the healthcare reform debate is really about deficit reduction. Deficit reduction means your ability to have healthcare coverage has a major barrier: **cost**. If we add additional data to the information seen previously, the impact of **cost** on **access** is very real. Now for the rest of the story!

Even those with insurance coverage through employers (15 percent) or government-provided healthcare (31 percent) find cost to be a burden to access. The uninsured suffer the greatest impact (62 percent). Women are impacted more than men when it comes to **cost**. Twenty to 32 percent of women did not access their physician for some variation of cost-related reasons, while 12 to 22 percent of men were impacted.[56]

And there are other logistical problems that create a barrier to **access** and ability to see the doctor of their choice.[57] And this impact occurs across socio-economic status. Regardless of socio-economic status, a quarter of women can't find time to go to the doctor. Not being able to find time off from work also plays a big role (18 to 19 percent), especially amongst low-income females (26 percent). Transportation is also a major factor that impacts lower-income women (18 percent) more than their sisters who make more money (4 to 9 percent). Childcare (11 to 15 percent) ranks between time off from work and transportation, but it also seems to impact poorer women the most (19 percent).

CHAPTER TWO *What Have We Learned?*

Our ability to understand **access** to American Healthcare in transition encompasses three components: *coverage, services,* and *timeliness.* Having healthcare coverage is the key.

The healthcare reform debate is really about deficit reduction. Deficit reduction means your ability to have healthcare coverage has a major barrier: **cost**.

Women are impacted more than men when it comes to **cost**.

Deficit reduction and other Administration approaches to healthcare reform will impact your **access** to healthcare and the ability to see the doctor of your choice.

CHAPTER THREE

Healthcare Costs

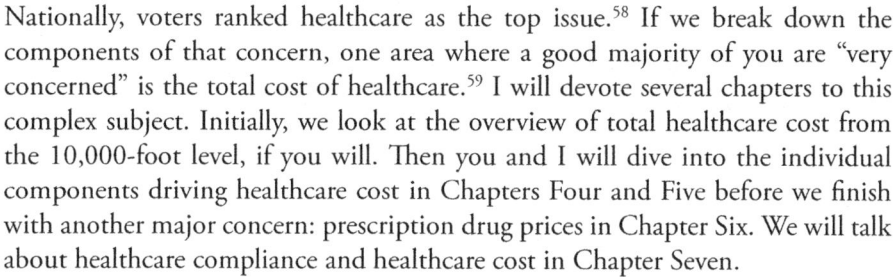

Nationally, voters ranked healthcare as the top issue.[58] If we break down the components of that concern, one area where a good majority of you are "very concerned" is the total cost of healthcare.[59] I will devote several chapters to this complex subject. Initially, we look at the overview of total healthcare cost from the 10,000-foot level, if you will. Then you and I will dive into the individual components driving healthcare cost in Chapters Four and Five before we finish with another major concern: prescription drug prices in Chapter Six. We will talk about healthcare compliance and healthcare cost in Chapter Seven.

TEACHING POINT: The cost of healthcare has increased. The usual way to track the cost of healthcare is either as a percentage of our Gross National Product or per-capita (or per person) spending. Gross national product (GNP) is an estimate of total value of all the final products and services turned out in a given period by the means of production owned by a country's residents.

PERCENTAGE OF GNP[60] versus PER-CAPITA SPENDING[61]

YEAR	%GNP	% CHANGE	PER CAPITA	% CHANGE
2014	17.1%		$9,403	
2015	17.7%	3%	$9,994	6%
2016	17.9%	1%	$10,348	3%
2017*	18.0%	0.5%	$10,724	3.6%
2018*	18.2%	1.1%	$11,193	9.6%
2025*	19.9%	9.3%	$15,365	37.2%

*expected/projected [62]

Since 1960, when the cost of healthcare was a mere 5 percent of our Gross National Product, national health spending will have increased to a projected 19.9 percent by 2025. In 2016, it was 17.6 percent. In personal terms (as in how that impacts you), your yearly bill (out-of-pocket cost) is now over $11,000 and climbing — talk about financial stress![63]

The **underinsured**, as you may remember, are the ones who have healthcare insurance, but the cost is so prohibitive that they rarely enter the ballpark, and when they do, it is usually the cheap seats. The **uninsured** spend their time in the parking lot and enter the healthcare ballpark during the seventh inning stretch to see the emergency room doctor as their rare interface with healthcare. In other chapters, I talk about this segment of our population in more detail. For now, you can see that the financial stress of healthcare cost impacts not only the uninsured (68 percent go without care due to cost, and 51 percent have outstanding medical debt) and underinsured (their numbers aren't much better at 53 and 45 percent, respectively), but those with healthcare insurance as well (31 and 21 percent, respectively).

TEACHING POINT: A Case Study in Variability

WHAT DRIVES HEALTHCARE COST?

1) Healthcare Services, or Variability in Provider billing

2) Healthcare Services, or Variability of the cost of Procedures

3) Medical Technology, or Variability of the cost of Medical Devices

4) Pharmaceuticals, or Prescription Drug Prices

5) Compliance

Lurking just below the surface are **administrative costs**.

At the end of the day, you, as the healthcare consumer, feel the impact of the increasing cost of healthcare. This is reflected in what you pay each year out-of-pocket (a subject we will discuss later) as well as the total cost for healthcare per person (per capita spending).

AN INTRODUCTION TO HEALTHCARE COST AND VARIABILITY

The first key concept here begins with variability. This is yet another example of the tectonic plates at work. Variability, in its simplest definition, means lack of consistency or fixed pattern. In the American healthcare "system" in transition, the variability can be seen in the examples already discussed and those yet to come.

Variation tells you how tightly your data is clustered around the mean (the average). This is called the Standard Deviation (SD). By that I mean, how much in line with the average (cost, access, quality) is the topic under discussion; the larger the SD, the greater the variability. An example of this would be the varying prices charged by providers of healthcare. American Healthcare in transition is a case study in variability.

The second key concept is actually a group of three interrelated factors: service intensity, higher prices, and administrative costs. Service intensity is the amount of work required for a healthcare procedure, examination, etc. Some providers (though not all) may "up-code" or overstate the amount of work actually done. This leads to higher prices. The administrative costs come from the hierarchy put in place in order to maximize the income for the work done or to review the work done to see where cost can be influenced (by up-coding for example).

Why is medical care more expensive in the United States?[64] It is not demographics that defines a patient population. It is not the illness burden or how sick a patient population may be. It isn't even the number of widgets, tests, procedures, etc., that are ordered by healthcare providers, which is called service volume.

It is the **variability**. This may be defined in terms of **service intensity**, which is a measure of the number, technical complexity, or attendant risk of services provided. It also measures how that intensity of service can be administratively manipulated with up-coding.

"Up-coding is fraudulent medical billing that costs us all money and possibly health. It refers to a practice in which a provider bills a health insurance payer (whether private, Medicaid or Medicare) using a CPT code for a more expensive service than was performed."[65] You got a taste of that specter when we briefly discussed its impact on you losing access to your doctor.

It can also be measured in how cost-effective the services rendered were (i.e. 'bang for the buck'), as well as results compared to the effectiveness of other services. As you can imagine, service intensity varies all over the map.

A second component of this variability is the **price**. As we will soon see, the price is not right or the same anywhere you measure it. Notice the range of prices. This is the **variability** we talked about earlier. Look at the wide swings of average cost for medical services in the U.S. for individuals with and without insurance.[66]

TYPE OF SERVICE	WITH INSURANCE	WITHOUT INSURANCE
Ambulance	$15-$100 copay	$400-$1,200+
Air Ambulance	$50-$500 copay	$2,000-$200,000
Emergency Room Visit	$50-$500 copay	$150-$3,000+
Urgent Care	$35-$100 copay	$50-$500
Blood Tests	$0-$30 copay 10%-50% coinsurance	$500-$3,000+
Blood Test-Cholesterol: at pharmacy; at home; Portable Digital Monitor	Blood Tests $0-$30 copay 10%-50% coinsurance $10-$50 copay 10-50% coinsurance	$5-$25 $15-$50 $75-$200
X-RAYS	$10-$50 copay 10%-50% coinsurance	$100-$3,000+ $1,000-$5,000+
Allergy Shots	$10-$25 copay per visit	$20-$100 per visit
Diabetes Medication	$10-$200 per month for multi dose	$200-$500 per month for multi dose
MRI	$20-$100 copay	$1,000-$5,000+
Sprained or Broken Wrist	Copays and coinsurance up to out-of-pocket minimum	Mild to moderate sprain or fracture $500; Surgery $7,000-$10,000
Sprained or Broken Ankle	$100 to out-of-pocket maximum	Non-surgical treatment $2,000+ Surgery-$11,000-$20,000+
Broken Leg	Copays and coinsurance up to out-of-pocket maximum	Non-surgical treatment $2,000+ Surgery-$17,000-$35,000+
Elbow Treatment and Surgery	Copays and coinsurance up to out-of-pocket maximum	Non-surgical treatment $500-$3,000; Surgery-$10,000-$16,000+
Hip Fracture	Copays and coinsurance up to out-of-pocket maximum	$13,000-$40,000+ Average cost-$26,912

CHAPTER THREE: Healthcare Costs

TYPE OF SERVICE	WITH INSURANCE	WITHOUT INSURANCE
Physical Therapy	$10-$75 copay 10%-50% coinsurance	$50-$350
Heart Rate Monitor; Blood Pressure Monitor	n/a	$30-$470 $18-$100+
Heart Surgery	Copays and 10%-50% of coinsurance	$30,000-$200,000+
Heart Valve Replacement	Copays and 10%-50% of coinsurance	$80,000-$200,000+
Heart Bypass Surgery	Copays and 10%-50% of coinsurance	$70,000-$200,000+ Average charge not including doctor's fee $177,094
Brain Surgery	Copays and 10%-50% of coinsurance	$50,000-$150,000+
Anesthesia	10%-50% coinsurance	$500-$3,500+
Baby Delivery	<$500-$3,000+	Vaginal $9,000-$17,000; C-Section $14,000-$25,000
Postpartum Maternity Checkup	$20-$30 copay per visit	$100-$200 per visit

Then there are those **administrative costs**, or the cost of doing business in order to make a profit. One comparison indicated that when applied to a health insurance company outside of a government agency, it can be as high as 18 percent plus a 3 percent profit margin. For comparison, administrative costs for Medicare are roughly 2 percent. The administrative costs for each provider of healthcare is roughly $83,000 per physician per year. In case you were wondering how that compares to Canada, what we pay in America is roughly four times the administrative cost for each physician as it is on the other side of our northern border.[67]

And we have plenty of administrators. There has been a 3,000 percent explosion of the administrative side of healthcare since 1970 versus a less dramatic physician increase.[68] In 2013, there were over 1 million doctors of medicine all over the United States. This figure included some 148,000 inactive and some 44,000 unclassified physicians. Practicing physicians in 2013 were 854,698. In 1970 there were 310,845.[69] This represents a 175 percent increase — not quite the same.

Other sources indicate that administration consumes up to 14 percent of our healthcare dollar.[70] And where does that money go? I modified a table that was initially created in an article written in 1992 by Kenneth Thorpe. It appears to still be relevant today, give or take a few modifications. It will serve as a snapshot of administrative expenses for the purpose of our discussion.[71]

Function/ Component	Health Insurance	Hospitals/ Facilities	Physicians	Firms/ Employers	Consumers/ Individuals
Transaction related	Claims processing	Admitting and billing	Billing	Tracking employee hires/ terminations	Submitting claims, appeals, analyzing the EOB
Benefits Management	Statistical analyses, quality assistance, plan design	Management information systems	Management information systems	Internal analyses	Tracking expenses eligible for reimbursement
Selling and Marketing	Underwriting, risk/ premiums, advertising	Strategic planning, advertising	Advertising	Flexible benefit programs (i.e. healthcare, etc.)	Search costs
Regulatory/ Compliance	Premium taxes, reserve requirements	Waste management	Licensing requirements	Filing summary plan descriptions, COBRA obligations	Mandated benefit laws
TECTONIC PLATES	80% of the billing-related costs in the United States are because of contending with this added complexity.[72]	25% of total hospital cost[73]	7 billing FTEs/10 MDs providing care[74]; MDs spend 3 hrs/wk doing administrative work[75]; 89% of physicians say the "business and regulation of healthcare" has changed the practice of medicine for the worse[76]	60% self-insured/open ended fee-for-service[77]; Costs up to $15,000/ covered beneficiary[78]	30% of healthcare is wasted with no benefit to the patient[79]

Where the American healthcare "system" seems to be running far beyond the power curve is in the cost of providing coverage. That said, in the United States, physicians' time is billed (and paid) at a more expensive level than their peers in other countries (which are the services). The same appears to be true for procedures, devices, and pharmacy, as well. In other words, cost drives coverage. Why is American healthcare so expensive?

In "The Healing of America," T. R. Reid* explored why American medicine falls behind other countries in quality while it races far ahead in cost of care. According to the Atlantic article on his work, "First, it really starts with the prices: the U.S. is unique in our reliance on for-profit insurance companies to pay for both essential and elective care. The absurd complexity of U.S. healthcare creates its own costs."[80]

Healthcare systems abound for just about every Tom, Dick, and Harry. Seniors. Veterans. Military personnel. Native Americans. Those in end-stage renal failure. Under 16 in a poor family. Over 16 in a poor family. Working for the federal government. Not to mention the ultimate example of variability — the myriad of private plans (healthcare plans offered by healthcare companies). "This is the fundamental fact of American healthcare: We pay much, much more than other countries do for the exact same things."[81]

TEACHING POINT

WHAT IS THE RETURN ON INVESTMENT (ROI)?

RETURN ON INVESTMENT

IN THE CURRENT AMERICAN HEALTHCARE "SYSTEM" IN TRANSITION:
Unlike" traditional **return-on-investment** models, in **health care**, benefits are frequently gained from cost avoidance rather than from revenue enhancement activities."

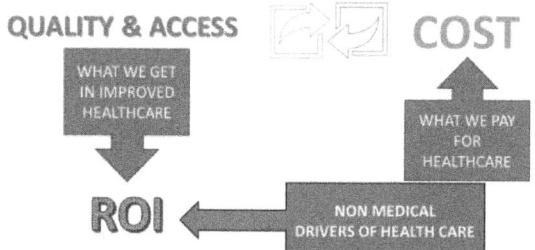

IN OUR AMERICAN HEALTHCARE "SYSTEM" IN TRANSITION:
We change the emphasis to the correct syllable. IMPROVED ACCESS and QUALITY of care AND incorporating the NON MEDICAL DRIVERS OF HEALTH CARE.

---

*T. R. Reid is an American reporter, documentary film correspondent, and author. He has also been a frequent guest on National Public Radio's Morning Edition.

This topic includes the issue of Return on Investment. We cannot leave an introductory discussion on cost without introducing the concept of **return on investment**, which is the next stop along this journey. It is a way to keep the major tectonic plates associated with having healthcare in mind: **cost**, **quality**, and **access**.[82] ROI is determined by the ability to impact the non-medical drivers of healthcare and access to healthcare.

Let us start a concept that shows our cost for healthcare in the United States as a percentage of our Gross Domestic Product (GDP). Data from 2013 clearly demonstrated that the United States spent far more on healthcare than the usual 'industrialized' suspects. This trend has continued. America spends much more on healthcare for each individual in the United States (per capita) than any other nation in the world and gets less health for it.[83] The latest updated data for 2016, published in June 2018, confirms this trend.[84] The United States' healthcare expenditure averaged 17.2 percent of the Gross Domestic Product. In second place was Switzerland at 12.3 percent, followed by France at 11.5 percent.

Simply put, the United States has a healthcare "system" that does not get the health status improvement one might expect. To put it bluntly, there is no bang for the buck. The Return on Investment, or ROI, would not be described as acceptable, especially if we look at life expectancy at birth amongst industrialized nations. Again, the United States ranks 25th in life expectancy worldwide, with an average life span of just over 79 years. The leaders such as Japan and Switzerland are approaching 84 years. But the basic issue may very well be the fact that the United States Healthcare "System" is not a functioning system at all, but rather is a hodgepodge of various interacting moving processes, or tectonic plates fueled by the business model of profit margin. Other causes of poor outcomes are relative lack of attention to non-medical drivers of health and non-coverage of a relatively large portion of the population.

NON-MEDICAL DRIVERS OF HEALTHCARE

What happened to lower the death rate from infectious disease from 1900 to 1980 and beyond?[85]

Did better healthcare lower the death rates? No, other forces were at work — in other words, **almost all economic, environmental, and public health changes.** What were they? Improved economics and less extreme poverty; a dozen people no longer shared the same tenement sleeping quarters and their tuberculosis; improved diets produced stronger immune systems; state Health Departments were established; there was a better management of human waste and disappearance of horse manure from the streets; centralized, purified, chlorinated, municipal water supplies appeared; screens on windows kept flies out of the kitchen and dining room and off of food; mosquito control began; and some vaccinations — pertussis (1914), diphtheria (1926), and tetanus (1938) — were combined in 1948 and given as the DTP vaccine.

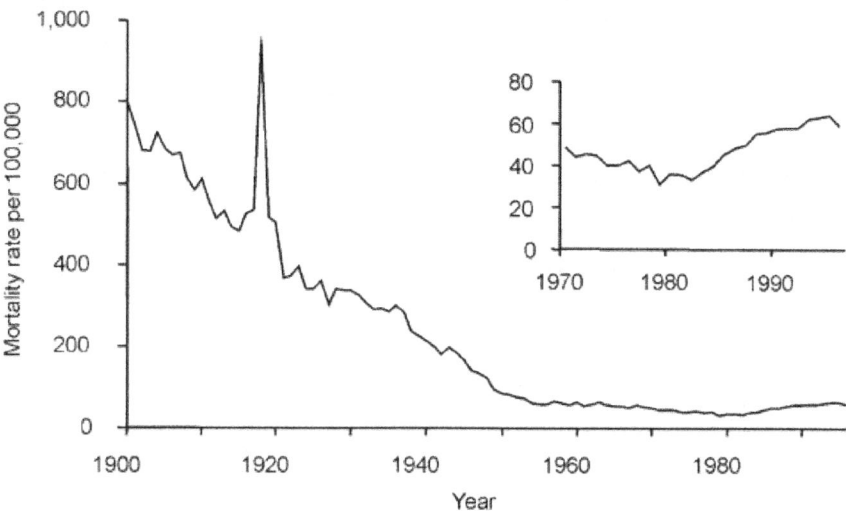

So, it could be argued that economic, environmental, and public health changes account for most of the improvement in a population's health. These factors must be addressed if we are to improve the ROI spent on healthcare. Of all of the confounding variables, how significant is medical care? **Medical care** is relatively less important than are other factors in determining health outcomes for a population. Of the 30-year increase in average U.S. life expectancy since 1900, only about two years, or 17 percent are attributable to better medical care. Socio-economic status (40 percent) and health behaviors (29 percent) have a greater impact. The three important social determinants of health (SDOH) are poverty, education level, and housing.

NON-COVERAGE OF A RELATIVELY LARGE PORTION OF THE POPULATION

A snapshot in time

There are two separate groups of patients to be reviewed in this section: those without insurance or the **uninsured**, and those who have insurance but can't or don't use it due to economic or other considerations, or the **underinsured**.[86]

So how does the United States do in terms of access to care? About 75 percent of Organization for Economic Co-operation and Development (OECD) nations* cover 100 percent of their populations. A higher fraction of U.S. residents go without health coverage than any other OECD country.[87]

Uninsured

In 2017,

1. The number of people without health insurance increased to 28 million, up from 27.3 million the year before.

2. The composite picture of this group is 19 to 64 years old (84.6 percent) and male (54.6 percent even though the U.S. population has more women than men).

3. They tend to have less than a high school education and/or have lower incomes.

4. About one-quarter of the uninsured people are 26 to 34 years old, and about 20 percent are ages 34 to 44. Fourteen percent are under 19 years old.

5. About 40 percent of uninsured people are non-Hispanic white (nearly 60 percent of people in the United States are non-Hispanic white).

6. The uninsured were disproportionately concentrated in the South[88].

In 2018 and 2019, this data is subject to change due to the current political climate in the United States, which places more Americans at risk for loss of their

---

*The Organization for Economic Co-operation and Development is an intergovernmental economic organization with 36 member countries, founded in 1961 to stimulate economic progress and world trade.

healthcare insurance in spite of the results of the 2018 midterm elections (see Chapters Eight and Nine for further details).

Underinsured

In 2018 and beyond,

1. Out-of-pocket costs, excluding premiums, over the prior 12 months are equal to 10 percent or more of household income

OR

2. Out-of-pocket costs, excluding premiums, are equal to 5 percent or more of household income if income is under 200 percent of the federal poverty level ($22,980 for an individual and $47,100 for a family of four)

OR

3. Deductible is 5 percent or more of household income[89]

What does that mean?

1. Twenty-three percent of 19- to 64-year-old adults are underinsured

2. This is an improvement from the 23 percent, or 31 million people in 2014.

3. As of late 2016, 28 percent of U.S. adults age 19 to 64 who were insured all year were underinsured — or an estimated 41 million people.

4. Half (51 percent) of underinsured adults reported problems with medical bills or debt of $4,000 or more than two of five (44 percent) reported not getting needed care because of cost.[90]

CHAPTER THREE *What Have We Learned?*

Healthcare cost has increased to 18 percent of our Gross National Product.

The yearly bill (out-of-pocket cost) for healthcare spread across the Amrican population is now over $10,000 and climbing.

Variability is the key cost driver.

Service intensity, price, and administrative costs fuel the variability, while demographics, illness burden, and service volume do not.

Simply put, the United States has a Healthcare "system" that does not get the health status improvement one might expect. To put it bluntly, there is no bang for the buck. ROI is determined by the ability to impact the non-medical drivers of healthcare and access to healthcare.

Medical care is relatively less important than other factors in determining health outcomes for a population. Of the 30 years increase in average U.S. life expectancy since 1900, only about two years are attributable to better medical care. In other words, the non-medical drivers of healthcare are almost all economic, environmental, and public health factors.

There are two separate groups of patients to be considered: those without insurance, or the uninsured, and those who have insurance but can't or don't use it due to economic or other considerations, or the underinsured.

CHAPTER FOUR

Healthcare Costs and Provider Variability

TEACHING POINT

How Providers of Healthcare charge for their services

Again, the constant theme in American healthcare is variability. That is why the prices in the United States are expressed as a range. "All of this means there are about as many price tags for that hypertension checkup as there are insurers and providers."[91]

There's one party — the provider —who provides the service. They each have their own master list of charges for different services, and these charge lists are different from provider to provider.

HOW PROVIDERS CODE

I will now take a minute to talk about **how providers code**. Why? Because you need to understand the coding process in order to understand this tectonic plate.

Coding an outpatient procedure or physician service

CPT 4-Procedure codes and HCPCS (Healthcare Common Procedure Coding System, Level II) are used to tell insurance companies what kind of procedure or service was performed. They also sometimes denote pharmacy and supply items, as well as capture physician visit times. Procedure codes must match up with diagnosis codes in order to get claims paid. Keeping up on procedure codes attached to charges is one of the most important areas for hospitals and physicians, yet it's probably the one that's overlooked the most.

Coding an inpatient hospital stay

The coding and payment process is referred to as the inpatient prospective payment system (IPPS). The code set used to report medical diagnoses on claims for services used by all providers is the ICD-10-CM diagnosis coding system. The Centers for Disease Control and Prevention (CDC) developed and maintains the code set.* Providers select codes based on documentation in the patient's medical record. These codes are primarily used to determine coverage. Inpatient providers report ICD-10-CM diagnosis and ICD-10-PCS procedure codes on claims, which are then used to assign discharges to the appropriate MS-DRG. Diagnosis-related group (DRG) is a system to classify hospital cases into one of originally 467 groups, now nearly 500. The DRG system was intended to identify the "products" that a hospital provides. Each case is categorized into a diagnosis-related group (DRG). Each DRG has a payment weight assigned to it, based on the average resources used to treat Medicare patients in that DRG.

DRGs have been around since 1975 when Yale University started grouping together patients with similar treatments and conditions for comparative studies. On October 1, 1983, DRGs were adopted by Medicare as a basis of payment for inpatient hospital services in order to attempt to control hospital costs. The original DRG system has been changed and there are various DRG systems in use. "Two of the main DRG systems currently in use are the Medicare Severity DRG (MS-DRGs) and 3M's All Patient Refined DRGs (APR-DRGs). Different DRG systems are used by different payers."[92] Variability!

Based on the multiple ways that a provider of services can code for the healthcare they provide, how they code determines how they get paid. The claims process starts when a healthcare provider treats a patient and sends a bill for the services provided to a designated payor after their internal process using the appropriate coding system as discussed above. The 'payor' or 'insurance provider' is usually a health insurance company, unless an individual does not have employer or government sponsored healthcare, in which case it is the individual. The payor then

---

*This is the U.S. agency charged with tracking and investigating public health trends. It is a part of the U.S. Public Health Services (PHS) under the Department of Health and Human Services (HHS).

evaluates the claim based on a number of factors, determining which, if any, services it will reimburse. If you are the payor, you have no such clout.

TEACHING POINT

PAYMENT MODELS

How do providers of healthcare get paid?

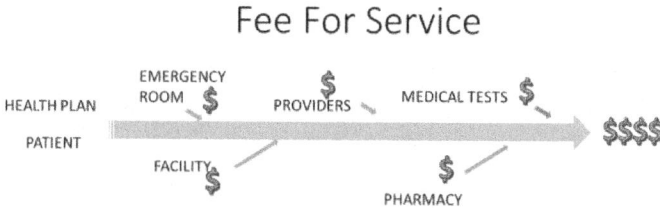

We will begin with the most traditional and cost-provoking healthcare payment model: **fee-for-service**. It requires patients or payers (the **third party**) to reimburse the healthcare provider (the **first party**) for each service performed.* While **access** is encouraged, there is no incentive to improve **quality** or contain **cost**.

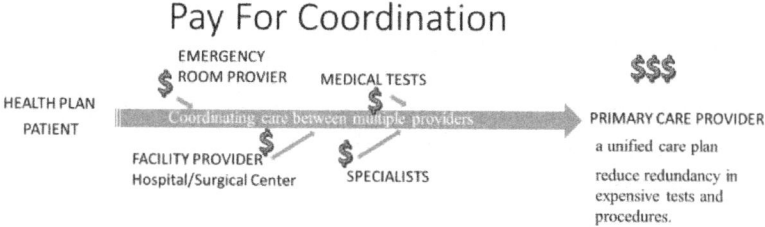

Pay-for-coordination is a small step beyond fee-for-service, as it coordinates care between the primary care provider and specialists (the **first party**). You still are churning widgets (services), however, coordinating care between the myriad of providers in a health plan can help reduce waste, which results in less expensive care. The emphasis here is on **cost** and perhaps a little on both **access** and **quality**.

---

*The inspiration for the illustrations of the payment models come from http://www.mckesson.com/population-health-management/resources/what-payment-models-exist/. Each diagram in this chapter was created by the author.

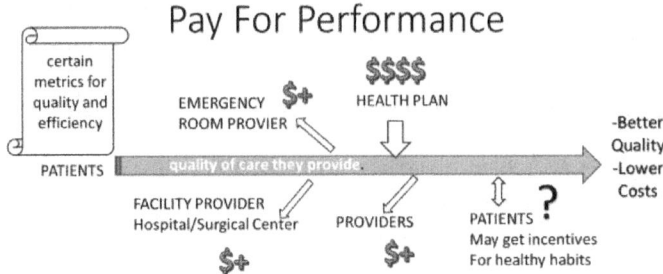

Quality of care is further served in pay-for-performance (P4P), or value-based reimbursement. Healthcare providers are only paid if they meet certain metrics for quality and efficiency. This is truly a direct link between **quality**, **cost**, and **access**.

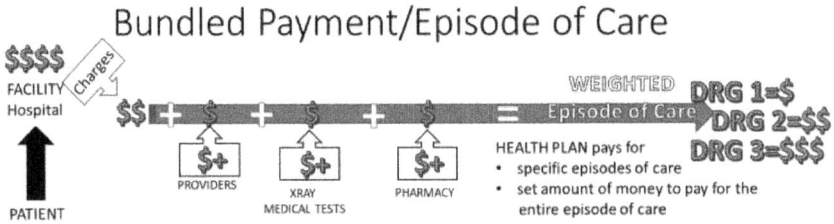

We take this a step further in bundled payments, in which providers are reimbursed for specific episodes of care. **Cost, access,** and **quality** of care are merged, as there is a certain finite amount of money to pay for the entire episode of care. **Cost** is given greater weight than **quality** or **access**. This is the Diagnostic-related Groups (DRG) model, which is a system used to classify hospital cases into one of nearly 500 categories. The intent of the DRG model was to identify the "products" that a hospital provides. This is how we pay **facilities** or hospitals and other inpatient providers.

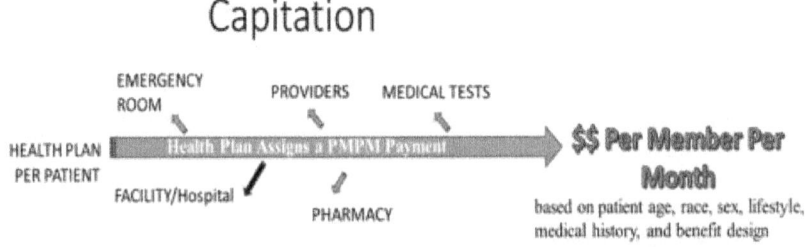

CHAPTER FOUR: Healthcare Costs and Provider Variability

In the capitation healthcare payment model, patients (the **second party**) are assigned a per member per month (PMPM) payment based on their age, race, sex, lifestyle, medical history, and benefit design. When fully capitated, this is another example of coordination between **cost** and **quality**, but **access** may suffer.

Global Budget

On the far end of the spectrum is the global budget, which is a fixed total dollar amount paid annually for all care delivered. It is capitation on steroids. Again, **quality** and **cost** may be addressed at the expense of **access**.

Risk Sharing

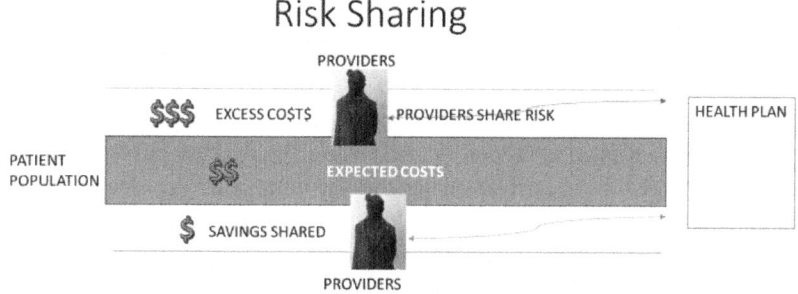

These next payment methods disperse the risk among the providers of healthcare. This program occurs with both Medicare and Commercial Health plans. There are two types of savings programs associated with risk sharing, "upside" and "downside."

The "Upside" Shared Savings Program is an incentive laden program to share the wealth (savings generated) only. This is the Medicare Shared Savings Program (MSSP) for Accountable Care Organizations.

The Downside" Shared Savings Program is where the participating plans suffer the good results (shared savings) with the bad (the risk of excess costs). All MSSP participants must move to a downside model after three years.

Sharing risk impacts **cost**, but safeguards must be instituted to preserve **quality** and **access**.

PHYSICIAN FEES

VARIABILITY: PHYSICIAN FEES

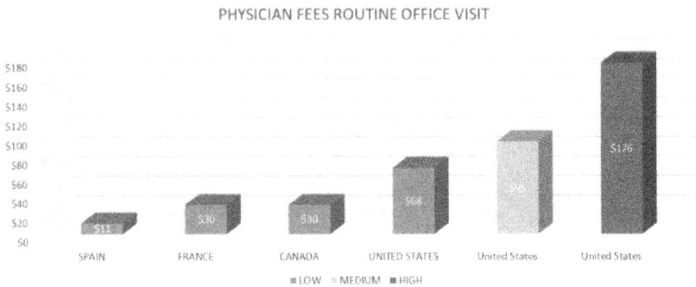

The net results? The wide variability of physician office fees. The United States leads the rest of the world by a large margin.[93] The variability comes from multiple factors as we have discussed. But primarily, the variability is built into the three-party process (plus decision-makers/administrators) I have described. The consumer of healthcare is no longer the decision maker or master of their own healthcare fate.

What is the point of all this? Doctors are among the highest paid professionals in the United States, frequently beating out lawyers, software developers, and finance managers, amongst other groups of professionals. "Doctors bank about $35,000 more each year then the next top earners — lawyers."[94] Their compensation varies based on the location and their specialty, as well as how well they (or their practice consultants) have learned to use the systems just described.

   Orthopedics $443,000
   Cardiology $410,000
   Dermatology. $381,000
   Gastroenterology. $380,000
   Radiology $375,000
   Urology. $367,000
   Anesthesiology $360,000
   Plastic surgery. $365,000
   Oncology $329,000
   General surgery. $322,000
   Emergency medicine. $322,000
   Ophthalmology. $309,000
   Critical care. $306,000

Pulmonary medicine $281,000
Obstetrics/gynecology $277,000
Nephrology $273,000
Pathology $266,000
Neurology $241,000
Rheumatology $234,000
Psychiatry $226,000
Internal medicine $222,000
Allergy $222,000
HIV/ID $215,000
Family medicine $207,000
Endocrinology $206,000
Pediatrics $204,000

How much do physicians make overall?[95] Orthopedists top the list with annual average compensation of $443,000, taking into account salary, bonus, and profit-sharing contributions, according to Medscape's 2016 physician compensation report. Cardiologists and dermatologists come in second and third for earnings, logging annual compensation totaling $410,000 and $381,000, respectively. The lowest earning doctors were pediatricians, who brought in about $204,000 annually.[96]

Physicians generate income for hospitals. Only about 31.4 percent of physicians identified as independent practice owners or partners in the 2018 Survey of America's Physicians.

In contrast, almost half (49.1 percent) of the over 8,700 physicians surveyed by the Physicians Foundation and Merritt Hawkins identified as hospital or medical group employees.[97] According to a Merritt Hawkins survey, physicians generated $2,378,727 in net revenue on behalf of the hospitals with whom they were affiliated.[98] Cardiovascular surgeons led the way.[99]

CHAPTER FOUR *What Have We Learned?*

There are three pieces to the puzzle:

1. First party: the provider of healthcare

2. Second party: you, the consumer of healthcare

3. Third party: the insurance company or Federal/State agency who pays the provider. Or you.

There is a disconnect between what the first party charges and what the third party pays because the third party has developed many types of payment models. This process fuels the **variability**.

The consumer of healthcare no longer drives the process, makes the decisions, or sets the policy.

CHAPTER FIVE

Healthcare Costs And Procedures

TEACHING POINT

THE COST OF PROCEDURES

The cost of your healthcare is dependent on where you live. There were huge ranges in prices even within the same state. In the example below, a colonoscopy (a procedure that allows doctors to look inside and see how healthy your large intestine, or colon might be) could cost anywhere from $202 to $1,966 in South Dakota.[100] Other ranges are shown based on a search of the literature.

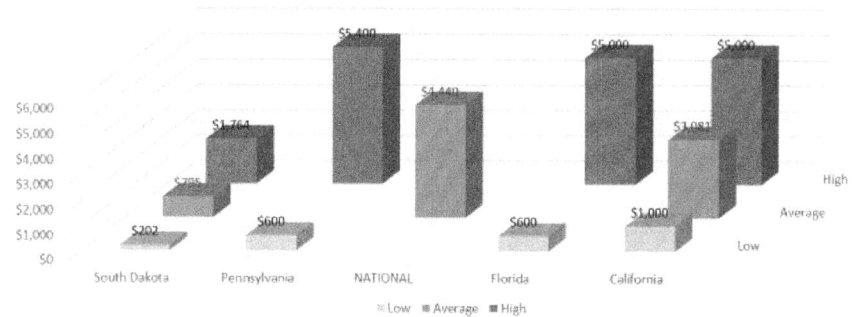

The Dartmouth Atlas of Healthcare addresses "unwarranted regional variation" where a surgical procedure *is* part of the treatment possibilities. Unwarranted variation is defined in the Atlas as differences in care that are not explained by patient needs or preferences. The Dartmouth project identified "unwarranted variation" in treatment of hip fracture, cholecystectomy (removal of the gall bladder), hip replacement, colectomy (removal of the colon), CABG (returning blood supply to the heart after a heart attack), back surgery, mastectomy for breast cancer, lower extremity revascularization (unclogging of arteries of the leg), carotid endarterectomy (opening up the artery in the neck), radical prostatectomy (removal of the prostate in men), and TURP for BPH (opening up the pathway from the bladder blocked by an enlarged prostate).

For many of these procedures, the medical evidence for doing the surgery was unclear. For many others, the risk of complications for surgery may be higher than the risk of the disease process. According to the Dartmouth Alas Project,* "many of these differences appear to be explained by differences in local medical opinion of the value of surgical care."[101]

The prices contracted and paid for all across the country, by region and even in the same region, by multiple healthcare plans to the army of healthcare providers is, you guessed it, variable! Let us look at one of the very same procedures the Dartmouth Atlas found to be suffering from "unwarranted variation."

Hip replacement:

> Average price in America: $26,489
> Average price in Australia: $26,297
> Average price in Argentina: $6,862

The American average price, the 50th percentile, for a hip replacement is $26,489. Hip replacements in countries such as Argentina, Spain, and the Netherlands all fall somewhere below on average. America's 25th percentile for a hip replacement is $16,622, and the 95th percentile is $53,644.

And now we will discuss the connection between procedures and devices. Artificial joint implants prices in the U.S. are exaggerated from the get-go because of

---

*For more than 20 years, the Dartmouth Atlas Project has documented glaring variations in how medical resources are distributed and used in the United States. The project uses Medicare data to provide comprehensive information and analysis about national, regional, and local markets, as well as individual hospitals and their affiliated physicians.

the few companies that manufacture them. Then the complexity of our American healthcare "system" in transition flares its ugly head: the prices are marked up several times by intermediaries, making artificial implants the single biggest cost of most joint replacement surgeries.

And the story is similar for CABG, also known as bypass surgery. The average price varies around the world as well:

- Average price in America $75,345
- Average price in Australia $42,130
- Average price in the Netherlands $15,742

It is readily apparent that there is a remarkable variation in our healthcare spending across regions and age groups. This is not new news. The Dartmouth Atlas project studied variations using Medicare data on people over 65, and the 2013 Institute of Medicine study showed an "inconsistent" association between spending and quality in both over-65 Medicare and under-65 private insurance markets. In other words, this project was the first to show that it was not demographics, illness burden, or service volume that drove our healthcare spending, but variability.

VARIABILITY

What does variability in procedures look like?[102]

VARIABILITY: PROCEDURES

Knee Replacement Surgery
Total Hospital & Physician Costs

- Spain: $7,827
- United Kingdom: $7,839
- Australia: $22,425
- United States: High $52,451, Medium $25,637, Low $16,379

NB: There is only one price for these services/procedures in other countries

■ Low ■ Medium ■ High

Quality does not always go up when you throw more money into healthcare services like procedures.

It was also the Dartmouth Atlas Project that looked at **cost** and **quality**. There is no direct cause or effect; quality does not always go up when you throw more money into healthcare services. The relationship would be described as inconsistent at best.[103]

In the search for solutions, the emphasis may not be on the correct syllable. Unfortunately, the emphasis for problem solving is different for those policy makers looking at variation in production — number of services provided — and those trying to solve pricing variation — the cost of doing business and making a profit.

TEACHING POINT
MEDICAL DEVICES

The Food and Drug Administration (FDA or USFDA) is a federal agency of the United States Department of Health and Human Services, one of the United States federal executive departments. It regulates medical devices. Remember, technology is one of the key drivers for the cost of healthcare. The definition of medical device is any "instrument, apparatus, appliance, software, material, or other article"[104] — regardless of how it is used or what gadgets and gizmos it contains, specifically for diagnostic and/or therapeutic purposes.

As mentioned earlier, there is a connection between procedures and devices. Artificial joint implants prices in the U.S. are exaggerated from the get-go because few companies manufacture them. Then the complexity of our American healthcare "system" in transition flares its ugly head: the prices are marked up several times by intermediaries, making artificial implants the single biggest cost of most joint replacement surgeries.

A 2007 WebMD article indicated that about 500,000 knee replacements and more than 175,000 hip replacements were performed annually. Hip replacements were expected to increase 174 percent in the next 20 years and knee replacements would rise even more at 673 percent.[105]

And the data supports the fact that we pay too much for these devices.[106]

CHAPTER FIVE: Healthcare Costs And Procedures

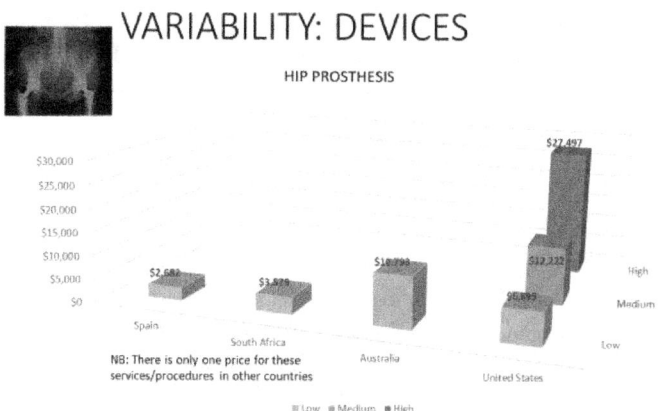

VARIABILITY: DEVICES
HIP PROSTHESIS

In recent years, the Centers for Medicare & Medicaid Services (CMS) and some private health insurance companies have begun switching to bundled-payment models. I talked about that model in Chapter Four. As you recall, under a bundled-payment model, an insurer reimburses hospitals a single, fixed amount for a common procedure and associated costs, rather than reimbursing for separately itemized services and supplies.

Let us talk about these medical devices. It is important to know how they are classified and approved as we head eventually into an important case study.

Medical devices are classified from the simple to the complex based on their intended use, indications, and need for patient protection. **Class I devices** include non-sophisticated elastic bandages, examination gloves, and hand-held surgical instruments. They are subject to the least regulatory control, or general controls.

Class II devices include a little more sophistication and potential for harm and include such tools as acupuncture needles, powered wheelchairs, infusion pumps, air purifiers, and surgical drapes. These devices require a little stricter oversight than the general controls to "assure safety and effectiveness."

Class III devices are "those for which insufficient information exists to assure safety and effectiveness when general or special controls are applied as these devices are usually those that support or sustain human life, are of substantial importance in preventing impairment of human health, or present a potential, unreasonable risk of illness or injury."[107]

Enter premarket approval, a scientific review to ensure the device's safety and effectiveness, in addition to the controls discussed above. **Premarket approval (PMA)** is the most stringent type of device marketing application required by the FDA.[108]

That is the evidence-based medical way. Unfortunately, there is another way in which medical devices are allowed to enter the marketplace. In my opinion, this is a little more like slipping in the back door. I will let you be the judge of that, however. **Premarketing Notification** (510(k)) is a 'fast-track' process. It must be similar to a device already on the market that has been previously approved. The FDA has only just recently begun to re-evaluate this idea after numerous recalls of devices that entered the marketplace based on this process.[109]

With Medical Devices as the background, I am going to present a case study to you. This is the case you saw as I was introducing the journey we would be taking together. This case involves a spinal cord injury, an event which often leads to the need for a medical device.

Spinal cord injuries

Before we discuss the next case and its particulars, we will go over some basic medical information to level the playing field.

Spinal cord injury (SCI) in the United States is a common event.[110] How common? According to the National Spinal Cord Injury Statistical Center, the distribution of the causes of SCI have changed drastically since 2010:

- Vehicular: 38 percent
- Falls: 30 percent
- Violence (primarily gunshot wounds): 14 percent
- Sports/Recreation activities: 9 percent
- Medical/Surgical: 5 percent
- Other: 4 percent

As of 2015, 12,500 new SCI occur each year. Between 240,000 and 337,000 people are currently living with SCI in the United States. The average age at injury which was 29 years old in the 1970s is now an older population at 42 years old in 2015. Conversely, the length of hospital stays is declining. In the 1970s it was 24 days. In

2015 the average hospital stay was 11 days. The same trend was seen in rehabilitation stays which have declined from 98 days to 36 in the same time period. [111]

The prevalence of <u>*nontraumatic SCI*</u> is estimated to be three to four times greater than traumatic SCI.[112] Nontraumatic Spinal Cord Injury (NTSCI) is any damage to the spinal cord that has not been caused by a major trauma. In other words, the spinal cord has been damaged in other ways such as infection, loss of blood supply, compression by a cancer or through a slow, degenerative process such as osteoarthritis.[113]

Medical complications after SCI are both common and severe. In other words, the chances of going back into the hospital is 50/50 over the first year after an SCI, and you have about a one in three chances of being hospitalized again each year. The most common reasons for this are:

- genitourinary (kidney or bladder)
- respiratory complications
- pressure ulcers[114]

Why is this important? Because our patient in the case study below suffered re-hospitalization from a kidney infection as well as the significant complication of depression.

A CASE STUDY
The Call To Arms

This case involves a middle-aged man who suffered an SCI but his seat at the ballpark was located behind the plate. This case will show that tectonic plates can be disruptive of the best-laid plans, even if they are made from the premier seating section in our healthcare stadium. So, this is a 'call to arms'. As we go through the case, keep in mind the SCI discussion that led us to our case study.

Why is this case a call to arms? The patient indicated the following:

"You work for a 'monopoly company' with one of the best healthcare packages around. So, you don't really look behind the facade to see what is really covered. No one is looking to have a catastrophic event. You trust the company; the health plan; the dental plan; routine things; the basic fundamentals; emergency room; common cold; basic dental work. You don't think about the long-term consequences of a major catastrophic event which may lead to a need for long term care."

Not being an informed healthcare consumer. You were set up to be a victim!

CASE NOTES:

1. Spinal cord injury (SCI) with complete paralysis below the waist.

2. Major complication-depression

3. Wake-up call to arms

This elite seat behind the behind home plate comes with free healthcare. The members do not pay anything into it. There is a small deductible. People took advantage and now healthcare doesn't start until a year on the job. But this case involves an employee of 26 plus years duration. His coverage began after a 90-day probationary period. There was no need to ask about the coverage because "the insurance is so good, you don't even worry about it." Only after a service, when the bill comes, are your responsibilities spelled out. (Author's note: This is the EOB, or Explanation of Benefits, which is a very useful tool as you move along the continuum from victim to informed consumer of healthcare. We will visit this again down the road.). Then the deductible is itemized. It is usually about $500 per year. If problems arose, you could always go to the union, and they would go to bat for you. If you were injured on the job, a position would be created to allow you to work until able to go back to your full-time job.

Our patient didn't have any real major medical issues for the first 26 years of employment. For 26 years, our patient didn't worry about covered benefits because all of his needs were met. Until D-day. The flexibility to create a modified position described above only occurs if you are hurt at work. But this injury didn't actually occur at work.

> "I was heading to work. It was daylight savings and got up to go to work found out that I was one hour early. I didn't realize it at home. When I got to the parking lot it was empty. Is it time to be at work? Is it Monday? Oh, it was daylight savings. I got a bite to eat and then laid back in the driver's seat until it was time to go to work."

> "I woke up to them (fire department) pulling me out. They asked me if I could move my legs. I think I told them I couldn't. Then they asked me if there was anybody they could call. I gave them my brother's name and my wife's name. I really didn't know what was going on. Other than the fact that I couldn't move my legs.

> "I asked them what happened, and they said I was in an accident. I was wondering how that could happen because I was parked. They said I was hit from behind. To be honest with you, I don't really remember how I felt. I don't remember the ride to the hospital. The next thing I remembered was that I was in the ICU."

The patient's brother had flown in and went to the hospital. The brother continues.

> "My brother was due for surgery in two hours. They didn't give me my brother's real name. They use a code. They gave him an alias for confidentiality until they could sort the evidence. The main doctor comes out and tells me about the procedure. He showed me the x-rays. He showed me where my brother had broken his neck and his back. They told me he was in an accident. My sister-in-law was there as well. She had gone to the police station because the police hadn't written up the report that is usually done after an investigation to determine cause."

"They haven't done that report to this day," interjected our patient.

The brother takes up the story.

> "It was a rainy day. The driver lost control. Speculation was that he was impaired. The police did not test the driver for impairment. The police indicated only that he was going at excessive speed on a rainy day."

At the end of the day, our patient suffered a neck injury and a partial tear in the spinal cord at T11/T12 (mid back). He has function in his upper body and trunk. He has some tone but no contractures (condition of shortening and hardening of muscles and tendons, which can lead to deformity and rigidity of joints). He had no bowel or bladder control. See the MRI below. "X" marks the spot.

The patient continues.

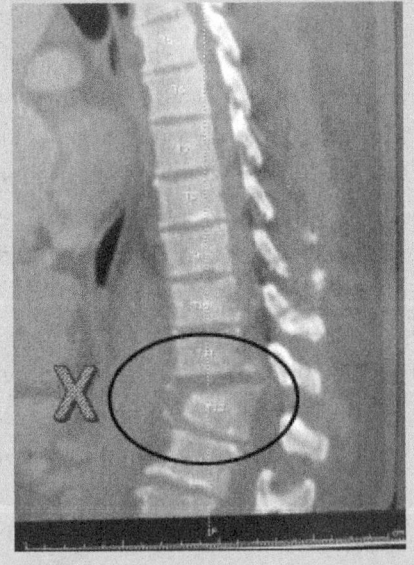

> "I was fortunate because of my insurance coverage to go to a first-class prestige rehabilitation hospital. I was 'medevaced' (medically-evacuated) from my home state to the state where the first-class rehab was. Both ways. The insurance paid for it. I got everything I needed to be entered back into society. Then I had to go back to my home. Then you don't have the necessary stuff (resources) to continue what you learned. Things are put on a waiting list. You wait. You lose faith and hope. You start to decline. I got a UTI (kidney-bladder infection), which resulted in a month-long hos-

pitalization and skilled nursing. It was there that I got some of the equipment I needed. But after that I was back 'on the street' without any support. You start to question yourself. Then you start questioning God.

"I started having a spiritual war. That becomes depression. Then you start second guessing your life. My mother died at that time and that made it worse. I just didn't care anymore. I just let it go. I didn't do any of the things that I was trained to do. On my six-month follow-up I was able to get some of the equipment I required. A standing machine. I started to do my work. But the negative started again. I started losing hope and faith. I didn't think I could go on. My brother invited me to come out. But I was afraid that it was the end. I decided to come out. He would be my last line of defense.

"I am now doing better. It has been a blessing, a call to arms. They basically saved my life. The next step is outpatient rehabilitation. The question is further insurance coverage. I didn't know anything about how the coverage would work. I still have my outpatient therapy hours, but at present they will not cover what I really need. We are in limbo."

In other words, this patient was a victim. He has now had his "call to arms" and is becoming an informed participant. It is unclear at this point what the future will hold, but the company nurse has been involved and the patient has been contacted by his employer. The battle to overcome the tectonic plates has moved forward.*

"Faith is returning," said our patient. "Throughout this entire ordeal, I have been blessed with the support of family, friends, folks at church, and even

---

*Pictures used by permission

the head honchos at work and the union." At the end of the day, there is always hope when you are an informed participant. Hope, faith, friends, and family are all important. Being informed is the linchpin!

And why did I drop this case study here under Medical Devices? This patient might benefit from a medical device. An excellent example of the FDA's Premarketing Notification (510(k)) notification process for approval.

CALL TO ARMS

CHAPTER FIVE *What Have We Learned?*

The cost of your healthcare procedures is dependent on where you live.

Quality does not always go up when you throw more money into healthcare services such as procedures.

The prices contracted and paid for all across the country is variable.

This process fuels the **variability.**

Medical devices are classified from the simple to the complex based on their intended use, indications, and need for patient protection.

Enter premarket approval, a scientific review to ensure the device's safety and effectiveness.

There is a dangerous loophole, however. Premarketing Notification (510(k) is a fast-track process that only has to show a preexisting approval to a similar device.

CHAPTER SIX

Healthcare Cost And Prescription Drugs

Nationally, voters ranked healthcare as the top issue.[115] If we break down the components of that concern, a majority of voters are "very concerned" when it comes to the total cost of healthcare. Voters were also "very concerned" about what was going on in the world of pharmacy as it impacts them, not only in regards to how much prescription drugs cost, but also how to lower those drug prices.[116]

I will address both of these topics in this chapter.[117]

TEACHING POINT

The Cost of Prescription Drugs

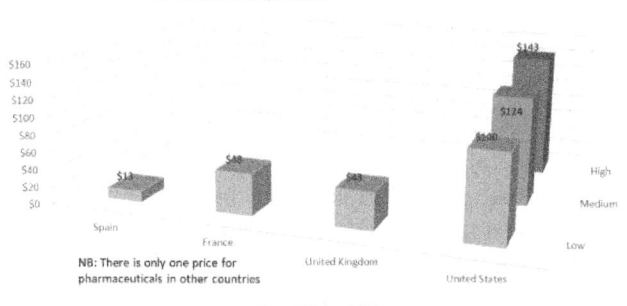

From 2005 through 2013 the annual retail price of therapy per drug increased from $4,140 to $11,341.[118] After doubling over seven years, this dramatic increase has now modulated.[119] Current trending has leveled off at just under 6 percent and is predicted to stay in that range through 2025.[120] So what are the cost driving culprits?

PRESCRIPTION COST DRIVERS

Here is a summary of pharmaceutical cost drivers based on the current situation.

Monopoly rights

Pharmaceutical drugs are the only major healthcare service in which the maker of the drug is able to set prices with little or no constraint. This price tag is largely driven by brand-name drug prices that have increased in recent years at rates far beyond the consumer price index.[121] Additionally, manufacturers are able to set such high prices because of market exclusivity, which is protected by monopoly rights awarded with the Food and Drug Administration (FDA) approval and patents.[122]

There is also the issue of the 319 drugs (as of December 29, 2017) that are on the FDA List of Off-Patent, Off-Exclusivity Drugs without an Approved Generic.[123] Many of the drugs on this list are for small patient populations, which might not be worth the risk to make the investment of selling generic versions. This allows drug companies who acquire these drugs to increase the price tag.

This is the sales strategy applied by "Pharma Bros," a personification of the medical industry gone bad.[124] That name applies to the bad actors, not the pharmaceutical industry as a whole. That said, it is an example of the business profit-first mentality that seems to permeate the pharmaceutical industry as a whole.[125] This is part of the healthcare industry phenomena of administration costs (to assure profit) that I mentioned in Chapter Three.

Enter the Pharma Bros, followed by huge price increases. Their drug companies can price new medicines, particularly orphan drugs,* beyond the reach of the individual patient and paid directly by an insurance company or the government. This is because they fall under legislation for drugs that treat rare diseases. A

---

*The FDA Office of Orphan Products Development's (OOPD) mission is to advance the evaluation and development of products (drugs, biologics, devices, or medical foods) that demonstrate promise for the diagnosis and/or treatment of rare diseases or conditions.

CHAPTER SIX: Healthcare Cost And Prescription Drugs

rare disease is defined in the United States as a condition that affects fewer than 200,000 patients.[126]

The public explanation offered by the creators of this strategy is simple and clever in that it appears to be related to the public good and how much value the medications have for altering patient lives for the better. In essence, they interfere with efforts by health plans to block access to drugs. And the "special sauce" to get those medicines into the hands of customers who need them is to have copays that are often zero (even for the higher priced drugs). They add "so-called specialty pharmacies to make it hassle-free for doctors and more affordable for patients."[127]

Medicare drug benefit

In 2003, Congress created the Medicare drug benefit. This legislation "prevented the country's largest single-payer healthcare system from negotiating drug prices."[128] The end result was that Medicare could not use its significant volume — and market negotiating leverage — to manage prescription drug prices.

An interesting part of this contradiction to common sense is that the government does employ pricing strategies for other government health programs such as the Veterans Health Association (VA), Department of Defense (DOD-Tricare/Tricare For Life), 340B program*, and Medicaid. Prescription drugs are a significant component of medical care for 59 million seniors and people with disabilities.[129] This accounts for $1 out of every $6 in Medicare spending, which was $110 billion in 2015. This amounted to 29 percent of the retail sale of prescription drugs in the United States. The majority of Medicare prescription drug spending is on drugs covered under the Part D prescription drug benefit. Medicare Part B also covers drugs "administered to patients in physician offices and other outpatient settings."[130]

The Medicare drug benefit also impacted generic drug availability. The force of this issue impacted Medicare by $12 billion in 2016. Part of the cost included 50 drugs whose manufacturers have withheld or refused to sell samples so generic counter-part medications can be produced.

---

*Requires pharmaceutical manufacturers to enter into an agreement, called a pharmaceutical pricing agreement (PPA), with the HHS Secretary. Under the PPA, the manufacturer agrees to provide front-end discounts on covered outpatient drugs purchased by specified providers, called "covered entities," that serve the nation's most vulnerable patient populations.

Availability of generic drugs

Legacy drugs, or retail prescription drugs, should move from patent and exclusivity to generic in a seamless unhindered fashion, but that is not the reality. This primary strategy for reducing prescription drug cost is constantly bucking the pharmaceutical industry headwinds of "numerous business and legal strategies."[131] This is how it is supposed to work: an innovator firm develops new drugs, which are then patent-protected, which gives the firm a protection on their investment by giving them the sole right to sell the drug while the patents are in effect.[132]

When patents or other periods of exclusive marketing for brand-name drugs are near expiration, manufacturers can apply to the Food and Drug Administration to sell generic versions. Roughly 44 percent of all prescriptions in the United States are filled with generic drugs. Yet in July of 2016, the FDA generic drug application backlog comprised 4,036 generic medications.[133]

There is a process. An Abbreviated New Drug Application (ANDA) is an application for a U.S. generic drug approval for an existing licensed medication or approved drug. By year's end in 2016, a record of 835 ANDAs were approved. In 2017, there were Food and Drug Administration (FDA) approved or tentatively approved 937 ANDAs. The FDA is on pace to approve a record number of abbreviated new drug applications (ANDAs) in FY2018. The average being 67 ANDA approvals and 16 tentative approvals each month.[134]

Physician prescribing practices

Another key contributor to drug spending is when a physician prescribes a specific choice when "comparable alternatives" are available at different costs. Doctors who received money or other perks from drug and device makers, even if it's just a meal, are prescribing a higher percentage of brand name drugs overall than doctors who didn't. Some states have even tried to legislate different aspects of Marketing and Direct-To-Consumer Advertising (DTCA), including advertising, marketing, and doctor-detailing and counter-detailing.

HOW IT'S DONE: MARKETING AND DIRECT-TO-CONSUMER ADVERTISING (DTCA)

In 2012, the pharmaceutical industry spent more than $27 billion on drug promotion — more than $24 billion on marketing to physicians and over $3 billion on advertising to consumers, mainly through television commercials. This approach is designed to promote drug companies' products by influencing doctors' prescribing practices.[135]

Direct-to-consumer advertising

In 1997, FDA-issued guidance that enabled pharmaceutical companies to more easily advertise to the public. These ads have encouraged one-third of respondents to speak to their doctors about the promoted drug and one-fifth to request the prescription.[136] The United States and New Zealand are the only member countries of the Organization for Economic Cooperation and Development in which drug companies can advertise prescription drugs directly to consumers.[137]

Indirect marketing

Medical professionals require continuing medical education in order to obtain re-licensure. Continuing Medical Education (CME): in 2011, the pharmaceutical and medical device industries provided 32 percent of all funding for continuing medical education courses in the United States — $752 million out of $2.35 billion.[138] To prevent these courses from functioning as veiled marketing, the Accreditation Council for Continuing Medical Education regulates them. However, a 2007 Senate Finance Committee report found that "drug companies have used educational grants as a way to increase the market for their products in recent years."[139]

Research and development

To be fair, there is a cost associated with research and development. The cost of developing a prescription drug that gains market approval was $2.6 billion recently. This represents a 145 percent increase, correcting for inflation, over the estimate made in 2003, which was $1.4 billion.[140] The cost to develop a new pharmaceutical drug exceeded $2.5 billion in 2014.[141] That said, "In a short period, development cost is more than recouped, and some companies boast more than a 10-fold higher revenue than R&D spending — a sum not seen in other sectors of the economy."[142]

A drug in the pipeline can take 10-plus years to reach production. Big pharmaceutical companies have turned more to mergers and acquisitions. The combination of investor pressure and a narrowing window of opportunity for making a return on their investment have driven this industry change in this direction.[143] Pharmaceutical companies have changed course as changing business wisdom seems to indicate that "mergers and acquisitions" are the only way to meet their investor's expectations on 'earnings.'"[144]

By that I mean, they buy the next blockbuster drug rather than doing it the old-fashioned way of developing it in-house. In their JAMA (Journal of the American Medical Association) article, Dr. Kesslhem et al (all MDs, MPHs, and PhDs) address the issue of the relationship between high drug prices and the cost of drug development. "Although prices are often justified by the high cost of drug development, there is no evidence of an association between research and development costs and prices."[145] In the United States, the price of prescription drugs are based primarily on the basis of what the market will bear.

Whether through research and development or mergers and acquisitions, when a drug company comes up with FDA approval, they bring the approved pharmaceutical to market with flourishes and ruffles. The results? The next case study tells that story.

CASE FILE
Pharmacy Cost

1. Inherited form of vision loss

2. Symptoms include night blindness, loss of peripheral vision

3. No cure[146]

4. Newly FDA approved gene therapy[147]

5. Cost $850,000

Retinitis pigmentosa (RP) comprises a complex group of inherited forms of vision loss characterized by progressive degeneration and dysfunction of the retina, primarily affecting photoreceptor and pigment epithelial function. The clinical manifestations of RP include night blindness, loss of peripheral vision from progressive loss of photoreceptors, and variably loss of central vision due to cataracts and macular edema.

CHAPTER SIX: Healthcare Cost And Prescription Drugs 81

> Although prior to this therapy there was no cure for RP, treatments were available for managing some aspects of its clinical manifestations. This therapy is the first of its kind in the United States to deliver a fucntional gene to replace the bad one.[148]
>
> New treatments are in active development, including gene therapy, transplantation, and implanted electrical devices. The case study's purpose is to point out that Spark Therapeutics said it would charge $850,000. As I mentioned earlier, there is a cost associated with research and development. The question for consideration is "where's the beef?"* Where is the math that justifies the price?

The "market value" of a drug

It would appear that determining the market value of a newly minted pharmaceutical takes both science as well as "the art of the deal." There is no prescribed evidence-based route available to determine the retail price of these blockbuster drugs. In the articles I have read, the spokesperson cites such considerations like how effective their pharmaceutical is in helping patients live longer or have an improved state of health. The other market-driven factors of variability that are also at work are usually not mentioned.

What are these market-driven factors of variability, also known as the real reasons? "How does it compare to competitors? Are there competitors? Will payers pay for the drug? Can patients afford the copay? What is the average copay for a patient? What are other drugs priced at? How much will the company have to give in government-mandated discounts, such as the 340B clause in Medicaid? What are the cost-of-doing-business discounts to PBMs or wholesales?"[149]

So, "where's the beef?" It would appear to be in the eye of the beholder.

And the tectonic plates keep coming. In future chapters, we will talk at length about specific tectonic plates. I will outline one here because we are talking about

---

*Clara Peller (August 4, 1902 – August 11, 1987) was a manicurist and American character actress who, at the age of 81, starred in the 1984 "Where's the beef?" advertising campaign for the Wendy's fast food restaurant chain, created by the Dancer Fitzgerald Sample advertising agency.

your interest in healthcare costs, and more specifically, prescription drug costs. This tectonic plate is a short step from our case study of the $850,000 biological injectible drug as it deals with prescription drug costs of biosimilar (generic) versions of high-priced biological pharmacueticals such as our gene therapy example.

THE TECTONIC PLATE

And the tectonic plates keep coming. In this example we are dealing with that specific type of pharmaceutical I mentioned above in the case study — a biological.

What is a biological product? According to our own FDA, biological products include a wide range of products such as vaccines, blood and blood components, actual cells, gene therapy, and the like. They can be bits of sugars, proteins, or nucleic acids or more complex combinations of these bits all the way up to "living entities such as cells and tissues."

At the end of the day, biologics are from "natural sources — human, animal, or microorganism." They are often produced by "biotechnology methods and other cutting-edge technologies" such as genetic and cellular. Like our first case study, biologicals often are "at the forefront of biomedical research, and may be used to treat a variety of medical conditions for which no other treatments are available."[150]

Another side of this issue is the "copycat" phenomena. The drug industry concentrates on replicating what has already proven to be successful ("copycat") as a substitute for truly "new" drug development and "therapies that are chemically similar to established drugs — rather than on riskier, novel drugs. Critics say this tendency helps explain why therapeutic breakthroughs are increasingly less frequent."[151]

The Trump administration has issued a policy change that could drive up prices of certain biologic drugs, implementing a new industry-backed measure that overturns existing regulations that promoted lower prices. This administration's emphasis appears to be elsewhere. Even in the face of escalating prescription drug prices, this policy is a win for the drug makers. In this case, we have a new policy that ends a well thought out and cost-reducing idea. The drug makers argued the old rule would discourage investment in the generic counterpart, called "biosimilars."

The beef here is that the biological products with no generic competition result in up to 75 percent of the cost, but only a third of administrations to patients. "Spending on expensive biological medicines dwarfs their usage among patients."[152]

At the end of the day, even though generics are prescribed, the percentage of the dollars still flowing into the coffers of the original manufacturer of the antecedent legacy biological dwarfs the dollars being spent on the biosimilars, in spite of the fact that the generics are prescribed to two-thirds of the patients on such medications.

TEACHING POINT

LOWERING DRUG PRICES

We discussed your concerns about the cost of prescription drugs previously. What I didn't do was offer some advice as to what might be done to lower these costs. Clearly, the present administration is going in another direction, which falls short of more far-reaching ideas. Even though there were 50 initiatives, they did not include importation of lower cost prescription drugs nor allowing Medicare to negotiate directly with drug makers. Here is a list of suggestions for addressing the cost of prescription drugs.[153]

1. Allow the federal government to negotiate with drug companies to get lower drug prices for Medicare

2. Make it easier for generic drugs to come to market, as this,

    a. removes the barriers being thrown up by the patent-holding companies

    b. increases competition

    c. reduces cost

3. Require full disclosure of how patent holding drug companies set their drug prices

4. Place maximums on what the patent holding drug companies can charge for high-cost drugs such as biologicals, cancer and hepatitis treatment

5. Create an independent oversight committee to monitor and adjust drug prices

6. Allow the purchase of imported drugs from places such as Canada as well as online ordering

7. Eliminate prescription drug advertising/marketing especially direct to the public

8. Encourage consumer awareness by requiring higher cost share if patients elect to choose similar, higher cost drugs

Another possible approach is to require Pharmacy Benefit Managers to pass drug rebates directly back to the customer, be it the employer, the payor (such as Medicare), or to the actual consumer. Drug manufacturers of brand-name drugs pay rebates to insurers and pharmacy-benefit managers (PBMs) to offset the retail prices. These rebates go toward lowering the PBM's cost and lowering the premiums they charge their employer clients. Why not send these rebates directly to the consumers who take the drugs? Currently, only a small fraction goes to offset your premiums or to reduce your out-of-pocket costs at the pharmacy window. [154] As the controversy deepens, the blame-game is now coming to the front. In a February 5, 2019 Wall Street Journal article, "Drug firms now blame middlemen (read pharmacy benefit managers) for prices[155]."

More tectonic plates. Activists "argue that drugmakers" copay offset programs, which cover part of the higher copays patients must pay for certain drugs, promote the use of pricier brands. Drugmakers say copay coupons help defray patients' out-of-pocket costs."[156] Check out the data in the example below. I think that the activists are correct!

THE ART OF THE DEAL
$10B/YR Program

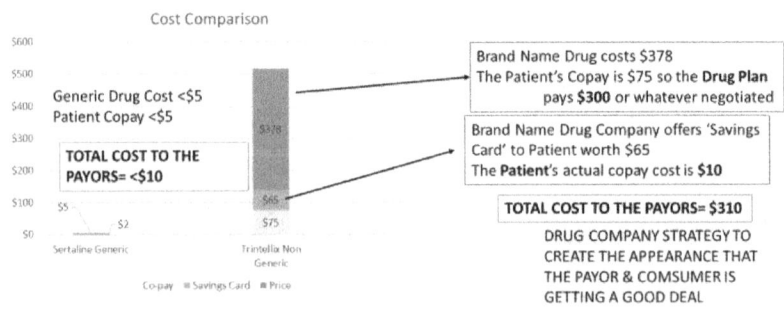

Setraline affects serotonin in the brain. Serotonin is a neurotransmitter. Antidepressants ease depression by affecting chemical messengers (neurotransmitters) used to communicate between brain cells. Setraline is a selective serotonin reuptake inhibitor (SSRI) that is frequently used as a first-line antidepressant because of its efficacy, tolerability, and general safety in overdose. In addition, SSRIs potently treat anxiety, which is often part of depressive syndromes. Trintellix is an atypical antidepression agent — it doesn't fit into other classes of antidepressants. It also works as an SSRI.

Let us compare these two head-to-head as far as cost and how the pharmaceutical industry manipulates to push the higher-priced non-generic medications over the less expensive generic drugs (see diagram above). In the brand name corner is Trintellix. In the generic corner is Sertaline. Let us see how the process works. Generally, by pretending to offer a great deal to consumers through copay off-set programs, the pharmaceutical companies will hope that nobody notices the higher cost being paid by the Second Party (Consumer) as well as the Third Party (Payor).

While the current administration may not be adequately addressing pharmacy prices, there are private (and wealthy) citizens who are. **The Institute for Clinical and Economic Review** (ICER) is a Boston-based independent nonprofit organization addressing Return on Investment (as we discussed in Chapter Three). "The ICER value framework proposes a budget impact threshold above which a drug or a product would likely contribute significantly to excessive growth in healthcare costs."[157]

CHAPTER SIX *What Have We Learned?*

Prescription drug costs more than doubled, 104 percent, between 2006 and 2013. These costs have increased 174 percent since 2005. Current trending has leveled off at just under 6 percent and is predicted to stay in that range through 2025.

Pharmaceutical cost drivers

- Monopoly rights: Pharmaceutical drugs are the only major healthcare service in which the producer is able to set prices relatively unrestrained.

- Medicare drug benefit: Congress created the Medicare drug benefit. This legislation prevented the country's largest single-payer healthcare system from negotiating drug prices.

- Availability of generic drugs: This primary strategy for reducing prescription drug cost is constantly bucking the pharmaceutical industry headwinds of numerous business and legal strategies.

- Physician prescribing practices: Physician prescribes a specific choice when "comparable alternatives" are available at different costs.

- Marketing and direct-to-consumer advertising (DTCA): In 2012, the pharmaceutical industry spent more than $27 billion on drug promotion, more than $24 billion on marketing to physicians, and over $3 billion on advertising to consumers, mainly through television commercials. This approach is designed to promote drug companies' products by influencing doctors' prescribing practices.

- Research and development: There is no evidence of an association between research and development costs and prices.

Tectonic Plates:
The Trump administration has issued a policy change that could drive up prices of certain biologic drugs, implementing a new industry-backed measure that overturns existing regulation that promoted lower prices.

The drug industry was relieved by the Trump administration's price proposal, which does not include importation of lower cost prescription drugs or letting Medicare negotiate directly with drug makers.

Some (legitimate) proposals to lower drug prices:

- Allow the federal government to negotiate Medicare drug prices
- Make it easier for generic drugs to come to market

CHAPTER SIX: Healthcare Cost And Prescription Drugs

- Full disclosure on drug prices
- Ceiling for charges on high-priced drugs
- Independent oversight of the drug industry pricing of prescription drugs
- Allowing Americans to buy imported drugs from Canada
- Eliminate prescription drug advertisement
- Healthcare consumer should be encouraged to buy lowest-cost drug
- PBM rebates should go to the healthcare consumer

CHAPTER SEVEN

Healthcare Cost and Patient Compliance

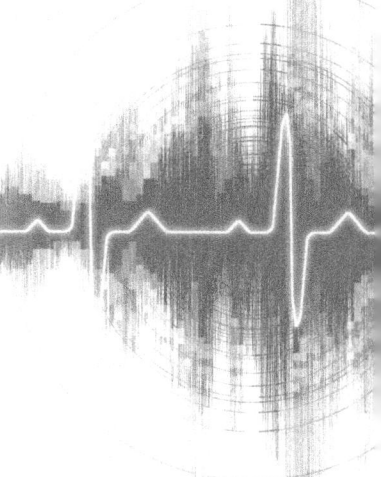

PATIENT COMPLIANCE

Nationally, voters ranked healthcare as the top issue.[158] If we break down the components of that concern, 65 percent of voters are "very concerned" about the total cost of healthcare.[159] This chapter is about a major driver of healthcare cost that has not received the attention that I believe it should: our own involvement in our healthcare and how compliant we are in doing the appropriate things to improve our health and, by extension, decrease the total cost of healthcare.

TEACHING POINT

COMPLIANCE ALONG THE HEALTHCARE CONTINUUM

The last variable we will take up before we close this discussion on concerns about healthcare costs is one that you, the reader and patient, can control: **compliance**.

In medicine, compliance describes the degree to which a patient correctly follows medical advice. Usually compliance is linked to medication or drug compliance, but for our discussion, it will apply to other situations such as any provider of healthcare (the **first party**) advice regarding your healthcare. It also applies to how well you take care of yourself. Both the patient and the healthcare provider affect compliance, and a positive physician-patient relationship is the most important factor in improving compliance. We discussed previously how important this relationship is and why your ability to access your physician is a key concern in Chapter Two.

In a piece published in The New York Times on October 31, 2000, a survey done by the Commonwealth Fund was analyzed and found that, "scores of people who have money, health insurance, and access to good medical centers are choosing not to go for checkups."[160]

CASE STUDY in Compliance

I was volunteering at the local YMCA when I began chatting with a fellow volunteer. One thing led to another and the discussion finally got around to healthcare. Imagine my surprise when my fellow volunteer explained to me that I had neglected a very important group of healthcare consumers: the healthcare consumer with good seats at the healthcare ballpark who are not encumbered by **cost**, but just do not get the healthcare they require. Here is the result of the research I did subsequently to correct my lack of knowledge. Does the case study example sound like anyone you know?

Mr. 'H. N.,' age 33, was a television producer in New York City. He avoided doctors for years until his new girlfriend insisted that he get a checkup for sexually transmitted diseases. In the article 'H. N.,' who no longer has a regular doctor, expressed many of the thoughts men have about obtaining healthcare. In this New York Times survey that 4,350 Americans completed in the year 2000, testimonials from 'H. N.' and many others indicated that one in three men and one in five women have no regular doctor. Cost remained central, but beyond that, denial and embarrassment played a key role, especially for men like 'H.N.'

Men and Compliance

Surveys show that nearly 60 percent of men won't seek medical services for a serious health problem because of underlying fear and a desire to come across as macho. Why, then, do some men refuse to go to the doctor regularly? Quotes from a **www.heart.org** survey might give us a clue:

- "I don't have a doctor."
- "I don't have insurance".

- "There's probably nothing wrong."
- "I don't have time."
- "I don't want to spend the money."
- "Doctors don't do anything."
- "I don't want to hear what I might be told."
- "I've got probe-a-phobia."
- "I'd rather tough it out." [161]

Women and Compliance

In the 2013 Kaiser Women's Health Survey of 3,000 women, doctors discussed the multitude of reasons why women don't go to the doctor.[162] The focus was meant to be on factors other than cost, yet that was still a concern about access and expense.

More than a quarter of women — 26 percent — delayed care in the past year because of cost, compared to 20 percent of men. Uninsured women were far more likely to face cost barriers than either insured women or those on Medicaid.

If we get past the **cost**, low-income women couldn't get time off work or weren't able to find childcare. Finding the time was a common reason for women across all income levels. For lower-income, female wage-earners, it often came down to not having sick days.

The Kaiser Women's Health Survey of 2017 updated the overall healthcare coverage data for women:

- Approximately 1 in 10 (12 percent) non-elderly adult women report being uninsured in 2017 (down from 18 percent in 2013);
- An additional 8 percent of women who were insured at the time of the survey had a lapse in coverage in the prior year;
- Most women are still insured through a private plan, either employer-sponsored or one they bought on their own;
- The greatest increase in coverage occurred through the expansion of the Medicaid program, which now covers 14 percent of women ages 18 to 64 (up from 9 percent in 2013).[163]

The Kaiser Women's Health Survey of 2017 demonstrated the overall demographics of the uninsured, low-income, and minority females who have been historically underserved:

- Nearly 3 in 10 women ages 18 to 64 live in households that are below 200 percent of the federal poverty level (FPL was $20,420 for a family of three in 2017);
- Nearly 2 in 5 women identify as racial and ethnic minorities (13 percent black, 16 percent Latina, and 9 percent Asian or other);
- Half are in their childbearing years;
- A sizable minority of women also report that their health is fair or poor (18 percent);
- Over 4 in 10 have a health condition that requires monitoring and treatment (45 percent).[164]

We are again discussing the social determinants of health (SDOH) previously discussed in Chapter Three. For these women in particular, access to healthcare is an essential and ongoing concern. Especially in light of those women who delayed care in the past year because of cost, couldn't find the time, couldn't get time off work, or weren't able to find childcare.

But there is another group of non-compliant healthcare consumers. Why are you or your fellow healthcare consumers with good seats at the ballpark not getting the healthcare they require? This major factor has yet to be addressed fully. In Chapter Three and Chapter Twelve, we have talked about or will discuss the uninsured and underinsured, those who do not have clear **access** to healthcare. As my fellow volunteer said, there was another group of folks who do not interface with the medical profession: the non-compliant patient. Keep in mind, a lot of the forces motivating this segment of the American population may be similar to those that impact the folks with social determinants of health (SDOH) whom we have called the underinsured and uninsured. But there is something different about this cohort.

There are numerous reasons for noncompliance, including the individual's personal feelings. Some common examples include:

- Lack of awareness regarding health-endangering vices
- Overly optimistic and convinced they will get better no matter what

CHAPTER SEVEN: Healthcare Cost and Patient Compliance

- Embarrassed to discuss symptoms
- Fear of finding out that they have a catastrophic health condition

COMPLIANCE ALONG THE HEALTHCARE CONTINUUM

Why is this subject so important? Compliance and healthcare cost go hand in hand. The Healthcare Continuum is the life cycle of healthcare as we go from "worried well" to seeking care before we hit the slippery slope of the common chronic diseases, which may ultimately end at becoming seriously ill. Each of the stops along the curve is associated with healthcare cost. By not taking care of ourselves, we are not compliant with the medical treatment being provided. That is a contributing variable to the cost of American healthcare in transition.

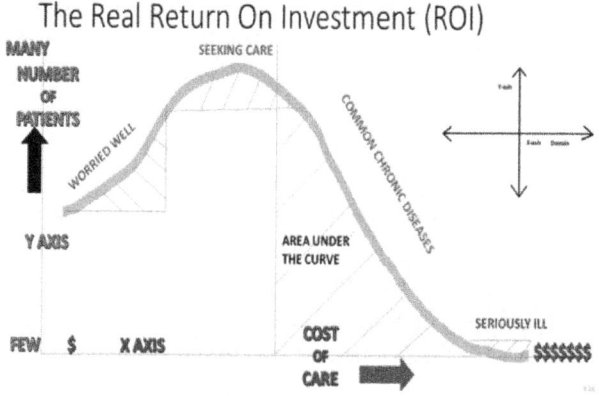

The Healthcare Continuum starts when we become concerned about staying healthy. I call this group the **worried well**. Did you get your mammogram? Have you had your lipid levels (healthy/non-healthy cholesterol among others) checked? Do you know what your blood sugar is? Your blood pressure? Do you exercise? Watch your diet? All of the things we each know are good for us but are difficult to do consistently. Most of us pay some sort of lip service to this, as we are busy living our lives.

It's important to know the projected impact of preventive services. I would recommend that you become familiar with the US Preventive Services Task Force (USPSTF) A and B Recommendations.[165] These are the evidence-based tasks (A and B refer to good evidence) that you can do as part of the **worried well** to improve your healthcare and minimize your downstream out-of-pocket healthcare costs. What might these things be? A wide array of pro-active activities from A through Z, which include preventing alcohol misuse, screening and counseling to diabetes screening, osteoporosis screening for women, and visual acuity screening for children.

Then we actually become concerned about a real medical issue that happens to wander into our lives — those darn tectonic plates again. A little elevated blood pressure; perhaps the cholesterol is a little high; some pain somewhere where it wasn't before; we get sick with anything from the flu to pneumonia. In other words, we transform from the **worried well** to actually **seeking care**. Those of us who are fortunate to remain in this position on the continuum will do so for longer periods of time. You and I have discussed **access** before (Chapter Two). We will visit this issue again throughout our journey.

Eventually, for all of us, we will have to move on to the next phase of the continuum, especially if we have been less than forthright attending to the issues that brought us to medical care in the first place. This is called **compliance**, but eventually we all enter that slippery slope on the curve called **common chronic diseases**. Care Management and improved compliance in the realm of chronic disease have a role to play on this slope of the continuum.[166]

This is where most of us live throughout our adult lives as we age. The shape of the slope will vary based on genetics and many other factors, but eventually we all enter this next phase of the Healthcare Continuum. Some of us will go on to become seriously ill with cancer or some other catastrophic medical issue. Even a relatively healthy adult who approaches the end of life will require more care. This is also the very end of the continuum, at which we become **seriously ill**.

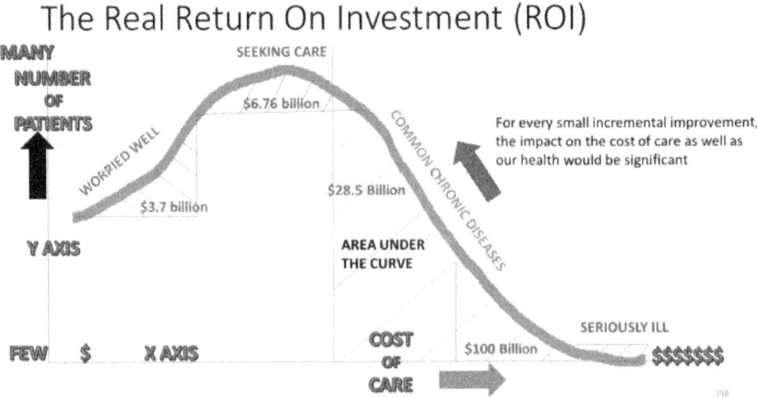

CHAPTER SEVEN: Healthcare Cost and Patient Compliance

The **area under the curve** is basically the quantity that is obtained by the product of the x and the y axis. Why is that important? Because it is a way to measure how significant any particular intervention might be along the Healthcare Continuum (or any curve for that matter). To be specific, if we are looking at healthcare cost (and we are), the **area under the curve** on our example above would represent the cost of healthcare for that particular segment. In this case, the representation of the cost of care for **worried well, seeking care, common chronic diseases**, and **seriously ill**.

In actuality, the cost of **common chronic diseases** represents a large portion of the cost of care that results, in part, from how well we as patients are compliant with taking control of our healthcare. Therefore, if we are **compliant** as **informed consumers of healthcare**, we can impact not only the state of our health but the cost of that care. Imagine if we were all compliant just a little bit more: we could inch our place on the Healthcare Continuum back toward the level of **seeking care**.

SCORECARD OF POTENTIAL SAVINGS

Worried Well	$3.7 billion
Seeking Care	$6.76 billion
Common Chronic Diseases	$28.5 billion
Seriously Ill	$100 billion

"Ninety percent of the nation's $3.3 trillion in annual healthcare expenditures are for people with chronic and mental health conditions.[167]" This is in actuality the blending of **common chronic disease** and the **seriously ill** with heart disease, stroke, cancer, and diabetes.

ARE YOU AN INFORMED CONSUMER?

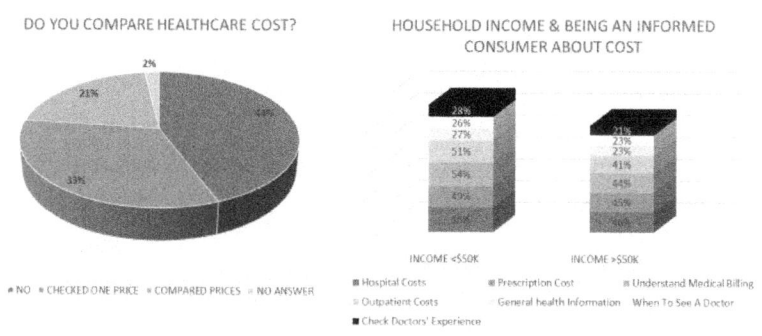

For every small incremental improvement, the impact on the cost of care as well as our health would be significant. A World Health Organization study indicated two trends: (1) only 50 percent of patients suffering from chronic diseases in developed countries follow treatment recommendations and (2) figures are even lower in respect to adherence rates for preventative therapies and can be as low as 28 percent in developed countries.[168]

How we choose to help ourselves along the Healthcare Continuum is the final and most important piece of the transformational process of victim to informed consumer. However, as the Wall Street Journal asks in an article title, "Can Consumers Be Smart Healthcare Shoppers?"[169]

I believe that we can.

CHAPTER SEVEN *What Have We Learned?*

Compliance is a healthcare cost that you, the reader and patient, can control.

Scores of people who have money, health insurance, and access to good medical centers choose to not go for healthcare. The most common reason appears to be for cost: 26 percent of women and 20 percent of men received delayed care for this reason. But 60 percent of men won't seek care just because of fear and male machismo.

The Healthcare Continuum is the life cycle of healthcare as we go from **worried well** to **seeking care** before we hit the slippery slope of the **common chronic diseases**, which may ultimately end at becoming **seriously ill**. Each of the stops along the curve is associated with healthcare cost. For every small incremental improvement on the Healthcare Continuum, the impact on the cost of care as well as our health would be significant, which is associated with compliance. Consumers can be smart healthcare shoppers if they comply.

PART B

The Law Of The Land

CHAPTER EIGHT

What Is Healthcare Insurance?

TEACHING POINT

SETTING THE STAGE: THE AFFORDABLE CARE ACT

Then came the Affordable Care Act, which had the purpose of improving affordability and accessibility and overseeing, coordinating, and governing the many pieces in play. It did, and it didn't. What it did do was stretch across both the private and public payor structure and add more Americans to the roles of the insured. It also brought controversy and the immediate call for repeal and replacement.[170]

The Affordable Care Act

Signed in March of 2010 by President Barack Obama, the original bill had added many reforms, about 400 sections in all. These reforms impacted all phases of healthcare and had far-reaching impact on how healthcare insurance and the industry providing it would be governed. I had the pleasure of listening to Tommy Thompson* discuss the ACA shortly after it was passed.

He also was pretty astute in his comments, questions, and predictions about the ACA, which he called "The Good, The Bad, and The Ugly."† In my notes from that discussion, the Good was summarized as an "action versus insurance com-

---

*Mr. Tommy George Thompson (Republican) went from state legislator in Wisconsin to 42nd Governor of Wisconsin (1987 to 2001). The United States Senate confirmed him as the 19th Secretary of Health and Human Services where he served until January 26, 2005.

†"The Good, the Bad and the Ugly" was a Western film directed by Sergio Leone and starring Clint Eastwood, Lee Van Cleef, and Eli Wallach as the namesake heroes and villains.

panies." Remember, it is the health insurance profit motive model with added administrative cost to assure profit and variability in American healthcare in transition, which is probably responsible for a fair share of the tectonic plates. That model certainly determines where you sit in the healthcare ballpark. Overseeing the insurance companies was a good thing.

The ACA extended dependent young-adult care with no limit on "damages" (insurance coverage). There were provisions for wellness and prevention. The act included Quality of Care Pay for performance (P4P) based on outcomes that would move from process to accountability for quality. It created the Centers for Medicare and Medicaid (CMS) "innovations", which included the IPAB or Independent Payment Advisory Board. The IPAB would be able to restrict the cost for Medicare as well as oversee the concept of Bundled Payments and change the way providers of healthcare would be paid. We discussed Provider Variability in Chapter Four.

As for the Bad? The law was passed as a "shell" that did not fit the statutes or law. Congress did not put the law together — the rules were still being written at the time of passage. To quote Mr. Thompson, "We really didn't know what was going on." Why was this important? He steadfastly maintained that, "We the people — subject matter experts, or SMEs — should let Washington know what is going on." It is difficult to do that when all you have is a "shell."

Mr. Thompson went on to say that constitutionally, the bill was being tested. At the time of his discussion, three states had indicated "yes" while two states had indicated "no." Ultimately, he predicted that the federal court system would decide, but that the current administration would not want that to happen in an election year. In summary, he stated: "52 percent of Americans confused."

And now for the Ugly. Nancy Pelosi, and by that, I mean her leadership in Congress, drove the process upon which Mr. Thompson had some observations. The Democrats were in power in 2008 and had replaced the heads of three powerful Congressional committees (including the Commerce Committee) and "dictated" the same healthcare bill being reported out by all three.

In spite of criticism from Republicans, there was pressure to pass the bill before Thanksgiving as the governors' races in 2009 were leaning heavily toward the Republicans. Why was this important? The states would be asked to expand Medicaid and Republican-held state houses would be less likely to. As a result, Congress stayed in session over Christmas to pass healthcare with the White House telling the Senate to "Pass it!" (Author's note: there are many similarities between

CHAPTER EIGHT: What Is Healthcare Insurance?

this process and the one which continues to occur in Congress and the current administration).

Deals were struck to pick up Senate support (including Medicaid deals). On the day before Christmas in 2009, the Senate passed the bill. However, the House and Senate were not ready for "prime time" and did not add the details. The result was that they passed a "shell", which was signed by the president. The Secretary of Health and Human Services, or HHS, was to write the rules.*

Mr. Thompson went on to make some predictions. He did not believe the law would be repealed and that the courts may change it, which they did. He also believed that presidential elections may influence it, which certainly was true with the 2016 election.

He then asked some very pertinent questions, ones that have played out in the discussions we have had in the earlier chapters:

- Will the states be able to handle the cost and volume of expanded Medicaid and the new healthcare exchanges? Mr. Thompson predicted 16 million new Medicaid patients and 16 million new healthcare exchange patients. He was correct about the first.

- Will individuals buy insurance or wait until they need it and pay the penalty? Some waited, and most paid a penalty.

- Will companies still continue to offer coverage versus paying the penalty and redistributing the difference? They did but may have influenced their employee's participation through manipulating hours as well as changing the playing field by adding more cost-sharing to their employees.

- Will hospitals and providers be able to survive in a bundled-payment environment that makes up the soon-to-come "Patient Centered Medical Home and the Accountable Care Organization? " The answer is yes for most providers, but some hospitals did not.

- Will hospitals employ providers? Again, the answer is yes.

- Will small practices survive? Even though consolidation is the norm, the answer is probably yes.

---

*United States Department of Health and Human Services or HHS is a cabinet-level department of the U.S. Federal Government. Their mission is to "[Protect] the health of all Americans and [provide] essential human services."

- Will we see concierge medicine? Yes, and many more innovations as well.

Ultimately, the former HHS Secretary saw the private sector as the best place to define the final rules and format of the ACA if we the people — patients, physicians, advocates — have a voice in the discussion, and those voices are heard. It is of interest to note the public swelling of pro-ACA support increased in volume as the political wrangling escalated in 2016 and beyond. As Tommy Thompson said, "a vacuum offers great opportunities."

A SUMMARY OF THE PROS AND CONS

The pros and cons that follow are adapted from an online healthcare guide.[171]

Pros

Did more Americans obtain health insurance? The answer is yes, as most estimates indicated that more than 16 million Americans obtained health insurance coverage within the first five years. It is of interest to note that the coveted age group of young adults — age 18-26 — appeared to be included amongst those newly insured. If a parent's health insurance plan covered dependents, young adults usually could be added to their parent's plan — either ACA marketplace or employer's — and stay on it until they turn 26.[172]

Was health insurance **more affordable**? Again, it would appear that the answer was mostly yes, but not for the obvious reasons. Insurance companies are required to spend over 80 percent of insurance premiums on medical care and improvements.[173] It is still not totally obvious if the ACA failed at the bare minimum of preventing insurers from making unreasonable rate increases or whether there were other causes.

The major positive was for people with **pre-exisiting medical conditions**. This segment of the population was no longer left out in the cold due to denial of coverage. No longer did preexisting medical conditions incumber coverage. You did run out of insurance coverage — until recently. Insurance companies previously "set limits on the amount of money they would spend on an individual patient called the **pre-set dollar** amounts."[174] After the ACA, insurance companies could no longer maintain that pre-set limit on the coverage. This is an important issue to you, the healthcare consumer. I will expand on this subject a little later on.

Preventative care received a boost as more healthcare screenings were covered. A long list of evidence-based screenings became available at little or no cost. **Lower prescription drug costs** — another one of your current concerns — became a reality as the number of prescription and generic drugs covered by the ACA grew every year. "Savings on prescription drugs exceeded $15 billion within the first five years of the ACA."[175] Yet, as we discussed earlier in Chapter Six, pharmacy costs remain a major issue.

Cons

Many people did indeed **pay higher premiums**. Cost went up as insurance companies provided a wider range of benefits and covered people with preexisting conditions. Premiums rose for a segment of the population who already had health insurance. If you didn't have insurance, your wallet became lighter due to the mandate.

Something to consider here: insurance cost strategy is based on getting a number of people who are healthy to pay premiums. This way, there are enough premium dollars to pay for those who are sick. What we may not be discussing in this debate is that by allowing children to remain covered by their parent's insurance up to age 26, it removes the premium dollars from the risk pool. Someone has to subsidize this premium loss.*

This was the downside risk to the understandable and basic important ACA goal of everyone carrying uninterrupted insurance because not having insurance passes healthcare costs on to everyone else. Yet, the requirement that the uninsured without an exemption must pay a modest fine was viewed in some circles as "government intrusion."

Taxes went up for segments of the American population. "The Affordable Care Act (ACA) made several changes to the tax code intended to increase health insurance coverage, reduce healthcare costs, and finance healthcare reform."[176] Excise taxes were to be applied to high cost health plans, health insurance providers, pharmaceuticals, and medical devices, but new taxes alone were not the only funding created; additional funding from Medicare payments was added. The American wealthy subsidized payments to cover the poor (high income surtaxes).

The **employer mandate** is something else to consider. "Some employer groups are urging the Trump administration to suspend enforcement of the Affordable Care

---

*Used with permission from Joel Brill MD, Chief Medical Officer Predictive Health

Act's (ACA) employer shared responsibility (ESR) rules and focus on working with Congress to repeal the requirements."[177] The ACA's employer mandate is still in effect at the time of this discussion. That said, there has been some movement toward changing the rules of engagement as to what defines a full-time employee, ergo impacting the number of employees that an employer with greater than 50 employees must cover.

The ACA currently requires employers with 50 or more full-time or full-time equivalent employees to offer minimum essential coverage to 95 percent of full-time employees and their dependents that is both affordable and meets minimum value as defined in the ACA. If not, employers will be assessed employer shared responsibility payments (ESRPs) as penalties for failing to comply with the healthcare law.[178]

As we headed into fall 2018, House Republicans entertained another effort to strip away the employer mandate of the ACA. According to a CBO report, the measure could cost $51.6 billion over the next 10 years.

What's in the bill?

- Retroactively lifts employer mandate penalty from 2015-2018;
- Changes definition of full-time worker who needs to be provided health insurance from 30 hours a week to 40 hours a week;
- Pushes back imposition of "Cadillac Tax" on high cost health plans until 2023.

Businesses were perceived to be manipulating payrolls through layoffs and cutting employee hours to avoid covering employees. The actual data indicated that there were no job cuts. There may have been some cutting of hours below the mandatory minimum to be considered a full-time employee and thus eligible for employer sponsored healthcare coverage.[179]

There was a **complicated enrollment process**. Not surprisingly, the newly launched ACA website had "technical problems" that created barriers to enrolling, which led to delays and enrollment falling below the levels predicted. Confusion permeated the choice process resulting in consumer complaints. "New sign-ups may be limited by lack of information about the plans and subsidies available, difficulties in navigating the sign-up process, or perceptions fanned by campaign rhetoric that the ACA is problematic or might disappear."[180]

The ACA has been under constant attack, blurring its future impact on the healthcare "system." The ACA weathered the threat of repeal and replacement. That said, Medscape published an excellent discussion on what repeal might mean to you. I have utilized the structure in that article to create the 'bones' to hang the 'meat' of each issue discussed below.* Keep an eye out for recurrent manipulations of the ACA by other administrative and legislative means. Because even without repeal and/or replacement, "Get ready for a bumpy ride."[181]

THE BUMPY RIDE: HOW THE ACA REPEAL MIGHT IMPACT YOU

Coverage for people with preexisting conditions

The subject of preexisting conditions has become an important sounding board and the primary tenant of the Affordable Care Act. Of American voters, 65 percent cite preexisting conditions as an important concern related to healthcare. I will not go into detail now about the current healthcare law of the land, as I will do so down the road in a section devoted to it. I will take a few minutes here to address this concern ahead of the detailed discussion down the pike.[182]

Newly insured adults with preexisting conditions

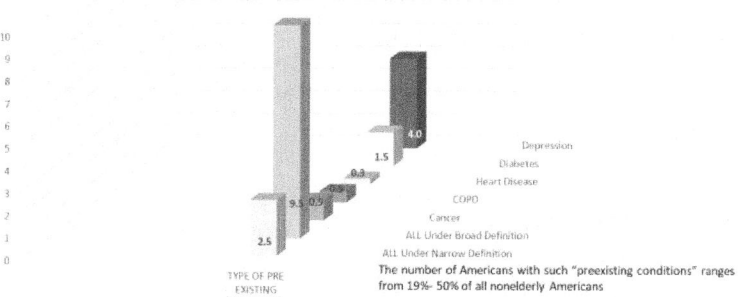

---

*The summary discussions that follow are modified from: Medscape: What's At Risk in Repealing the ACA? How Will It Affect You? Leigh Page, February 23, 2017. Additional information added along with other cited sources. Used by permission.

Health insurers cannot deny coverage or alter a plan offered to people with preexisting medical conditions.[183] A preexisting medical condition is any medical situation that is excluded from coverage by an insurance company because the health issue was believed "to exist prior to the individual obtaining a policy."[184]

"Twenty-seven percent of adult Americans under 65 years of age who have preexisting medical conditions might lose healthcare coverage (52 million people in a 2016 estimate)."[185] If those under 18 are included, a 2017 estimate indicated that, "about half of nonelderly Americans have one or more preexisting health conditions, according to a recent brief by the U.S. Department of Health and Human Services (130 million Americans who have a preexisting health condition)."[186]

There is one exception: individual health insurance policies purchased before March 23, 2010 that have not been changed to reduce benefits or increase costs to consumers will be grandfathered in.

People with Preexisting Health Conditions Can No Longer Be Denied Coverage

A preexisting condition, such as cancer, made it difficult for many people to get health insurance before the ACA. Most insurance companies wouldn't cover treatment for these conditions because the illness or injury occurred before you were covered by their plans. Under the ACA, health insurers cannot deny coverage, charge more, or make coverage exclusions for people with preexisting health conditions, such as asthma, diabetes, or cancer.[187]

Health Status Premium Underwriting

Insurers are barred from considering health status as a factor in setting a household's premium.

Relief for High Risk Individuals

This establishes two transitional programs:

- Reinsurance and Risk Corridors that run from 2014-2016 to provide funding to mitigate insurer losses that come from serving a high number of high risk individuals

CHAPTER EIGHT: What Is Healthcare Insurance?

- Establishes a permanent Risk Adjustment program that transfers money between insurers based on the risk levels of their enrollees.[188]
- In other words, those plans with sicker patients will get part of their costs subsidized by those plans with a healthier patient population.

Impact

Up to 130 million people could be adversely impacted in the healthcare insurance arena if coverage for preexisting conditions were eliminated. "Nationally, the most common preexisting conditions were high blood pressure (44 million people), behavioral health disorders (45 million people), high cholesterol (44 million people), asthma and chronic lung disease (34 million people), and osteoarthritis and other joint disorders (34 million people)."[189]

Mandates to buy insurance

WHO: individual Americans as well as employers with 50 or more full-time employees (usually working 30 or more hours a week) "must buy healthcare insurance or face monetary penalties."[190]

The data:

- Mandates are unpopular;
- In 2015, 7.5 million people or 4.5 percent of taxpayers[191] paid a fine (through income tax review) for not purchasing the required insurance (calendar year 2014) at a cost of $210/person. Flat dollar amount limit was $325.
- In 2016, 6.5 million people paid a fine (through income tax review) for not purchasing the required insurance (calendar year 2015) at a cost of $470/person (20 percent fewer than the year before).[192] Flat dollar amount limit was $695.
- In 2017, 2.5% of applicable income or $695 flat dollar amount limit adjusted for inflation
- In 2018, 2.5% of applicable income or $695 flat dollar amount limit adjusted for inflation
- 2019 and beyond 0.0 percent of applicable income or $0[193]

If removed,

1. The individual marketplace could be disrupted;
2. The risk pool would decrease and narrow to contain more ill individuals as healthy individuals delay purchasing insurance;
3. Cost for healthcare insurance would go up.

Here is the **crux of the affordability issue**: In order to lessen the exposure of risk pools for pricing insurance, younger and healthier people need to be in those pools. Without the penalty payments for not having insurance, costs for those sicker individuals in the pool will increase. Why?

1. Major innovation in U.S. public policy
2. Central pillar of health reform
   a. The CBO has projected potential losses in Americans covered by healthcare insurance;
   b. Over two-thirds of the ACA coverage increase over the last eight years, with data through the beginning of 2018, would be lost;
   c. The resultant increased risk pools of covered beneficiaries would be magnified by a predicted employer-sponsored insurance loss — due to healthy people opting out — which is estimated to be four times the current rate of employed people eligible for that coverage who choose not to carry it;
   d. This would be accompanied by an estimated potential maximum increase in premiums for ACA Individual Market Exchange Plans by 40 percent.

See Chapter Nine for a more detailed discussion of this and other ACA provisions versus the current tectonic plates.

Other insurance market reforms

There are 10 categories of services health insurance plans must cover under the Affordable Care Act. Specific services may vary based on each state's individual and particular requirements. I will list nine of those services here:

1. Ambulatory care
2. Inpatient care
3. Pharmacy
4. Rehabilitation
5. Laboratory and x-ray
6. Maternity
7. Emergency care
8. Mental health services
9. Pediatric care

Lifetime or annual payment limits

WHAT: "The current law prohibits health plans from putting annual or lifetime dollar limits on most benefits you receive."[194] In other words, no caps on what the insurance payment will be for each service or condition associated with that service.

Age bands

WHAT: The ACA limits age bands, meaning there is a limit to how much insurers can charge older people compared with younger people.

What are age bands?

1. Older age is thought to equate with higher healthcare costs for care and treatments.

2. By 55 years of age, we cross the $3,000 per year healthcare cost line. By 69 years of age, we hit the $4,000 per year cost line. By 75 years old, we are nearing healthcare costs of $12,000 per year. By 80 years old, we are nearing $15,000. It goes up exponentially from there.

3. Enter the age band rating, which governs what healthcare insurers can charge by way of higher premiums from older consumers over younger, healthier ones as a means of covering that expected increased cost of healthcare.

4. Prior to the ACA, the age band rating was at a 5:1 ratio, meaning that insurers "cannot charge seniors more than five times what younger patients pay in premium value."[195] The ACA limits this to a 3:1 ratio.

5. Costs comparisons can be drawn across age, race, gender, occupational groups, categories of injuries and illnesses.[196]

If these other market reforms are removed,

1. Premiums could be lower, but coverage would be less;
2. Annual or lifetime payments would be limited;
3. The likelihood of patients obtaining these services decreases.

Cost-free preventive services for patients

This next provision is really aligned with the one above. Think of it as the teeter-totter of healthcare coverage (only a pediatrician would think of that metaphor). The two are provisions that cover nine categories of care and preventative care are fundamentally linked in an inverse relationship. Messing with one impacts the other.

WHAT: The United States Preventive Task Force services previously mentioned lists the screening tests, counseling services, and preventive medicine[197], which have been shown to be effective in preventing illnesses before they cause you symptoms or problems.

1. Cost-free preventive services must be covered;
2. The goal is to:
    (a) Provide the patient and their family with "the most accurate and up-to-date information on ways to prevent illness and improve health and well-being"[198];
    (b) Provide a pathway for doctors, nurses, and other primary care professionals to render the recommended preventive care for their patients — you the healthcare consumer.

If this is removed, the risk is that people will wait until their disease is more advanced. This means more cost and lower life expectancy. See Chapter Six for further discussion about the Healthcare Continuum.

Medicaid expansion

WHAT: This linchpin issue has become how to maintain insurance coverage obtained under the ACA, as Medicaid has become the largest source of funding for medical and health-related services for people with low income in the United States. How does Medicaid expansion work?

- States get subsidies for expanding Medicaid. Although this figure is up to 133 percent of the federal poverty level (FPL), because of the way this is calculated, it turns out to be actually 138 percent.[199]
- Medicaid eligibility expanded to include eligible childless adults who were previously excluded in many states.

Other factors besides income that enter into the eligibility discussion include household size, disability, and family status, but eligibility rules differ amongst the various states. Generally, "Medicaid recipients must be U.S. citizens or legal permanent residents, and may include low-income adults, their children, and people with certain disabilities."[200]

1. In 2012, the Supreme Court weighed in, much like Mr. Thompson predicted, and eliminated the mandatory aspect of it, making expansion voluntary at the state level.[201]
2. By 2017, Medicaid expansion provided health insurance to 74 million low-income and disabled people" with 32 states, including Washington, D.C., participating.
3. In 2018, Idaho, Utah, Nebraska, and North Carolina were taking a second look at expanding their Medicaid programs.
4. There is also a debate about Medicaid expansion playing a central role in the midterm elections in Florida, Georgia, and Kansas.[202]
5. The Virginia General Assembly approved expansion of Medicaid.[203] Their governor is expected to ink his name to the bill.
6. This is unlike Maine, where the head of the state government has absolutely refused to endorse this legislative initiative even after Maine voters voted overwhelmingly to approve Medicaid expansion.[204]

If this is removed, the Congressional Budget Office (CBO) and the Joint Committee on Taxation (JCT) estimate that enacting the repeal legislation would result in an increase in the number of people who are uninsured by 18 million in the first year following enactment of the bill. After the elimination of the ACA's expansion of Medicaid eligibility and of subsidies for insurance purchased through the ACA marketplaces, that number would increase to 27 million and then to 32 million in 2026.[205]

Subsidies in the market place

WHAT: Subsidies to buy healthcare insurance are available to eligible beneficiaries, or those households with incomes up to 400 percent of the Federal Poverty Level (FPL).[206] Here is the scoop on subsidies.

1. Two types of subsidies:

    (a) premium tax credit

    (b) cost sharing subsidies

2. Subsidized Coverage: how much money is enough to guarantee that there is adequate subsidy money and tax credits to offset the impact of any changes in this mandate? [207]

3. There are calculators available to assist people.[208]

If this is removed,

1. The CBO estimated in June 2017 that "the number of people with health insurance would decrease by 4 million in 2019 and 13 million in 2027;"[209] and

2. Might also "spell the end of the Individual Healthcare Marketplace, which relies heavily on subsidies."[210]

Or would it? According to the Henry Kaiser Family Foundation, premiums would be affected in 2018, but the ACA marketplace would survive. "These results are generally consistent with a KFF estimate released in April 2018 projecting that silver marketplace premiums would have to increase by 19 percent on average to compensate for the loss of Cost Sharing Subsidy (CSR) payments, with the amount varying substantially by state."[211] Please see Chapter Nine for further details.

CHAPTER EIGHT: What Is Healthcare Insurance?

Innovation Center and value-based payments

WHAT: The Centers for Medicare and Medicaid Innovation (CMMI)

1. The "capstone" for moving away from Fee-For-Service Medicare payments to value-based payments (See Chapter Four);
2. Focus on Cost/Quality/Outcomes

If this is removed,

1. A simple Senate majority could strip the agency of its funding, which amounted to $1.4 billion to operate in 2015 fiscal year, according to the Centers for Medicare & Medicaid Services, or CMS, budget report.[212]
2. Congress would lose potential savings of $34 billion that the agency is expected to generate from 2017 to 2026.[213].

Closing the Medicare prescription drug 'donut hole'

WHAT: ACA gradually reduces the 'donut hole' until it disappears in 2020.

Before the ACA,

- "Medicare Part D drug coverage ended after a certain dollar amount;
- Drug payment would resume only when catastrophic coverage was triggered".

Here is how the donut hole works:[214]

The Donut Hole

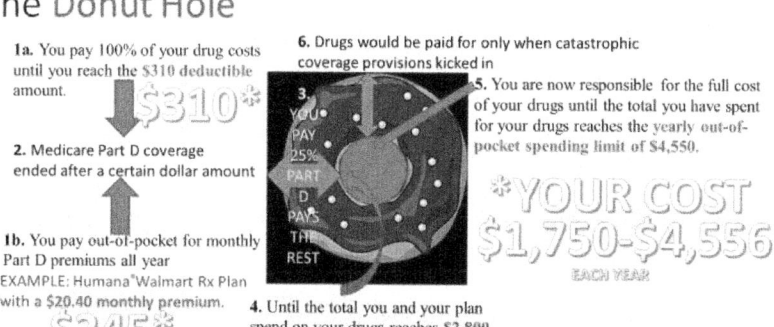

Taxes funding the ACA

WHAT:

The government

1. "Levies significant taxes on:
   (a) pharmaceutical manufacturers,
   (b) medical device manufacturers,
   (c) health insurers,
   (d) wealthy citizens,
   (e) tanning booths;
2. Taxes help to pay for coverage expansion and the Centers for Medicare and Medicaid Innovation (CMMI) expenses;
3. Reduced payments to Medicare Advantage Plans;
4. Cuts Medicare Disproportionate Share Hospital payments, which compensates hospitals for providing care to non-paying patients.[215] This federal law requires that state Medicaid programs make "Disproportionate Share Hospital (DSH) payments to qualifying hospitals (3,109 hospitals) that serve a large number of Medicaid and uninsured individuals." The ACA expansion of Medicaid "aimed to reduce funding for the Medicaid DSH program by $17.1 billion between 2014 and 2020."[216]
5. Starting in 2020, the ACA levies an annual 40 percent excise tax on plans with annual premiums that exceed $10,800 for individuals or $29,500 for a family to be paid by insurers."[217] These are the so-called Cadillac Health plans.

If these taxes are removed,

1. The ACA would lose funding for coverage expansion placing that at risk;
2. Some other source of funding sources would need to be found to fund replacement plans for the ACA.

Independent Payment Advisory Board

WHAT:

1. The Independent Payment Advisory Board, or IPAB, is a

    (a) United States Government agency consisting of 15 members;

    (b) With a goal of Medicare savings "without affecting coverage or quality."[218]

2. It was not triggered in 2017.

3. The IPAB doesn't

    (a) Reduce current Medicare benefits, premiums, or co-payments;

    (b) Raise taxes.

4. The IPAB does

    (a) Impact spending by decreasing provider/device makers/drug company Medicare payments;

    (b) Send the "recommended reductions to Congress to trigger an expedited review"[219].

5. If Congress doesn't legislate the cost savings, the IPAB's recommendations will go into effect automatically.

6. The IPAB has flaws:

    (a) No accountability to elected representatives/ voters; and

    (b) Cannot enact reform or structural change in healthcare.

If the IPAB is removed, another way to control federal healthcare spending would need to be initiated in its stead.

THE CHALLENGE CONTINUED

This war against the ACA is generally out of sight from the general public, unless someone goes looking. There has been a conservative strategy with the cooperation of Congressional Republicans to "cut the budget, impose debilitating regulations, track the subsequent missteps, and then attack the program as a failure."[220]

In 2014, House Republicans challenged the constitutionality of cost-sharing reductions (CSRs) in federal court. "On May 12, 2016, Judge Rosemary Collyer of the federal district court for the District of Columbia decided that the Obama administration cannot constitutionally reimburse insurers for the costs they incur in fulfilling their obligation under the ACA to reduce cost sharing for marketplace enrollees with incomes below 250 percent of the poverty level. Judge Collyer found that Congress has not specifically appropriated money for this purpose"[221].

1. The Obama Administration appealed this ruling;
2. With the election of Trump in 2016, everything was placed on hold;
3. In July 2017, state attorney generals were allowed to become involved;
4. On October 12, 2017, the Trump administration announced that it would not defend the CSRs as the administration felt them to be illegal;
5. As of that date, the payments were stopped[222].

"The move could actually force the government to dole out almost $200 billion more on health insurance over the next decade" as consumers still received the premium tax credit and insurers raised premiums to offset the loss of the subsidy.[223] As a result, discontinuing the insurer cost-sharing subsidies led to the premium tax credits being pushed higher. Consumer premium tax credits are far bigger than the cost-sharing subsidies given to insurers making this appear to be an extremely costly trade.

CHAPTER 8 *What Have We Learned?*

The Affordable Care Act's purpose was to improve affordability and accessibility and to oversee, coordinate, and govern the many pieces in play. It did, and it didn't. What it did do was stretch across both the private and public payor structure and add more Americans to the roles of the insured. It also brought controversy. And the immediate call for repeal and replacement.

There were pros and cons:

Pros:

- 16 million more Americans have health insurance
- Health insurance is more affordable for many people
- People with preexisting health conditions can no longer be denied coverage
- No time limits on care
- More screenings are covered
- Lower prescription drug costs

Cons:

- Many people have to pay higher premiums
- You can be fined if you don't have insurance
- Taxes are going up
- The wealthy are helping to subsidize insurance for the poor
- Enrolling can be complicated
- Businesses are cutting employee hours to avoid covering employees

Preexisting conditions
Under the ACA, people with preexisting health conditions can no longer be denied coverage.

Somewhat more that a quarter of adult Americans with preexisting conditions may be at risk of losing coverage or have their coverage become extremely expensive and/or prohibitive. This number may be closer to 130 million.

Another tectonic plate is shifting toward a preexisting condition near you. There is a war going on outside of the failed Republican attempt to repeal and/or replace the ACA. Whether by presidential fiat, Congressional legislation or Republican state governors' and attorneys' general actions, you, the healthcare consumer, need to be aware of its clandestine existence and the potential impact on you.

CHAPTER NINE

Tectonic Plates

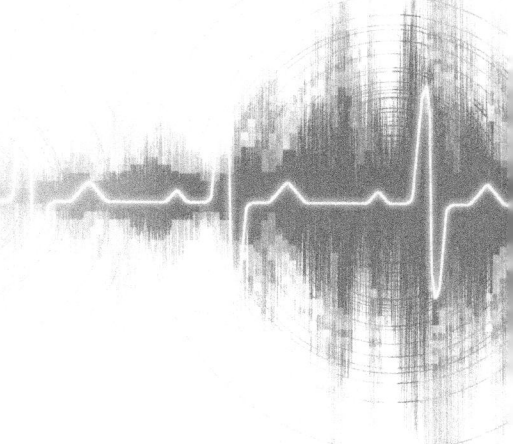

HEALTHCARE CONSUMER'S CONCERNS ABOUT THE ACA
(THE GOOD, THE BAD, AND THE UGLY)

As previously mentioned, voters ranked healthcare as the top issue.[224] If we break down the components of that concern, one area where a good majority of voters are focused is the Affordable Care Act. This chapter is about that major driver of consumer concern with some emphasis on preexisting conditions, repealing the ACA, and stabilizing the ACA marketplace.[225]

In a July 2018 poll, the Democrats' healthcare message was resonating with critically important blocs of midterm voters, according to Axios/SurveyMonkey polling. The big picture was that Democrats were moving left on healthcare and embracing the Affordable Care Act. Candidates were increasingly accepting a bigger role for the federal government. The voters they needed most in the 2018 midterm elections — including white suburban women and millennials — were largely on board.

"**The bottom line:** The ACA helped Republicans win previous midterm elections — and now the repeal effort has given the Democrats a weapon to use to motivate their base and reach out to independents."[226] The Wall Street Journal published an article on September 4, 2018 based on a Kanta Media/GMAG survey. Political advertising was tracked to determine the number of mentions for each topic of interest in the campaign. Healthcare dominated the messaging from the Democratic candidates, with 155,393 advertising mentions of healthcare in 2018 as of mid-August 2018. It was by far the No. 1 advertising message. Republican candidates on the other hand only had 48,125 advertising mentions. Trump (90,314), taxes (79,456), and immigration (73,919) were the major Republican hot buttons.[227]

In this chapter, we will discuss the tectonic plates impacting the ACA.

THE TECTONIC PLATES

Just when you have taken your seat and felt that you were going to enjoy the ballgame, the ground begins to shake beneath you. In actuality, those tremors occur on a regular basis, but until you actually sit in the ballpark of healthcare coverage, you probably won't notice them; not until something untoward happens, like you get sick and need healthcare, and the shade of the overhanging bleachers that you took for granted suddenly isn't protecting you from the sun anymore.

This fact is not dissimilar to the impact of healthcare coverage decisions or the uncertainty of politics on each of us as patients, providers, or advocates. I have discussed this before, but it is an important concept and needs to be addressed once again. Basically, the rigid outer crust of the planet is divided into seven or so primary plates which slide along each other. When that flow is impeded, pressure mounts up. The ground begins to shake, and we have earthquakes. For our discussion think of them as being the unstable relationship we have in this country with how healthcare is acquired and paid for — the unstable relationship of American Healthcare in transition and **cost, access,** and **quality**! The untoward results of deficit reduction and the health insurance for-profit model our American healthcare in transition is based upon. We will address them all.

TEACHING POINT

TECTONIC PLATE IMPACT ON THE AFFORDABLE CARE ACT (ACA)

ACA revamp must include conservative values

This Republican mantra includes,

- letting insurers charge higher premiums to older people;
- supporting a permanent congressional appropriation for subsidies to insurance companies who decrease deductibles and copays for lower-income consumers in exchange for explicit exclusions on abortion coverage;
- allowing for the renewal of short-term plans that don't comply with the health law;
- block funding from organizations that may have a role in abortion insurance coverage or procedures;

- changes to health-savings accounts, which are tax-free accounts used by consumers who have insurance policies with high deductibles;
- blocking billions of dollars in subsidies that insurers were getting to help pay for subsidies for lower-income consumers; and
- a proposed rule that would loosen restrictions on short-term health plans that don't provide the same consumer protections as ACA compliant plans.[228]

Preexisting conditions

Why should this issue be important to you as an informed consumer of healthcare? Another tectonic plate is shifting toward a preexisting condition near you.[229]

Short-term insurance policies

- Exclude those with preexisting conditions;
- Don't have to offer comprehensive coverage; and
- Impose annual/lifetime limits.[230]

Association health plans (AHP)

- Executive order from President Trump;
- Bid to expand healthcare coverage to small business owners, entrepreneurs, and their employees as well as the self-employed;
- Under an AHP, coverage could be less robust, which would mean that the plans would be more likely to attract healthier people.[231]

And to shake the ground even more, lawsuits abound concerning the constitutionality of the ACA. Based on the Trump administration's earlier action of eliminating the individual mandate (see below) and proposing short-term insurance plans without coverage for preexisting conditions, Republican governors joined the fray. They were supported by a Justice Department brief supporting the lawsuit of the 20 state attorneys suing to end the ACA on the grounds that it is unconstitutional without the mandates and preexisting condition coverage.[232]

Here are some key facts to know about the case:

- The Justice Department filed a brief in this lawsuit;
- The administration wants an end to ACA guarantee of coverage of preexisting health conditions;
- The administration wants to raise limits on how much insurance companies can charge seniors and women;
- It impacts the individual marketplace and employer-paid health insurance;
- It allows employers to impose waiting periods before new hires' health insurance kicks in; and
- Employers could opt-out of covering new hires' preexisting medical conditions.

A Commonwealth Issues Brief spelled out the following information:

- Between 2013 and 2015, 16.5 million non-elderly adults gained coverage following full ACA implementation;
- Of these people, 2.6 million had preexisting conditions and were otherwise precluded from coverage because of discriminatory denials and pricing;
- Another 9.4 million had conditions that could have otherwise affected insurance cost; and
- The proposals to replace current protections for people with preexisting conditions with high-risk pools are unlikely to maintain the ACA's gains.[233]

Coverage mandates

The individual mandate was modified under the 2017 tax package passed by the Republican-controlled houses of Congress and enacted on December 22, 2017. Although the penalty was in effect for 2018, the law effectively eliminated the penalty associated with the individual mandate beginning in 2019[234].

Individuals and employers with 50 or more full-time workers have to buy insurance or face financial penalties. These mandates are quite unpopular. This was the ACA's inducement to get young and healthy people to buy insurance. Without it, healthier people were expected to drop out of the market with resultant increased insurance premiums but savings for the federal government (deficit reduction).

Defanging the individual mandate would result in 13 million fewer Americans having health insurance and the federal government saving $338 billion over the next 10 years[235]. Premiums in the unsubsidized ACA Individual Exchange Plans will be 6 percent higher than if the individual mandate had not been removed[236].

It was initially supposed to be an executive order, but Congress used tax reform to remove it in 2017.

Now, 20 Republican state attorneys are suing the federal government to end the ACA. Their premise is that if the penalty is no longer applicable, then the individual mandate is illegal. This, in turn, makes the ACA unconstitutional. As I mentioned above, it has been extended to include the preexisting conditions as well. The Justice Department will not defend the mandate in court (see above — same lawsuit indicating unconstitutionality, just different justification).

And at the time of this writing, House Republicans were preparing a new vote concerning the ACA employer mandate.

1. The bill,

- Retroactively lifts employer mandate penalty from 2015 to 2018;
- Changes definition of full-time worker who needs to be provided health insurance from 30 hours a week to 40 hours a week;
- Pushes back imposition of "Cadillac Tax" on high-cost health plans until 2023.[237]

2. House GOP bill delaying key parts of the ACA will cost over $50 billion.[238]

It's another nail in the coffin as far as the Republicans suing to end the ACA are concerned, as they believe the ACA to be unconstitutional now that the Republican administration has removed key elements by fiat and tax bill.

On December 14, 2018, a federal judge in Texas ruled the ACA unconstitutional on the very grounds that if you remove the individual mandate that everyone needs to have health insurance (remember our broken For-Profit Healthcare Insurance Model?), the ACA is unconstitutional. "The ruling, while invalidating the law, didn't immediately block enforcement of the ACA, a situation that could trigger widespread uncertainty in the near term. Some states could stop enforcing or administering the law, including Medicaid expansion, starting January 1, when the elimination of the penalty takes effect."[239]

Remember, the Supreme Court upheld the ACA in 2012 as a tax, and as such, enacting it was in the purview of Congress. There now becomes the question whether this ruling will be allowed to stand as Congress, through its inability to repeal and replace the ACA in 2017, left most of the ACA intact.

"Our analysis shows that if the entire law were eliminated, the number of uninsured people would increase by 17.1 million, or 50 percent, in 2019; this estimate reflects coverage losses over and above the losses associated with setting the individual mandate penalties to $0."[240]

Other insurance market reforms including cost-free preventive services

Per the ACA, insurers must cover 10 categories of essential benefits.[241] Insurers must cover certain preventive services with minimum cost-share to the patient.[242] Insurers are also prohibited from putting lifetime or annual payment limits on these benefits. The ACA limits age bands, meaning that there's a limit to how much insurers can charge older people compared with younger people.[243] "The HHS Assistant Secretary for Planning and Evaluation (ASPE) estimated approximately 137 million people (55.6 million women, 53.5 million men, and 28.5 million children) have received no-cost coverage for preventive services since the policy went into effect."[244]

The Trump administration continues its assault on the ACA by introducing "Short-term" health plans. Originally designed to cover employees changing jobs for a 90-day window only, Republicans are determined to offer them for up to three years duration as an alternative to the ACA. "Short-term plans don't include all routine medical needs. Two important exclusions are preexisting conditions and maternity coverage. Often, drug coverage and services for preventive, dental, vision, and mental healthcare are also excluded."[245]

In a review of existing "Short-term Insurance Policies," the Kaiser Family Foundation found the following information:

CHAPTER NINE: Tectonic Plates

SHORT TERM HEALTH PLANS

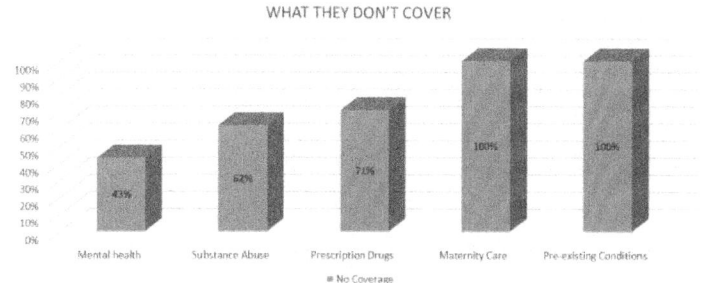

Covered benefits:

- Does not adhere to the ACA Protections of Preventive Services/10 Essential Health Benefits
- Giving healthy consumers more choice to the detriment of those with healthcare needs
- Giving consumers lower premiums but greater risk for out-of-pocket costs

Consumer beware:

- What isn't covered
- Potential downstream out-of-pocket cost[246]

And the hits keep coming: "More employers can opt out of providing contraception coverage to their employees under final regulations from the Trump administration that narrow the Affordable Care Act's contraceptive mandate[247]."

Medicaid expansion

This is the joint federal and state program that helps with medical costs for some people with limited income and resources that are insufficient to pay for healthcare. It offers benefits not normally covered by Medicaid, like nursing home care and personal care services.[248] Here is the Medicaid Data.[249]

WHO IS IN THE PROGRAM

- Children through CHIPS
- Newly-eligible adults
- Existing beneficiaries without disabilities under 65 yo
- People with disabilities
- Aged (over 65 yo)
- Includes Veterans
- NB: groups tend to merge with some beneficiaries being in multiple buckets
- Including Dual eligible Medicare/Medicaid beneficiaries

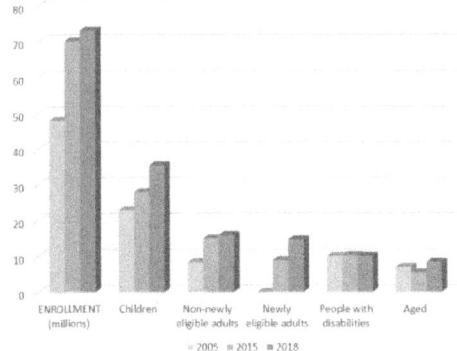

Adopted from multiple sources to include CMS.gov, Kaiser Family Foundation and others

In the ongoing battle over Medicaid, the Republicans want to shrink it (cut its spending and add restrictions so that it serves fewer people). The Democrats want to expand it (increase its funding and reach so it serves millions more people).

The Medicaid expansion program had been tremendously popular, adding millions to the Medicaid rolls. The CBO estimated up to 14 million would lose coverage. The actual numbers vary somewhat depending upon whether the AHCA or BCRA is used as the model. This puts strain on emergency departments and federally funded community health centers, which could also lose their ACA funding.

As of March 2016, the Centers for Medicare and Medicaid Services (CMS) reported that nearly 72.5 million individuals were enrolled in Medicaid/CHIP. Since the beginning of the ACA's first Open Enrollment Period in October 2013, Medicaid/CHIP enrollment has grown by 20 million individuals.[250]

Subsides in the marketplace

On the ACA's state-based healthcare marketplaces, subsidies to buy insurance are available to people who have household incomes of up to 400 percent of the federal poverty level.[251] There are two kinds of subsidies: one for premiums, the other for healthcare expenses.[252]

New tectonic plate changes would leave vulnerable constituents — patients like you — without important protections. At the end of the day, you generally qualify for Medicaid if you are at 44 percent of the Federal Poverty Line (FPL) and for individual insurance marketplace subsidies from 100 to 400 percent of the FPL. This still leaves a large portion of the population without subsidies in the states that did not expand Medicaid coverage, between 44 and 100 percent of the FPL.[253]

But first a reminder about what we are talking about.

HEALTHCARE 101 How Health Care Insurance Flows

THE EOB

PREMIUM
PREMIUM TAX CREDITS

COVERAGE
BENEFIT COVERAGE
IN NETWORK
DEDUCTIBLE

Must Be Met First Before Your Health Insurance Kicks In

Must Actually Be A Covered Benefit

MEDICAL NECESSITY
EXPERIMENTAL

Must Actually Be Supported By Evidence Based Process

EXPLAINATION OF BENEFITS
1. Billed By Provider
2. What Plan Covers
3. Your Possible Bill
COINSURANCE

COPAY
Paid At The Time And Place Of Service

MONEY OUT OF YOUR POCKET
COST SHARING REDUCTIONS

Halting some ACA cost-sharing

There are consequences with keeping the premium tax credit while insurer cost-sharing subsidies are discontinued:

- without subsidies, healthcare would cost the same for everybody;
- premium tax credits are not stopped;
- ACA Mandated Cost-sharing Reductions: as previously discussed, the Trump Administration halted these in 2017;
- insurers raised prices;
- taxpayer pays for the increased premium tax credit;
- increased premium for those who do not qualify for subsidies; and
- paradoxical lower total costs for people who get premium tax credits.

So, at the end of the day what was the result of Trump's decision to stop the cost-sharing subsidies?

"President Donald Trump is halting some ACA cost-sharing subsidies. Big money saver for taxpayers, right? Wrong. The move could actually force the government to dole out almost $200 billion more on health insurance over the next decade."[254]

There was also a downstream impact.

Insurers exit from ACA marketplace

- The Republicans claim that there is a need to appeal/replace ACA;
- The tectonic plates we have been discussing have led to insurer's exiting from some markets and/or having rate increases;
- The Democrats claim that insurers are reacting to the uncertainty created by the Republicans.[255]

The exodus was heavy in 2017. As we turned the page to 2018 and beyond, there were signs of some insurance carriers returning to the marketplace.[256] More insurers are participating in the ACA marketplaces in 2019.[257]

Premium increase for the ACA marketplace

The CBO estimates that:

- the individual marketplace will not implode secondary to changes in subsidies;
- additional government funding estimated at $7 billion in 2018;
- would raise premiums for mid-priced plans;
- leaves slightly more people without an insurer[258].

"Although 2019 premiums for plans in the ACA marketplaces are flat or falling in many places, they would be substantially lower still if not for several key policy and legislative changes."[259]

Premium Impacts from Legislative and Policy Changes to the ACA

Legislative or Policy Change	Average percent by which 2019 unsubsidized premiums are higher than would be the case without change
• Individual mandate penalty repeal • Expansion of AHP*/STLD**plans	6% (all premiums on/off exchange)
• Loss of CSR*** payments	10% (silver exchange premiums)
Combined Impact: • Individual mandate penalty repeal • Loss of CSR payments • Expansion of AHP/STLD plans	16% (silver exchange premiums)

*AHP=Association Health plans **Short-term Limited Duration Health plans
***Cost Sharing Reduction (CSR) for out-of-pocket expenses

Insurers lose suit to recoup loses

Risk corridors were created to make sure that insurers who enrolled a sicker patient population would not be penalized, and the insurers who enrolled a healthier population would not reap windfall profit. This provision was to level the playing field so that insurers would not leave the marketplace. Instead of sharing the risk, here is what happened:

- Administration collected money from insurers;
- This money was redistributed with more going to insurance companies that lost money in the Individual marketplace;
- Government didn't collect enough to cover all cost;
- Government promised to cover certain insurance company costs even with this shortfall;
- The administration had disallowed payments because Congress didn't authorize;
- Insurance companies have filed multiple lawsuits and lost one at the time of this discussion.[260]

Fortunately, as of this writing, the administration has restarted these payments.[261] But stay tuned — tectonic plates have a way of changing.

TEACHING POINT

ADDRESSING YOUR CONCERN ABOUT STABILIZING THE ACA MARKETPLACE

Here is the ideal point in our discussion to add the ACA Individual marketplace into the mix.

This is for those of you who, with or without qualifying for subsidies, are considering buying healthcare coverage on the ACA individual marketplace. That is assuming that the lawsuit to make the ACA unconstitutional does not remain confirmed after appeal.

The cost burden created has hit the unsubsidized previous enrollees in the wallet. They have to pay the whole cost on their own. The data? The Henry J. Kaiser Family Foundation, or just Kaiser Family Foundation (KFF), is an American non-profit organization, headquartered in San Francisco, California. It focuses on major healthcare issues facing the nation, as well as U.S. role in global health policy. You have seen data from them throughout this book. The Kaiser Family Foundation analysis found the following:

- The individual marketplace increased by 64 percent to 17.4 million people in 2015 following implementation of the ACA;
- The individual marketplace remained "relatively unchanged" in 2016 (17.0 million people);
- In 2017, there was a 12 percent decline (15.2 million people);
- Enrollment has continued to fall in early 2018:
  - First quarter enrollment had declined by 12 percent
  - When the dust settled however, 14.4 million people enrolled as of the first quarter of 2018.[262]
  - This figure is greater than the 10.6 million people enrolled in 2013.[263]

Due to a surge in the last week of the ACA 2019 sign-ups on Healthcare.gov, nearly 8.5 million people enrolled in a health plan for 2019 on the federal insurance marketplace. Enrollment had been lagging 10 to 15 percent behind last year's numbers for most of the enrollment period. After a strong final few days, they closed just 300,000, or 4 percent, shy of 2018's totals.[264]

Remember that this does not include the totals from the individual state sites that remain functioning. Those numbers should be added to the Healthcare.gov site figures for the final tally. Here is that list of state exchanges:

- California 1.5 million
- Colorado 162,000
- Connecticut 114,000
- District of Columbia 19,000
- Idaho 94,000
- Maryland 153,00
- Massachusetts 267,000
- Minnesota 116,000
- New York 253,000
- Rhode Island 33,021
- Vermont 28,000
- Washington 243,000[265]

CHANGES IN THE INDIVIDUAL MARKETPLACE PREMIUM AND OUT-OF-POCKET COSTS

Let us begin with a brief introduction to the ACA marketplace and the plans being offered. I euphemistically call them the Precious Metal Plans.[266]

ACA exchange plans

Bronze
- Lowest monthly premium;
- Highest costs when you need care;
- Bronze plan deductibles — the amount of medical costs you pay yourself before your insurance plan starts to pay — can be thousands of dollars a year;
- Good choice if you want a low-cost way to protect yourself from worst-case medical scenarios, like serious sickness or injury. Your monthly premium will be low, but you'll have to pay for most routine care yourself.

Silver
- Moderate monthly premium;
- Moderate costs when you need care;
- Silver deductibles are usually lower than those of Bronze plans;
- Previously, if you qualified for cost-sharing reductions you had to pick a Silver plan to get the extra savings. You could have saved hundreds or even thousands of dollars per year if you used a lot of care;
- The cost-sharing reductions have been discontinued by the administration;
- Used to be a good choice if you qualified for "extra savings" or were willing to pay a slightly higher monthly premium than Bronze to have more of your routine care covered.

Gold
- High monthly premium;
- Low costs when you need care;
- Deductibles are usually low;
- Good choice you're willing to pay more each month to have more costs covered when you get medical treatment. If you use a lot of care, a Gold plan could be a good value.

Platinum
- Highest monthly premium;
- Lowest costs when you get care;
- Deductibles are very low, meaning your plan starts paying its share earlier than for other categories of plans;
- Good choice if you usually use a lot of care and are willing to pay a high monthly premium, knowing nearly all other costs will be covered.

Note: Plans in all categories provide free preventive care, and some offer selected free or discounted services before you meet your deductible.

Your premium can be lower, based on your income.

And what about the premiums?

Premiums

The reality of the 2016 marketplace premiums

Average Monthly Premiums in 2016 SILVER (UNDER ACA)

Individual Age Premium	2016 Avg.	2015 Avg.	Premium Difference
30-year-old	$312.00	$283.16	10%
40-year-old	$351.02	$318.48	10%
50-year-old	$490.75	$445.33	10%
60-year-old	$744.99	$675.76	10%[267]

The second-lowest silver plan is one of the most popular plan choices on the marketplace and is also the benchmark that is used to determine the amount of financial assistance individuals and families receive. From 2015 to 2016, the premium increased 10 percent.

Increases in Lowest Marketplace Silver and Gold Premiums, 2017–2018 monthly premiums are for a 40-year-old nonsmoker[268]:

MEASURE LOWEST SILVER PREMIUMS	2017	2018	Percentage Change
U.S. AVERAGE	$342	$444	32%
MEASURE LOWEST GOLD PREMIUMS	2017	2018	Percentage Change
U.S. AVERAGE	$439	$518	19.1%

Some of you will qualify for low- or zero-insurance plans based on your income versus the Federal Poverty Level and the impact of the president's manipulation of the subsidies. If you remember, the president ended the cost-sharing subsidies, which resulted in an increase in the premium tax credit that reduce premiums. Remember the Benefit Coverage Circle?

IMPACT OF THE TECTONIC PLATES ON THE ACA INDIVIDUAL MARKETPLACE

Premiums

2018

If your income is 250 percent of the Federal Poverty Level (FPL) or less, you stand a good chance of finding a zero-premium plan on the individual marketplace, which is usually a Bronze or Silver plan. It may also be age-dependent.

Most ACA Individual Exchange enrollees didn't see high prices. About 83 percent of consumers across the nation had their premiums reduced by the premium tax credit. "The average Healthcare.gov enrollee who received a premium tax credit paid about $89 per month for coverage, down from $106 in 2016."[269]

If you do not qualify for the subsidy, the burden remains. Here, you may be looking at a 17 percent increase in Bronze plan premiums, almost a 20 percent jump for a Gold plan, and a whopping 35 percent increase in premiums for a Silver plan for a 40-year-old single individual not eligible for federal aid.[270] "An analysis of CMS data shows that the average 2018 premium across all states was a bit higher at $631 per month." [271]

In other words, while the new expanded Bronze plans had slightly lower premium than the standard Bronze plans, they still represented over a 20 percent increase in average premium as compared to 2017. When reviewing all plans made public for 39 states, the average Silver plan premium is 31 percent more expensive in 2018 as compared in 2017. The highest increase when comparing increases for the four standard ACA plans was 31 percent[272].

2019
There may be some relief for 2019 as many insurers are reporting plans for single-digit gains or, in some cases, decrease in premiums. "For individual coverage offered under the ACA, premium increases have also slowed as health insurers become more familiar with the population buying such coverage. Individual ACA market premiums are forecast to increase just 3.1 percent for the 2019 coverage year,"[273] according to consulting and health research firm Avalere Health.*

Here are the discussion points for what premium increase/decrease look like in 2019. The discussion below comes from the Kaiser Family Foundation, which used the Silver level plan for a 40-year-old man, not the 27-year-old benchmark utilized by the Department of Health and Human Services as the actual pool of beneficiaries is older. [274].

---

*Avalere Health is a consulting firm headquartered in Washington, D.C., specializing in strategy, policy, and data analysis for life sciences, health plans, and providers. The company also publishes research studies on healthcare issues and the healthcare reform debate in the United States.

CHAPTER NINE: Tectonic Plates 135

DISCUSSION POINTS:

1. The average premium will decline after the pattern previously discussed of raising costs for coverage.

2. Who should take credit? Remember that these changes are occurring in the face of continued pressure from the current administration to remove younger, healthier people from the risk pools through Short-term Insurance and Association Health plans and removal of the mandate. Remember our previous discussion that indicated that these changes actually increased premiums 16 percent.

3. It looks like the for-profit health insurance model has reached the profit return point.

4. As we discussed above, the premium prices are still higher than they have been in years past! But there is a wide variability. Some States (Tennessee -26.4 percent) had a negative percentage increase. Others were not so fortunate (Delaware +21.3 percent increase).[275]

Out-of-pocket costs under the ACA

Out-of-pocket costs include the rest of the items described in the coverage circle: the deductible, in-network providers, medical necessity, coinsurance, copayments.

The amount of out-of-pocket cost is defined by the ACA. The ACA uses the term "affordable" as the reference point. The ACA counts affordable as 9.7 percent of an individual's income. If you are paying more than 9.7 percent of your income for out-of-pocket healthcare costs, that would not be considered as affordable healthcare. To determine if your out-of-pocket costs are affordable, use the following math:

> Divide your out-of-pocket costs by your income to get your percentage. If it is more than 9.7% your out-of-pocket costs would not be considered affordable. Then you can compare what your current out-of-pocket costs might be versus the data below.

Average 2016 Out-of-pocket Costs SILVER Plan

Deductibles only

- Individual - $3,117 (6 percent increase)
- Families - $6,480 (8 percent increase)

Maximum Out-of-Pocket Cost (all out-of-pocket cost)

- Individual - $6,110
- Families - $12,270

Out-of-pocket maximum/limit

After you spend this amount on deductibles, copayments, and coinsurance, your health plan pays 100 percent of the costs of covered benefits. The out-of-pocket limit doesn't include your monthly premiums. It also doesn't include anything you spend for services your plan doesn't cover.[276]

According to Healthcare.gov, the maximum out-of-pocket you have to pay for covered services in a plan year for a Marketplace plan is as follows:

2017 plan year: $7,150 for an individual plan
$14,300 for a family plan

2018 plan year: $7,350 for an individual plan
$14,700 for a family plan

For 2019, the ACA out-of-pocket maximum (OOPM) limits will be $7,900 for self-only coverage and $15,800 for family coverage (or anything other than self-only coverage).[277]

Tectonic Plate Alert!

On January 17, 2019, the Centers for Medicare and Medicaid Services proposed raising the out-of-pocket maximum for employer-sponsored plans beginning in 2020 by $200 to $8,200 annually, and the maximum for family coverage would increase by $400. "The plan would also change a calculation that determines how much people pay if they buy insurance from the ACA exchange and get credits to reduce their monthly premiums. The change could raise premiums next year for many of the roughly 9 million people who get the credit."[278]

The impact?

1. 100,000 fewer people being covered on the ACA exchanges
2. Net premium increases totaling $181 million

On top of this, CMS has "...signaled that it is reviewing automatic re-enrollment for consumers with plans on the exchanges, a move that could significantly reduce enrollment, because that is how many people sign up under the ACA each year (about 75 percent of consumers in 2018 actively shopped for a policy, while the rest were automatically renewed). No changes are planned for 2020." [279]

We have discussed previously how the Administration's decision to stop the cost-sharing subsidies had led to insurance companies raising the premiums for the ACA exchanges. As the tax credits for premiums were not impacted, this practice of "silver loading," or raising premiums on certain plans, resulted in increased tax credit subsidies on premiums, effectively lowering those premiums for the healthcare consumer who remained eligible for subsidies, while increasing the For-Profit Health Insurance company's income.

To counter this increased cost to the government, CMS has proposed reducing the fees insurers pay to help fund the exchanges. The goal? Lower premiums that would ultimately lower the increased cost to the government brought on by Trump's own decision to end the cost-sharing subsidies. You will recall that the government uses the Silver Plan prices to determine the tax credits.

After all is said and done, the only clarity is that the tectonic plates are rumbling, and untoward, unexpected, and unusual changes have occurred in the individual marketplace.

Tax provisions

The ACA levies hefty taxes on pharmaceutical manufacturers, medical device manufacturers, health insurers, and wealthy citizens. These taxes have been helping pay for the law's coverage expansions and such expenses as the Center for Medicare and Medicaid Innovation (CMMI). Similarly, the ACA reduced payments to Medicare Advantage plans, which are managed care plans for beneficiaries that were thought to be overpaid. It also cut Medicare Disproportionate Share

Hospital payments, which compensate hospitals for providing care to low-income patients.[280]

The Tax Provisions of the ACA took a big hit with the passage of the 2017 Tax Bill.

TAX PROVISIONS

- Enacted as part of Tax Reform Bill in 2017
- Removal of the ACA Taxes
  - Medical Devices
  - Cadillac Plans
  - Health Insurance Industry

David Blumenthal* writes in the Harvard Tax Review "the tax bill will be the most important healthcare legislation enacted since the Affordable Care Act (ACA) in 2010."[281] As a new tectonic plate, wealthy earners will also get a tax cut, as will segments of the medical and drug manufacturing industry as part of the 2017 tax bill. The resultant increase in the federal deficit has been estimated at $1.45 trillion.[282] As a result, expect increased targeting of the usual deficit reduction suspects of Medicare, Medicaid, and the ACA.

As of this writing, the tectonic plates are at it again. The House voted to repeal a 2.3 percent excise tax on medical devices. This tectonic plate was bipartisan in nature.[283]

"NOBODY DIES BECAUSE THEY DON'T HAVE ACCESS TO HEALTHCARE."

That said, let us look at one more question before we leave this chapter. The Pew Trust asked the question about health insurance and death rates.[284]

One gentleman, a Congressman who voted for the GOP's repeal and replacement of the ACA, made the comments at a town hall in his home district. While taking

---

*David Blumenthal is an academic physician and healthcare policy expert, best known as the National Coordinator for Health Information Technology in the period 2009-2011 during early implementation of the Health Information Technology for Economic and Clinical Health Act provisions on "meaningful use."

questions and comments such as "you are mandating [that] people on Medicaid accept dying." He replied, "No one wants anybody to die … nobody dies because they don't have access to healthcare."[285]

I will address this subject in two parts: Literature Review and my own research.

Literature Review:

In 2002, the National Academy of Medicine (formerly the Institute of Medicine) estimated that the "death rate of the uninsured is 25 percent higher than for otherwise similar people who have health insurance." The same study reported that 18,000 excess deaths occurred each year because 40 million Americans lacked insurance.[286] In January 2008, the Urban Institute updated the aforementioned study. "Subsequent research has continued to confirm the link between insurance and mortality risk. The true number of deaths resulting from un-insurance will be 'significant.'"[287]

A 2009 rebuttal study by the Health Research and Education Trust found that "when adjusted for health status and other factors, the risk of subsequent mortality is no different for people who lack insurance than for those who are covered by employer-sponsored plans[288]." There was a second conclusion from this work: "With health status excluded, the uninsured have a 10 percent higher mortality rate than similar insured persons."[289]

Massachusetts enacted healthcare reform in 2006 to expand insurance coverage and improve access to healthcare[290]. The Harvard researchers compared 2001-2005 death rates in Massachusetts to the four-year period after the new healthcare law was enacted and found that the mortality rate had decreased by 3 percent between 2006 and 2010. More access to healthcare may have prevented as many as 320 deaths per year and extending health coverage to 830 uninsured adults prevented one death per year[291].

I mentioned briefly the other government-sponsored insurance programs such as Tricare, the VA and the Indian Health Service in Chapters One and Two. Here is one of the reasons why. Data from those sources will help us understand the topic at hand.

1. The Indian Health Service (IHS) indicated that it that some deaths have occurred as a result of the care they are not receiving, as well as the care they are receiving.[292]

2. 307,000 veterans may have died awaiting Veterans Affairs healthcare. In 2013, there were 21,882,153 total veterans, of which the VA hospitals served 5.69 million as patients. There are 8.92 million people enrolled in VA healthcare system. Those numbers indicate that 3 percent of the VA eligible patients may have died due to some impediment to receiving healthcare.[293]

Now, let us extrapolate some data based on the impediments placed on getting healthcare by the American Healthcare Act. The Congressional Budget Office originally predicted that 22-24 million Americans would lose healthcare.[294] If 3 percent of these Americans presumably died because of this impediment to receiving healthcare, then 720,000 Americans might have died because of that lack of healthcare over time.

But that may be only part of the story. What about the well documented fact that only "50 percent of patients suffering from chronic diseases in developed countries follow treatment recommendations"?[295] That would also be considered an impediment to having healthcare. This becomes another potential at risk population for death of an additional 375,000 people. And that is only the **non-compliant** population.

The New England Journal of Medicine in 2012 published a study that analyzed the effects of Medicaid expansion on adult mortality in several states. They found a connection between access to Medicaid and reduced mortality-exact figure was a 6.1 percent reduction in mortality.[296]

The Center for American Progress projected what would happen if the NEJM results were applied to the states that had not expanded Medicaid. "In these states alone more than 12,000 lives per year could potentially be saved if state governments agree to expand their Medicaid programs."[297] Let us not lose sight of what is really at stake in the battle over Medicaid. Deficit reduction at the cost of healthcare consumers' lives.

My Research

The impact on lives lost without healthcare coverage is significant. And what is the potential bottom line relating to this tectonic plate projecting actual causes of death in the vulnerable populations?[298]

I used literature-reported figures for risk of death due to lack of healthcare and Congressional Budget Office Analysis of the various healthcare reform bills and then applied them to the National Vital Statistics Report for 2014[299] and calculated the projected yearly avoidable deaths from lack of healthcare insurance.

POPULATION	UNINSURED		UNDERINSURED	MENTAL ILLNESS	NONCOMPLIANT
DISEASE DEATHS	MEDICAID	EMPLOYED	EXCHANGE BASED	DEPRESSED	
Heart Disease	23,380	11,690	50,100		?
Cancer	22,568	11,284	48,360		
Chronic Lower Respiratory	5,670	2,835	12,150		
Stroke	5,068	2,534	10,860		
Other 'Internal' Causes	18,690	9,345	34,920		
Suicide				1,983	
TOTAL	75,376	37,688	156,390	1,983	
DEATHS NO INSURANCE					
three percent	2,261	1,131	4,692	59	
six percent	4,598	2,299	9,540	121	

So, the congressman was wrong. Around 28 million Americans are currently uninsured, and millions more could lose coverage under policy reforms proposed in Congress and actions by the administration[300]. "A growing number of policy leaders have called for going beyond the Affordable Care Act to a single-payer national health insurance system that would cover every American. "In 2002, an Institute of Medicine (IOM) was the first to link the lack of insurance with mortality. The evidence strengthens confidence in the Institute of Medicine's conclusion that health insurance saves lives, as "the odds of dying among the insured relative to the uninsured is 0.71 to 0.97."[301]

That said, we can't provide much in the way of guidance for the action of tectonic plates that are yet to come. On July 27, 2017, one potential earthquake fault was quieted for the moment due to the vote of the Senate. Will the subject of healthcare reform come up again? Most certainly! Healthcare Reform has already been impacted through executive decisions and with tax reform at the end of 2017. The Speaker of the House has said publicly that if the Republicans maintain control of Congress there will be another appeal attempt of the ACA.[302]

Both the president and certain Republican members of Congress have addressed healthcare again in 2018 and beyond, even in the face of the mid-term election results. How will the Democrats respond? "Republicans have often won support in recent elections by promising to repeal the Affordable Care Act. This year, Democrats hope to turn the tables by pushing the opposite goal — not just keeping the health law but expanding government's role in healthcare.[303]"

The Republicans are already blaming the ACA on rising premiums — something their political activity regarding healthcare has actually contributed to, as we have seen. Democratic candidates are responding to a push from party activists to move beyond the ACA and expand coverage further. They believe the law has flaws which should be fixed, not discarded.

Expect to see more uninsured and underinsured. Even those folks with good seats in the ballpark may be impacted by changes in the depth of coverage. This case study was a discussion of the potential seismic impact. For now, let us concentrate on the more mundane and predictable tectonic plates that have already raised their ugly lithospheres and caused measurable ground movement.

CHAPTER NINE What Have We Learned?

Each provision of the ACA continues to be rocked by **tectonic plates**.

TECTONIC PLATES

1. **ACA revamp must include conservative values**

2. **Preexisting conditions:** Short-term insurance policies and other alternative coverage plans which turn back the clock to the detriment of those with preexisting conditions

3. **Coverage mandates:** Removed with the 2017 tax bill and being used as the spear to have legal invalidation of the ACA

4. **Other insurance market reforms including cost-free preventative services:** Short-term insurance policies and other alternative coverage plans which turn back the clock in order limit or remove the 10 types of services covered under the ACA

5. **Medicaid expansion:** In the ongoing battle over Medicaid, Republicans want to shrink it (cut its spending and add restrictions so it serves fewer people). Democrats want to expand

it (increase its funding and reach so it serves millions more people).

6. ***Subsidies in the marketplace:*** There are two kinds of subsidies: one for **premiums**, the other for **healthcare expenses**. By eliminating the second, the federal government took on additional expense as the first were increased. Downstream impact included increased premiums, and chaos in the individual marketplace. By eliminating the cost-sharing aspect that levels the playing field for the risk pools for healthcare insurers, more chaos will ensue, and costs will go higher for those who remain in the marketplace.

   6A. *Insurers exit from ACA marketplace*

   6B. *Premiums increase for the ACA marketplace*

   6C. *Insurers lose suit to recoup losses*

   6D. *Addressing your concerns about the ACA individual marketplace*

   After all is said and done, the only clarity lies in that the tectonic plates are rumbling, and untoward, unexpected, and unusual changes have occurred in the individual marketplace.

7. ***Tax provisions:*** Mostly removed.

   Republicans opposed to the Affordable Care Act are showing interest in proposals to shore up the health law and lower premiums.

8. ***Yes, Mr. Congressman, you can die from lack of healthcare coverage.***

PART C

The Tectonic Plates You May Not Have Known About

So far, we have been discussing what you, the consumer, are concerned about when it comes to healthcare. Did you know that there are other tectonic plates lying in wait that you may not have known about? In this section, I will suggest some issues that should be on your radar.

CHAPTER TEN

Hospitalization

To Be or Not To Be? That is the Question

TEACHING POINT

WHEN TO HOSPITALIZE? WHEN TO OBSERVE?

Have you ever been admitted to the hospital? Did you get a bill? It was almost as painful as the reason for admittance, wasn't it? Especially if it was an unexpected bill from non-network providers associated with your in-network hospital. One area that has come to the forefront in recent years is when to admit a patient to the hospital, when should a patient be hospitalized or admitted for observation? This tectonic plate first surfaced under Medicare. Medicaid, although a state-by-state responsibility, often follows Medicare guidelines in determining healthcare coverage. The private sector often follows suit. As a rule of thumb, remember that as goes Medicare, often so go the other tectonic plates.

Medicare has crafted the oft-discussed two-midnight rule. This rule has created a tectonic plate where **observation** and **inpatient** collide. When you are being treated in the hospital, you will be assigned either an **observation** or **inpatient status**.[304]

1. Observation status: If you are too sick to get your care at your doctor's office or your doctors aren't sure exactly how sick you are, you will be "observed" in the hospital to see if you will require inpatient admission (if your condition warrants it). You can be sent home within 48 hours if you are stable or improved.

2. You're assigned inpatient status if you have severe problems that require highly technical, skilled care. There is an inpatient-only list, but what happens if the diagnosis does not fall on that list?

Making this interface more difficult is that the place of service is not the deciding criteria. Observation, as well as inpatient care, can occur in the Emergency Department, the hospital, on the same hospital wards, and even in the ICU. Some facilities have an "observation" unit. It seems that the guiding principle is not where the care is provided but whether the patient requires further treatment as a hospital inpatient or can be discharged safely and reasonably.[305]

The "two-midnight rule"

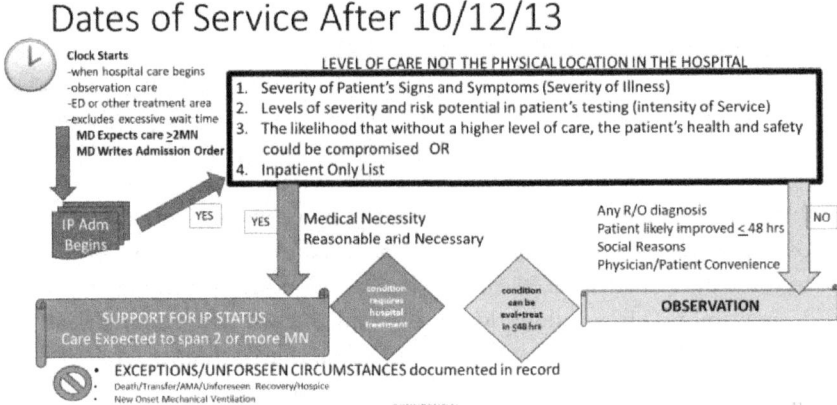

There are three key criteria.

1. **Severity of Illness:** "Severity of the patient's signs and symptoms at the time of admission."[306] How sick is the patient when they present for care?
2. **Intensity of Service:** "There are levels of acuity and risk potential involved in the patient's testing."[307] The testing will be complicated and may even pose a risk to the patient.
3. "The likelihood that without a higher level of care, the patient's health and safety would be compromised."[308]

And if that weren't enough, for cases after October 12, 2013, an additional set of clarifications was added.[309] If the admitting physician expects care to take greater than two midnights, he or she writes an order indicating the same. The reason for the admission must be reasonable and necessary and documentation must support inpatient status. The admission must have clinical documentation which supports the medical necessity of the admission.

Then there are the Get Out of Jail Free wildcards, or "Exceptions/Unforeseen Occurrences.[310]" These must be documented in the record as to why the expected "two-midnight stay" did not occur. These exceptions/occurrences include death, a transfer to another facility, the patient signing out against medical judgment (AMA), hospice, or unforeseen recovery. At last, some potential wiggle room.

"The Secretary of Health and Human services, or HHS, expected that in FY 2014, the two-midnight rule would result in a net shift of 40,000 encounters from outpatient to inpatient status. The Secretary determined that this shift would cost the Medicare program an additional $220 million over the course of the fiscal year.[311]" The Secretary and CMS used its exceptions and adjustments authority under the Medicare Act to reduce the operating Medicare inpatient standardized amount and other payments under the IPPS.*

But the private sector pushed back. The American Hospital Association (AHA) and several hospitals filed suit in federal district court in 2015. Per the Federal District Court's order, the CMS proposed to remove the payment cuts and reimburse providers for the payment reductions in FYs 2014, 2015, and 2016. The two-midnight rule remains in force and the payment cut with its previous financial impact have been eliminated.

With this well-intentioned shift from inpatient to outpatient — as well as some other tectonic plates — hospitals are losing patients, which is good news as far as **access**, **quality**, and **cost** are concerned. Right? In reality, this has become an unwitting tectonic plate driving up your healthcare cost, as the amount of payment received by the facilities is dependent upon the status. Inpatient payments are limited by the DRG system we discussed previously. On the observation side, there is no such constraint, and the providers of that observation care can and do charge to the maximum.

---

*The Inpatient Prospective Payment System (IPPS) standardized amount is the base payment rate for Medicare inpatient services prior to adjusting for diagnosis-related group (DRG) relative weights.

"Hospital systems seek heft to cut costs and do battle with managed-care firms over their future role and payment rates. Meanwhile they continue to invest in their own outpatient settings, looking to capture more of the patients their main facilities may lose[312]." Here is where your plan design adds to your out-of-pocket health cost risk: what the plan does not cover because you are under observation and were not an inpatient, you become responsible for. And that can be one large, expensive tectonic plate.

"More than 20 hospitals have filed for bankruptcy since 2016, three-fourths of them in rural areas."[313] "The days of the hospital as we know it may be numbered. In a shift away from their traditional inpatient facilities, healthcare providers are investing in outpatient clinics, same-day surgery centers, free-standing emergency rooms and microhospitals, which offer as few as eight beds for overnight stays.[314]" This has led to many rural hospitals either closing or finding a safe harbor under the 1997 Medicare Hospital Flexibility Program and the becoming critical access hospitals (CAHs) to provide short-term care. There are approximately 5,000 short-term care hospitals in the United States, and more than 53 percent are CAHs.*

Hospitals are fighting back. The profit motive in the healthcare insurance model of American healthcare is in transition. "Dominant hospital systems use an array of secret contract terms to protect their turf and block efforts to curb healthcare costs."[315]

Here is the short list of those contract demands:

- demand insurers include them in every plan and discourage use of other alternatives (such as rival hospitals and provider systems) which may be less expensive;
- mask prices from consumers;
- limit audits of claims;
- add extra fees;
- block efforts to exclude healthcare providers based on quality or cost.

---

*Critical Access Hospital is a designation given to eligible rural hospitals by the Centers for Medicare and Medicaid Services (CMS). Different hospital types exist to meet the varied needs of the patients and communities they serve.

One final note: be aware that Emergency Departments and other non-network or contracted physicians called in to see you while debating hospitalization or observation may not be in your network even if the hospital is. This will result in you getting a bill for their services to compensate what, if anything, your health insurance plan covers.

THE ISSUE OF READMISSION

TEACHING POINT

Going back into the hospital once discharged.

The Affordable Care Act established the Hospital Readmissions Reduction Program (HRRP), which required CMS to reduce payments to Inpatient Prospective Payment System (IPPS)[316] hospitals with excess readmissions, effective for discharges beginning on October 1, 2012.[317] Readmissions are a major problem in U.S. healthcare. By that I am referring to the following definition: "a patient admitted to a hospital within 30 days after being discharged from an earlier or initial hospitalization."[318] This is considered an "All-Cause" definition as it includes hospital readmissions to **any hospital** for **any reason**. One in five Medicare patients is readmitted, with between 50 and 75 percent of these re-admissions being considered preventable by CMS.

POTENTIAL IMPACT OF MEDICARE HOSPITAL READMISSIONS PROGRAM

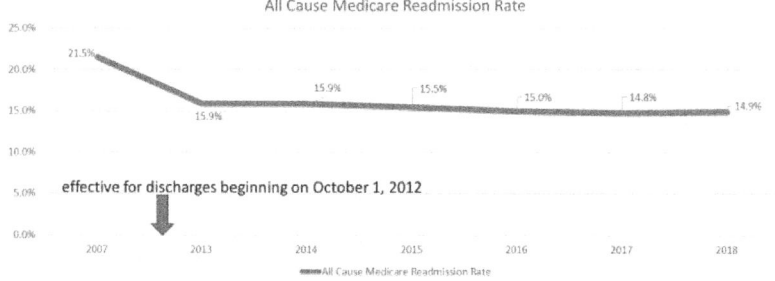

Hospital readmissions within 30 days after discharge became the subject of policy attention because they were accounting for more than $17 billion in what were considered to be avoidable Medicare expenditures that were associated with poor outcomes.[319] The conditions initially reviewed were acute myocardial infarction, heart failure, and pneumonia. Total hip or knee replacement and chronic obstructive pulmonary disease (COPD) were added later[320]. The program has been successful.[321] "From 2007 to 2015, readmission rates for targeted conditions declined from 21.5 percent to 17.8 percent, and rates for nontargeted conditions declined from 15.3 percent to 13.1 percent."[322] The "all cause" combined rate seems to have plateaued overall at around 15 percent.

Yet, there may be a downside risk to this program. "Among Medicare beneficiaries, the HRRP (Hospital Readmissions Reduction Program) was significantly associated with an increase in 30-day post discharge mortality after hospitalization for HF (heart failure) and pneumonia, but not for AMI (acute heart attack)[323]. "Some suggest that these findings might bring into question that the program is a reliable measure of hospital quality and basis for financial penalties."[324]

IMPACT ON THE SECOND PARTY?

What is the potential impact on you, the consumer of healthcare?

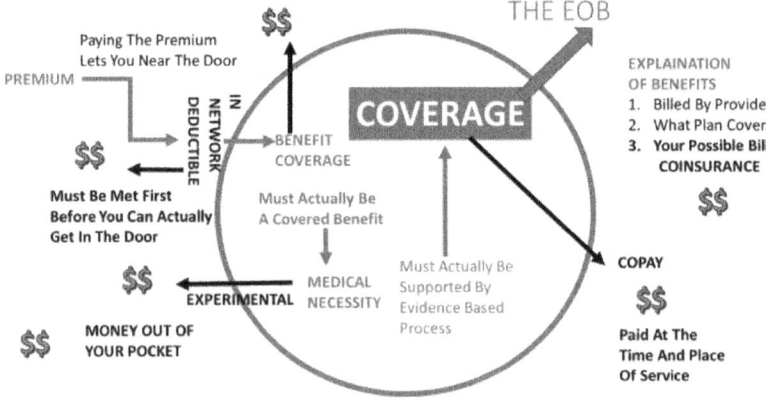

Regardless of where your seat may be in the healthcare ballpark, these tectonic forces may impact you as the patient. As we discussed previously, your insurance will pay what the plan includes, then you may pick up the rest of the tab. Remember the Coverage Benefit Circle: these out-of-pocket expenses are defined as a "copayment" (a fixed amount) or a "coinsurance" (a percentage of the cost of the service).

Hopefully you will have your own "Get Out of Jail Free" card and will be held harmless as part of the reimbursement process. For example, in Tricare parlance for hold harmless, certain varieties of coverage are mandated to protect the patient from reimbursement claims as the providers of healthcare are not permitted by law to pass along any unpaid portion of their bill.

Hold harmless

Before delivering care, network providers must notify patients if services are not covered. "The beneficiary must agree in advance and in writing to accept financial responsibility for non-covered services."[325] The agreement must document the specific services, dates, estimated costs, and other information.

However, Hold Harmless may not protect certain Medicare beneficiaries. If you are new to Social Security or high income, you may not be held harmless.[326] The difference can be seen in the PART B premium.

	STANDARD PART B	FOR BENEFICIARIES WITH HOLD HARMLESS
2016	$121.80	$104.80
2017	$134.00	$109.00

CHAPTER TEN What Have We Learned?

Admission or **observation** is decided by the two-midnight rule.

The severity of the patient's signs and symptoms at the time of admission are very crucial to determining inpatient versus observation status. There are levels of acuity and risk potential involved in the patient's testing. The greater the potential harm to the patient, the greater the probability that inpatient status is appropriate. And the sine qua non (indispensable and essential action, condition, or ingredient) for establishing the need for inpatient admission? Simply put, there is the likelihood that without a higher level of care, the patient's health and safety would be compromised.

There are exceptions that will transfer any admission into inpatient status. If these have occurred the patient (and their physician and hospital) receives a "Get Out of Jail Free" card and the admission is considered in patient rather than observation.

These exceptions/occurrences include death (unfortunate for the patient), transfer to another facility, the patient signing out against medical judgment (AMA), hospice, or unforeseen recovery.

"All Cause" Hospital Readmissions Reduction Program
Any readmission from any previous hospitalization within 30 days will not be covered.

Both could have a downhill financial impact on the healthcare consumer unless you have your own personal "Get Out of Jail Free" card. That specific agreement that you the patient will not be held responsible for the bill unless you agree in advance and in writing to accept financial responsibility for non-covered services. Before delivering care, network providers must notify patients if services are not covered. This won't help you with unexpected out-of-network provider charges.

Tectonic Plates:

- Beware of the added cost to you under **observation** status vs. **inpatient**.

- Beware the added cost of out-of-network providers even if your hospital is in-network.

CHAPTER ELEVEN

Quotes on Mental Illness & Addiction

TEACHING POINT

MENTAL HEALTH

There are several key reports documenting the inadequacy of healthcare available to the mentally ill.[327] Adults with severe mental illness have poorer access to and quality of general healthcare compared to people without mental illness.[328] Adults with severe mental illnesses have higher rates of chronic general medical conditions. Our highly fragmented medical delivery system has a challenge with clinical information capabilities, which highlights the "poor outcomes that result from lack of coordination."[329] The mentally ill perceive more barriers to obtaining general healthcare services and report that providers of care often dismiss their physical complaints as 'somatic,' or made up.

Yet mental health is well recognized. The Surgeon General's report in 2000 reported that,

> (m)ental health is fundamental to health, and mental disorders are real health conditions. On the basis of these findings, the Office of the Surgeon General recommended that people seek help if they have a mental health problem or think they have symptoms of a mental disorder.[330]

However, despite their "higher burden of chronic general medical disorders," adults with severe mental illnesses have poorer access to and quality of general healthcare compared to people without mental illnesses.

It is essentially because the U.S. healthcare system is "a highly-fragmented delivery system" with "lack of coordination" that the care provided to the "125 million chronically ill Americans remains poorly integrated."[331] There is greater separation between general and mental healthcare compared with other specialty medical sectors. Coordinated healthcare is less likely for people with severe mental illnesses than for other populations.

Now that we have established that Americans with mental health issues are treated often as second-class citizens, let us look at a case study in mental health.

CASE STUDY
Suicide Attempt by Any Other Name

CASE NOTES:

1. Intense social anxiety around a birth defect

2. Suicide attempt while intoxicated, not for the first time

3. Required admission for detoxification

4. Transferred to Acute Inpatient Psychiatric Facility

5. The strict reading of the rules: Plan considered this a readmission not a transfer

6. Rehabilitation denied

This late 30-something male had a past medical history of significant hypospadias. Hypospadias is a general description for abnormal formation of the male genital system. He had multiple repairs, resulting in intense social anxiety. He was admitted after presenting to the Emergency Department with a suicide attempt while intoxicated. The patient had previously tried to hang himself about four years ago after a divorce. He was also involved in a significant motorcycle crash and had a subdural hematoma in the past.

He admitted to drinking since age 17. His alcohol intake had increased dramatically over the past few months. The patient was drinking excessive amounts of wine and beer over the week prior to the admission and was described as being depressed. The patient was self-administering anti-depressive drugs as well. About two hours prior to the admission, the patient attempted suicide by slicing his left wrist with a straight razor. The blood alcohol level was at 0.223 (percent of alcohol in bloodstream).[332] Most states have now set .08 percent blood alcohol concentration (BAC) as the legal limit for driving under the influence (DUI) or driving while impaired (DWI).[333] His blood alcohol level would classify him as legally intoxicated in all states. This would place him as very drunk with severe impairment. As a habitual drinker, the impact would be somewhat less than on a social drinker.

There was a large laceration that was repaired, and the patient was admitted for detoxification and depression. The additional diagnosis of post-traumatic stress disorder (PTSD) was added. He was transferred to inpatient rehabilitation to gain insight into his addiction and to develop coping mechanisms to prevent further relapse.

While in rehabilitation, the patient attended group sessions and gained insight into the addiction process, triggers, and coping mechanisms. His attention and concentration and mood improved on the appropriate medications. Upon discharge, he remained anxious but had no further suicidal/homicidal thoughts. The patient was discharged to outpatient follow-up focused on subsequent outpatient rehabilitation. The plan did not permit admission to an inpatient rehabilitation unit. Plan short sightedness is a tectonic plate. "One of every 100 suicide attempt survivors will die by suicide within one year of their index attempt, a risk approximately 100 times that of the general population.[334]"

Suicide attempt while intoxicated
This patient's previous history and relapse, as well as the actual previous suicide attempts, supported the need for the transfer (not readmission) to an inpatient rehabilitation program.

The strict reading of the rules of the road led the plan to consider this a readmission and not a transfer as the rehabilitation was in another hospi-

> tal other than the one in which he was initially hospitalized for the medical care. Remember we discussed the "all cause" definition of readmissions for Medicare? For Medicare, this time-period is defined as 30 days, and includes hospital readmissions to any hospital, not just the hospital at which the patient was originally hospitalized.
>
> The tectonic plates have reared their ugly sliding surfaces once again. Common sense would seem to indicate that the move from an acute medical inpatient setting for detoxification to an acute psychiatric inpatient setting to address addiction for a patient such as this should be a seamless evidence-based pathway, especially given the data on suicide attempts. The plan saw otherwise.

TEACHING POINT

HOW PREVALENT IS ALCOHOLISM?

North Dakota/Wisconsin (just shy of 25), Alaska/Montana (22.5), and Illinois (21) had the highest excessive alcohol rate per 100,000 people in 2015. The whole United States had an average of 17.5.

GENERAL ALCOHOL STATISTICS

- Alcohol poisoning kills six people every day. Of those, 76 percent are adults ages 35-64, and three of every four people killed by alcohol poisoning are men.
- The group with the most alcohol poisoning deaths per million people is American Indians/Alaska Natives (49.1 per 1 million).
- Alcohol-impaired driving accounts for more than 30 percent of all driving fatalities each year.
- More than 15 million people struggle with an alcohol use disorder in the United States, but less than 8 percent of those receive treatment.
- More than 65 million Americans report binge drinking in the past month, which is more than 40 percent of the total of current alcohol users.

CHAPTER ELEVEN: Quotes on Mental Illness & Addiction

- Teen alcohol use kills 4,700 people each year, more than all illegal drugs combined.
- Drunk driving costs the United States $199 billion every year.
- Kids who start drinking young are seven times more likely to be in an alcohol-related motor vehicle accident.

If we break this data down into various component parts, the next two graphics spell out the snapshot for 2017.[335]

EXCESSIVE DRINKING IN U.S. 2017

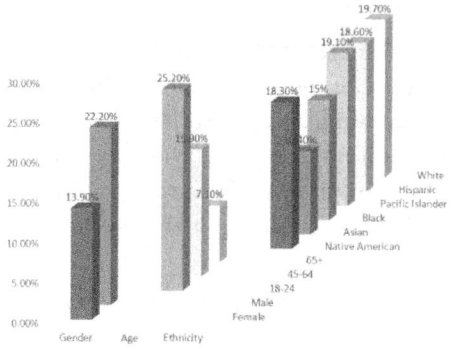

EXCESSIVE DRINKING IN U.S. 2017

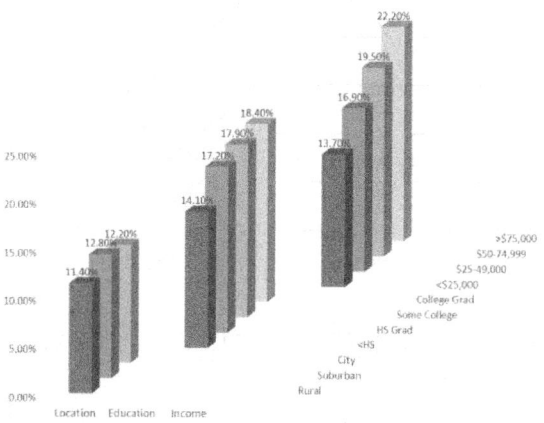

TEACHING POINT

THE ISSUE OF DRUG ADDICTION

What is addiction? Not a simple question to answer. "Addiction is defined as a **chronic, relapsing** brain disease that is characterized by **compulsive drug-seeking** and **use, despite harmful consequences**. It is considered a brain disease because drugs change the brain; they change its structure and how it works."[336]

Simple right? It's just a little change in brain chemistry if we look below the surface. "Addictive drugs directly or indirectly target the brain's reward system" flooding the circuit with dopamine (neurotransmitter present in regions of the brain that regulates feelings of pleasure).[337] Overstimulation rewards our natural behaviors and produces the euphoric effects sought by people who use drugs and teaches them to repeat the behavior.

What is the cost? In terms of dollars, abuse of and addiction to alcohol, nicotine, and illicit and prescription drugs cost Americans more than $700 billion a year. This figure is the sum of increased healthcare costs, crime, and lost productivity. In terms of finality of health outcome, the data is starker. Illicit and prescription drugs and alcohol contribute to the death of more than 90,000 Americans. The use of tobacco products may cause up to an estimated 480,000 deaths per year.[338]

Blue Cross and Blue Shield analyzed medical and pharmacy claims data for more than 30 million of its plans' commercially insured members. This study found that rates of opioid use disorder had "skyrocketed, with a 494 percent increase in opioid disuse disorders from 2010 to 2016."[339]

How significant has this become? A 2018 article in the JAMA Open Network indicated rates of addiction from greater than 10.85 percent to less than 20.33 percent of populations by county in the United States.[340] "The Centers for Disease Control and Prevention estimates that the total 'economic burden' of prescription opioid misuse alone in the United States is $78.5 billion a year, including the costs of healthcare, lost productivity, addiction treatment, and criminal justice involvement."[341]

The National Institute on Drug Abuse issued revised data in March 2018. What do we know about the opioid crisis?[342]

- Roughly 21 to 29 percent of patients prescribed opioids for chronic pain misuse them.[343]
- Between 8 and 12 percent of patients develop an opioid use disorder. An estimated 4 to 6 percent who misuse prescription opioids

transition to heroin. About 80 percent of people who use heroin first misused prescription opioids.[344] [345] [346]

Opioid overdoses increased 30 percent from July 2016 through September 2017 in 52 areas in 45 states. The Midwestern region saw opioid overdoses increase 70 percent from July 2016 through September 2017. Opioid overdoses in large cities increase by 54 percent in 16 states.[347]

The issue of overdose and death

The Centers for Disease Control and Prevention (CDC) reported that there were "more than 40,000 unintentional drug overdose deaths in the United States in 2011, a 118 percent increase since 1999.[348] More than 22,000 people die every year from prescription drug abuse, more than heroin and cocaine combined."[349]

West Virginia (32.5), New Mexico (just under 25), Kentucky (24), Utah (22.5), and Rhode Island (21) had the highest opioid related drug death rates per 100,000 people in 2015. The United States average was 14. Every day, more than 115 people in the United States die after overdosing on opioids.[350]

Decline in U.S. life expectancy

Drug-overdose deaths drove a decline in U.S. life expectancy in 2016 for the second year in a row. Deaths from drug overdoses surged 21 percent to more than 63,600 in 2016. Those deaths were the main factor causing life expectancy for Americans born in 2016 to fall to 78.6 years, down from 78.7 and 78.9 in previous years.[351]

"Significant increase in death rates for younger Americans — particularly those 15 to 44 — helped drive life expectancy down, with drug overdoses contributing heavily to those deaths[352]". The death rate fell in 65 and older. Drug deaths also boosted "unintentional injuries" into the number 3 slot for causes of death, up from number 4 in 2015. Unintentional injuries also included car crashes, accidental firearm deaths, and medical errors.[353]

The following data is taken from the CDC's 2017 report.[354]

- Number of deaths per year from heart disease: 635,260
- Number of deaths per year from cancer: 598,038
- Number of deaths per year from accidents (unintentional injuries): 161,374

Relapse

Relapse rates are common in many health conditions as well as drug abuse and addiction.[355] In fact, drug addiction has a higher relapse rate than Type I diabetes (40-60 percent to 30-50 percent) but less than hypertension or asthma (50-70 percent). "Drug addiction should be treated like any other chronic illness, with relapse serving as a trigger for renewed intervention[356]. Health and Human Services (HHS) launched the Five-Point Opioid Strategy in 2017 without funds. In September of 2018, funding was established.[357]

The Five-Point Opioid Strategy:

1. Better addiction prevention, treatment, and recovery services
2. Better data
3. Better pain management
4. Better targeting of overdose reversing drugs
5. Better research

Is this enough?

CHAPTER ELEVEN What Have We Learned?

Mental healthcare has been neglected in the healthcare system. The ACA mandated that mental healthcare be brought up to a par with other medical coverage.

There is a significant opioid epidemic in the United States:

- Deaths are increasing; for two years in a row, life expectancy dropped
- Unintentional injuries are now the third leading cause of death
- Drug addiction should be treated like any other chronic illness

Tectonic Plate: No request for funds from the administration to fight opioid addiction epidemic until very recently.

CHAPTER TWELVE

The View from the Parking Lot

TEACHING POINT

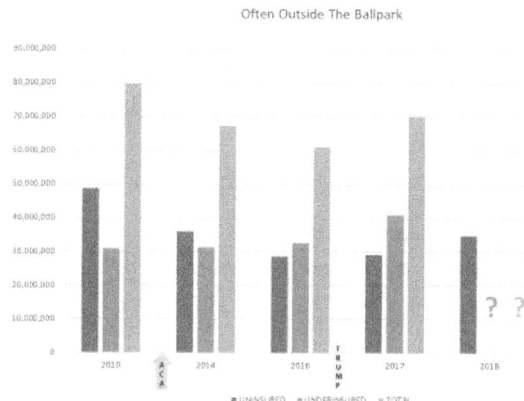

THE UNINSURED

I have mentioned those folks who do not have a seat at the ballpark — the uninsured. While a disadvantageous place to be, not having a permanently assigned stadium seat does not mean that you can't enter the ballpark. There is the so-called Seventh Inning Stretch, or the Emergency Room (ER) or Emergency Department (ED). Yet the common wisdom may not be correct when it comes to Emergency Department use by the uninsured.

"There is a popular perception that insurance coverage will reduce overuse of the emergency department."[358] There is evidence that insurance coverage increases ED use instead of decreasing it. Insured and uninsured adults use the ED at very similar rates and in very similar circumstances. The uninsured use the ED substantially less than the Medicaid population. While the uninsured do not use the ED more than the insured, they do use other types of care much less than the insured.

Relationship between cost and access

"Going without coverage can have serious health consequences for the uninsured because they receive less preventive care, and delayed care often results in serious illness or other health problems. Being uninsured also can have serious financial consequences."[359]

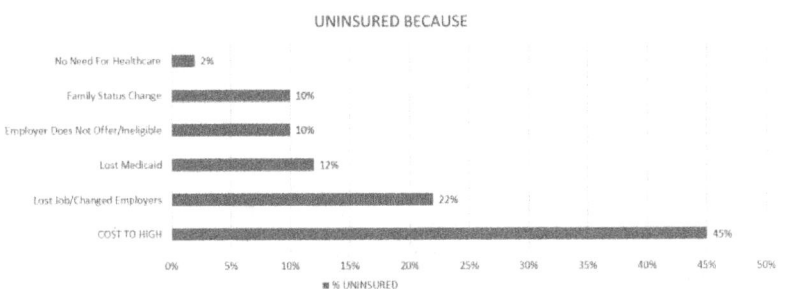

Characteristics of the uninsured

In 2016, 86 percent of the uninsured had at least one full-time or part-time worker in their family. Family income ranged from <100 percent of Federal Poverty Level to 400+ percent of FPL in almost equal percentages across the board. However, over 75 percent of those uninsured were <400 percent of the FPL. Ethnicity was white (44 percent), Hispanic (33 percent) and black (15 percent) primarily.[360] In just another example about the interconnectivity between non-healthcare related factors and the tectonic plates involves with American Healthcare in transition, individuals below poverty are at the highest risk of being uninsured. In terms of the adverse health effects of low socio-economic status, we should not be surprised that it has impact.

Barriers

"The uninsured are less likely than those with insurance to receive preventive care and services for major health conditions and chronic diseases."[361] This situation impacts **quality** of care in that outcomes are worse. As there is no usual source of care, **access** suffers. But at the end of the day, the constant barrier remains **cost**.

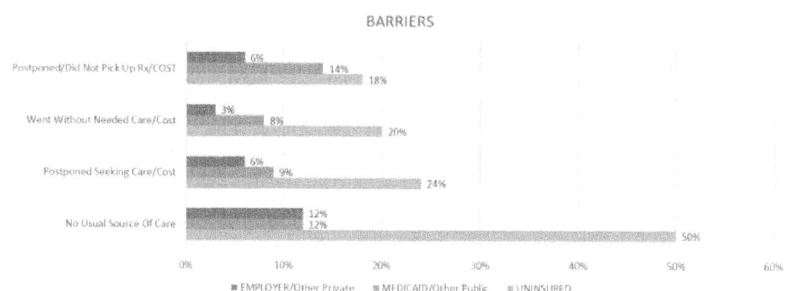

UNDERINSURED

The other side of the uninsured coin is the underinsured. What causes people to be underinsured? Health insurance is moving toward greater patient cost-sharing. In other words, such high out-of-pocket costs or deductibles relative to patient's incomes appear to be the major cause.

Underinsured defined:

- Out-of-pocket costs, excluding premiums, over the prior 12 months are equal to 10 percent or more of household income; or

- Out-of-pocket costs, excluding premiums, are equal to 5 percent or more of household income if income is under 200 percent of the federal poverty level ($22,980 for an individual and $47,100 for a family of four); or

- Deductible is 5 percent or more of household income.[362]

What Does That Mean?

- 23 percent of 19- to 64-year-old adults are underinsured, equal to 31 million people in 2014;
- Half (51 percent) of underinsured adults reported problems with medical bills or debt of $4,000 or more;
- More than two out of five individuals (44 percent) reported not getting needed care because of cost.[363]

Our Healthcare Ballpark now has an additional group of folks who enter the park on an irregular basis, find seats where they can — and are often obstructed — and are more vulnerable to the tectonic plates. What might happen moving forward (national gains) if all states achieved top rates of insurance coverage and eliminated the underinsured?[364]

1. 18 million more adults/children insured (beyond the maximum gains of the ACA before tectonic plates began to rumble);
2. 14 million fewer adults not getting care because of cost;
3. 26 million more adults with access through a usual source of care;
4. 11 million more adults getting recommended cancer screening;
5. 837,000 more vulnerable children receiving all recommended vaccinations;
6. 1 million less Medicare beneficiaries receiving a high-risk (Beers List-Chapter 13) prescription drug;
7. 440,000 fewer hospitalizations;
8. 5.7 million fewer non-emergent emergency department visits that are better treated in primary care doctors' offices;
9. 89,000 fewer avoidable deaths as diseases are treated;

    Performance benchmarks are set at the level achieved by the top-performing state with available data for this indicator. Estimate based on working-age population, ages 18-64, with employer-sponsored insurance, and Medicare beneficiaries aged 65 and older.

For the individual marketplace

Where will **cost** go from here? It has been projected that the poor and elderly will be the most impacted with their out-of-pocket costs projected to be even higher.

Remember our Benefit Coverage Circle? Based on information from Healthcare.gov, I have taken the liberty of annotating the diagram to apply relevance to the Individual marketplace. This will not be the only marketplace for the underinsured due to all of the manipulations, or tectonic plates, we have discussed, as well as state-by-state solutions and things like Short-Term Insurance Policies (Chapter Nine).

The projected impact of this tectonic plate will be to siphon off the healthy, leaving a sicker population using the ACA Individual marketplace. Without the documented impact of those nebulous plans currently coalescing into reality, here is what the Individual marketplace holds as we speak. The full impact of short-term insurance plans is yet to be seen. Also keep in mind the ongoing additional tectonic plates being added to the mix by this administration. I am referring to the **tectonic plate alert** in Chapter Nine.

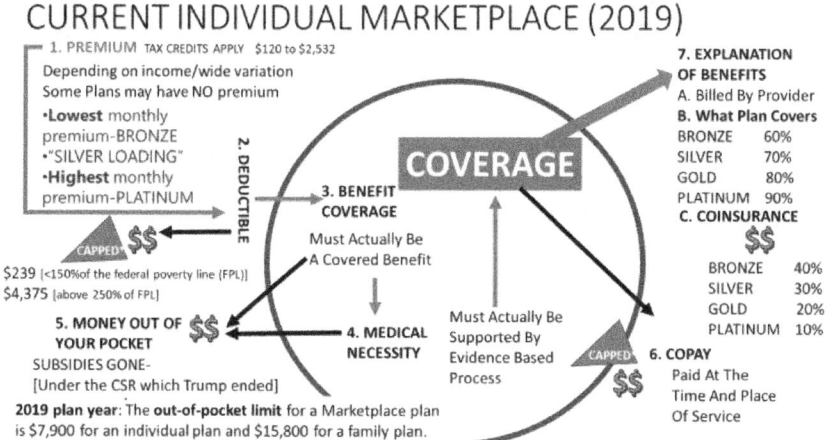

CHAPTER TWELVE *What Have We Learned?*

The number of persons under age 65 who were uninsured at the time of interview: 28.2 million

While the uninsured do not use the ED more than the insured, they do use other types of care much less than the insured.

No usual source of care, or **access** to care, appears to be as important as **cost**.

Health insurance is moving toward greater patient cost-sharing, which has resulted in many being underinsured.

Tectonic plate: Healthcare reform is really about deficit reduction, and the true victims are the underinsured. The tectonic plate of short-term insurance plans will further influence this group of healthcare consumers.

CHAPTER THIRTEEN

Medical Errors and Torts: Death From Medical Care Itself

TEACHING POINT

To err is human.

The data below are from the inpatient, or hospital, side of the ledger. Death is the ultimate tectonic plate. We have talked in some detail about the association of death with the lack of healthcare insurance in Chapter Nine, but the Grim Reaper can also raise its ugly head even for those who have access to medical care.

MEDICAL ERRORS

Regardless of the treating provider's intent (or assumed intent), something untoward happens to the patient that causes an "inaccurate or incomplete diagnosis or treatment." Essentially, a medical error is an "unintended act (either of omission or commission) or one that does not achieve its intended outcome, the failure of a planned action to be completed as intended (error of execution), the use of a wrong plan to achieve an aim (error of planning)."[365] This would include any treatment that is not indicated, or even contraindicated. In my mind, they are examples of an error of planning.

Another way to look at medical error is as a "deviation from the process of care that may or may not cause harm to the patient."[366] Regardless of how you define it, the final pathway leads to a Potential Quality Issue, or PQI.

TEACHING POINT

QUALITY ASSURANCE

Quality assurance includes monitoring and improving the quality of care provided to the patient. In the United States, two nonprofit groups dominate the performance-measurement field.

National Committee for Quality Assurance (NCQA) accredits health plans, provider groups, and various medical businesses.

Joint Commission focuses on hospitals, laboratories, and many types of medical institutions. The Joint Commission and NCQA measure quality in different ways. I will discuss accreditation more fully in Chapter Sixteen.

A word about Potential Quality Indicators *(PQI:)*

These are the monitoring measures that can be used with hospital inpatient discharge data to assess quality of care. They are also applied to outpatient care, which can result in potentially preventing the need for hospitalization. Think of it as an early intervention system to prevent complications or more severe disease or even death.[367]

Through this monitoring, potential quality indicators (PQI)[368] come to light. Think of these as suspected provider qualities of care or service issue that have the potential to affect the level of care being provided to the patient. When a PQI has been reviewed and investigated and determined to be a quality issue that requires further action to resolve, it is called an Actual Quality Issue (AQI).

Most healthcare organizations will have their own Professional Quality Management Committee (PROQMC, or another similar process regardless of what they might name it) consisting of plan quality and medical personnel as well as community physicians with specific specialties as needed. Committees such as these will review identified quality issues and establish final severity levels as well as suggest corrective action plans.

Severity Levels
0 Following investigation, there is no quality issue finding

1 Quality issue is present with minimal potential for significant adverse effects on the patient

2 Quality issue is present with potential for significant adverse effects on the patient

3 Quality issue is present with significant adverse effects on the patient

4 Quality issue is present with the most severe adverse effects and warrants exhaustive review

Provider Levels
Assigned to individual providers for PQIs opened after February 1, 2018

P1 Most experienced, competent practitioners would have managed this case in a similar manner

P2 Most experienced, competent practitioners might have managed this case differently

P3 Most experienced, competent practitioners would have managed this case differently

Sentinel Event
A sentinel event is a patient safety event (not primarily related to the natural course of the patient's illness or underlying condition) that affects a patient and results in any of the following:

- Death
- Permanent harm
- Severe temporary harm

Severe temporary harm is critical, potentially life-threatening harm that lasts for a limited time with no permanent residual but that does require transfer to a higher level of care/monitoring for a prolonged period of time; transfer to a higher level of care for a life-threatening condition; or additional major surgery, procedure, or treatment to resolve the condition.

Some examples of severe temporary harm might be hemolytic transfusion reaction, unintended retention of a foreign object in a patient after an invasive procedure (sponge, forceps, etc.) or severe neonatal hyperbilirubinemia or jaundice (bilirubin >30 milligrams/deciliter).[369]

Serious Reportable Events
National Quality Forum "never events" as defined in December 2011

A "never event" is a serious and reportable occurrence that is unambiguous and never should have occurred. The definition is as follows:

- Adverse or bad outcome;
- A problem in the safety system where the event occurred;
- Is a creditable event and one to which the "public" should hold the system accountable;
- Both healthcare providers/professionals and the public consider the event important;
- A clearly identifiable and measurable event;
- An event which should be included in a reporting system;
- The policies and procedures of the healthcare facility clearly are a contributing factor to the event.

"Serious Reportable Events include both injuries occurring during care management (rather than underlying disease) and errors occurring from failure to follow standard care or institutional policies and procedures."[370]

But quality actual starts before physicians and other healthcare providers are even brought into a Healthcare Organization's (Plan) "network." This is the Credentialing Process. Again, a committee of the Plan's provider service and medical personnel with representation to include the network's practicing physicians will meet and review healthcare providers being credentialed for the first time or recredentialed for continuation in the network.

There are two types of provider reviews. If the healthcare provider has not previously applied to be part of the network, that review is considered an initial review. Following initial acceptance into the network, providers are recredentialed at least every three (3) years.

Clean files are files which are acceptable under standard credentialing practices and that do not have any issues that require committee review. These are presented in a list format for review and approval. Non-clean files are files that are not acceptable under credentialing standards but that have one or more issues requiring

CHAPTER THIRTEEN: Medical Errors and Torts: Death From Medical Care Itself

review and discussion by the Credentialing Committee. The files are considered non-clean if there are problems falling into one or more of the following criteria:

A. A professional liability claims history falling into one of three categories:

1) a claim for wrongful death that resulted in either a settlement or a judgment against the physician (defendant);

2) a claim that resulted in payment of $1 million ($1,000,000) or more in either judgment or settlement; or

3) a series of five or more lawsuits resulting in either a settlement or judgment of any amount against the physician (defendant) in a five year period (or based on whatever accreditation process has been used for the healthcare organization)

B. Revocation, suspension, or termination (voluntary or involuntary) of any state, federal, or national license or certification that reflects performance within the scope of clinical practice

C. License is not full, current, and unrestricted in the state or states where services will be delivered;

D. Medicare or Medicaid sanctions;

E. Information contained in the National Practitioner Data Bank (NPDB) that is not included in any of the above, such as Board Actions, Criminal Actions, etc.

The final decision to accept or deny the provider into the Plan's network is generally based upon the provider's pattern of behavior. Each voting member has a red flag level and will raise it during the discussion. Then a vote is taken, and the majority will make the final decision. There is an appeal process for providers who were initially credentialed and then denied credentialing later.

CASE NUMBER
Space, The Final Frontier

This case is also an amalgam rolled into one case example. I have had a seat at the table for many a credentialing meeting. The format below used for reviewing the essential data is my own and does not reflect any of the established processes of any particular Plan.

PROVIDER NAME: Leonard "Bones" McCoy, MD

Initial credentialing

Date of Birth: January 20, 2227

Specialty:

"I'm a doctor, (Jim) not a(n)..."

Not Board Certified (as far as anyone can determine)

Education and Training: The University of Mississippi; obtained an MD and did a Rotating Internship 2248-2253

Star Fleet Academy 2262-2264 after his divorce left him with "nothing but his bones."

General Medical Officer

Work History: Unknown prior to 2262; chief medical officer of the Enterprise 2266

Star Fleet Medical Academy, San Francisco, Earth, Federation of Planets

Instructor after stepping down from the Enterprise

Malpractice History

CHAPTER THIRTEEN: Medical Errors and Torts: Death From Medical Care Itself 175

Case #1:

Date of Service: October 23, 2267

Date of Closure: January 31, 2275

Amount Paid: 400,000 Quatlooms

Death: None

Case history: Operated on an unusual silicon-based Horta without doing a complete pre-surgical workup; extenuating circumstances; Horta survived to rejoin its fellows apparently totally recovered

Criminal Action: Commander Spock transferred his "katra" — his knowledge and experience — into Dr. McCoy's mind before dying (see Board Action #1 below). This caused mental anguish for McCoy which led to consumption of banned Romulan Ale with subsequent DUI. He was arrested and then released on Spock's recognizance.

Board Action #1:

As is appropriate, Dr. McCoy has declared someone or something deceased with the statement, "He's dead", "He's dead, Jim", or something similar. However, he refused to pronounce First Office Spock dead after an encounter with archnemesis Khan. McCoy warned his superior officer, Captain Kirk, (the aforementioned "Jim") against opening the engineering doors while Chief Engineer Montgomery Scott (Scotty) said, "He's dead already," — clearly a dereliction of duty. The Intra/Inter Galactic Medical Board, chaired by Dr. Gene Roddenberry fined Dr. McCoy 100 Quatlooms and ordered 20 hours of Continuing Medical Education (CME) in the form of a script rewrite.

License Revocation-Mississippi State Medical Board revoked his License temporarily sometime between 2253 and 2262 because the passionate, sometimes cantankerous McCoy frequently argued with his colleagues about how they were mistreating their patients.

> RECOMMENDATION: In spite of frequent issues, Dr. McCoy invoked many extenuating circumstances. He has had only one malpractice case over his long career, and that incident was more than 15 years prior to his credentialing. One can be given a little leeway knowing that he carried a Vulcan's "katra" around in his head. That type of irrational behavior that led to the DUI would not be reproduced as evidenced by the stellar career Dr. McCoy went on to have at Star Fleet. Approve initial accreditation for three years.
>
> *For those of you who are not Trekkers (a fan of the U.S. science-fiction television program, Star Trek), please excuse the format utilized as we continue our journey over the tectonic plates and navigate the American Healthcare "System" together. Although the content of the physician credentialing profile shown above is fictitious, the need for a Quality of Care process is not. At the end of the day, it is the Quality Improvement System that offers hope to you, the patient, as you transform from victims to informed utilizers of healthcare. Each of the case studies and its accompanying evidence-based discussion is an example of such a quality improvement process.*

By improving quality and reducing the cost of unnecessary services and the excessive use of expensive technology, perhaps there could be a redistribution of funding by the decision-makers instead of deficit reduction. Even if The Affordable Care Act, Medicaid, and Medicare are modified or replaced in the foreseeable future, by decreasing our cost for healthcare in the United States (as a percentage of our Gross Domestic Product), there might just be enough money to go around to improve all the seats at the healthcare ballpark as well as open the turnstiles to those who are currently on the outside looking in.

After all is said and done, in spite of the best credentialing processes and Quality Management, deaths from medical errors occur. In 1999, the Institute of Medicine (IOM) reported 44,000 to 98,000 deaths annually.[371] At the 152nd annual meeting, the membership of the National Academy of Sciences voted to change the name of the Institute of Medicine to the National Academy of Medicine effective July 1, 2015.

CHAPTER THIRTEEN: Medical Errors and Torts: Death From Medical Care Itself

Subsequent studies have indicated the potential for 140,400 annual deaths. In 2004, the Agency for Healthcare Quality and Research (AHQR) reported 195,000 deaths a year from the Medicare population.[372] In 2008, the Inspector General reported 180,000 deaths of Medicare patients.[373] A 2013 published peer-reviewed journal article by Claussen et al. reported in patient medical error a death rate of 1.13 percent.[374] This means there are over 400,000 per year, more than four times the estimate put out by the then named IOM.

If the methodology and other evidence-based requirements are truly met by these papers, and these reported data are accurate, then the roll call order of the leading causes of death in the United States is about to change. The Center for Disease Control (CDC) released the following data for the top three causes of death in the United States in 2013:

- Heart disease: 611,105 deaths
- Cancer: 584,881 deaths
- Chronic Respiratory Disease: 149,205 deaths[375]

The newly calculated figure for medical errors puts the category of accidental deaths behind cancer but ahead of respiratory disease. The leading causes of death remained the same for 2014. It now appears that, thanks to medical errors and the opioid epidemic, accidental deaths is now the third leading cause of death. Yet, in and of itself, if all cases were accurately counted — there is no accurate coding for death by medical error — I believe that medical errors would have equal billing. Let me show you my thinking on this.

2014 leading causes of death:

1. Heart Disease deaths: 611,105
2. Cancer deaths: 584,881
3. Inpatient medical error deaths: estimated 400,000
4. Accidental Deaths (Chapter Eleven): 161,374
5. Chronic Lung Diseases deaths: 149,205[376]

The above[377] would then represent this potential "sea-change"* (an English idiomatic expression which denotes a substantial change in perspective, especially one that affects a group or society). In fact, the number of inpatient deaths attributable to medical error may be underreported. As I mentioned above, there is no separate category for medical error on death certificates, making it difficult for the CDC or anyone else to track these types of deaths. "In one case, a study noted, a botched test caused liver damage and subsequent heart failure. The patient's cause of death was listed as cardiovascular, when in fact it was medical error."[378]

CASE STUDY
Medication Error Resulting in Death

CASE FILE:

1. Medicare-aged male who was admitted to an inpatient psychiatric setting due to increasing agitation, aggressive behavior, and hallucinations; possibly suffering from Alzheimer's

2. Treated as needed with medications

3. Transferred to the ICU setting due to sudden onset of confusion and excessive sedation

4. Patient died in the ICU setting

A word about the Beers Criteria:

These criteria were initially developed to target nursing home patients. The Beers Criteria has progressed to become a list of medications considered inappropriate for older patients because of ineffectiveness and a high risk for adverse events. The criteria were updated in 2012 to report the drug-related issues and adverse side effects in older adults.[379] In 2015, the American Geriatrics Society (AGS) crafted these criteria as a list of

---

*Suggested by Dr. Joseph McMenamin, a university-trained internist and practicing emergency physician before being admitted to the bar. He holds medical and law degrees.

CHAPTER THIRTEEN: Medical Errors and Torts: Death From Medical Care Itself **179**

potentially inappropriate medications to be avoided by older adults. This is an example of the use of evidence-based medicine.

THE CASE STUDY

The patient is a '70-something'-year-old demented male who was admitted to an inpatient psychiatric setting for increasing agitation, aggressive behavior. While in the inpatient setting, he was treated as needed with medications including Haldol, Thorazine, and Ativan, owing to ongoing agitation. Owing to sudden onset of confusion and excessive sedation, he was then transferred to the ICU and eventually died there. Looking at the medication dosage schedule, the effect of the medications, the transfer to the ICU, and the cause of his eventual death become very apparent.

DRUG	Amount	DATE	TIME		DATE	TIME		DATE	TIME	
		DAY 1	1408	2026	DAY 2	0830	0900	DAY 3	1551	1630
Ativan	2 mg									
Thorazine	25 mg									
Haldol	5mg									

Ativan is a medication used for seizures. It is in a class of medications called Benzodiazepines.[380]

Thorazine is an antimanic agent.* It is considered a "first-generation"† (typical) antipsychotic.‡ The drug is a Phenothiazine derivative. The drug is used "off-label"§ for psychosis and agitation associated with dementia,

---

*Antimanic drug, or any drug that stabilizes mood by controlling symptoms of mania, the abnormal psychological state of excitement

†A first- generation drug is the first one to show the desired activity. Later generations are a successive line of derivatives of these original drugs.

‡Antipsychotics, also known as neuroleptics or major tranquilizers, are a class of medication.

§Denoting a drug prescribed for a particular indication even though the drug has not yet received approval from the Food and Drug Administration for that disease, condition, or symptom

which is what this patient had. Thorazine is considered a "high-risk" medication for the senior patient population. In fact, it is listed in the Beers Criteria:

> *Antipsychotics* are identified in the Beers Criteria as potentially inappropriate medications to be avoided in patients 65 years and older with dementia because of an increased risk of mortality, cerebrovascular accidents (stroke), and a greater rate of cognitive decline (thinking) with use; avoid antipsychotics for behavioral problems associated with dementia or delirium unless alternative nonpharmacologic therapies have failed and patient may harm self or others.[381]

There is evidence of increased mortality in elderly patients with dementia-related psychosis.

Haldol is considered a "first-generation" typical antipsychotic and is a high-risk medication for geriatric patients. It carries the same Beers Criteria warning on antipsychotics as above.[382]

Outpatient Setting

Although there is no outpatient data readily available to document the potential for death due to medical error in the outpatient setting, there is some indication that "if we can improve the hand-off of patients from the inpatient to the outpatient setting, the risk for consequent medical errors would be lessened."[383]

TEACHING POINT

MEDICAL MALPRACTICE CASES, OR TORTS

A second tectonic plate related to the issue of medical errors is that of the legal system's proclivity to pursue the medical profession for its alleged sins. "Americans file more than 17,000 medical malpractice lawsuits a year, recent data show." And some medical specialties are targeted more than others, according to a new study

CHAPTER THIRTEEN: Medical Errors and Torts: Death From Medical Care Itself

published in the New England Journal of Medicine.[384] Which ones are in the crosshairs the most?

Which physicians get sued (percentage of doctors who face a claim each year):

1. Neurosurgeons: 19.09 percent
2. Thoracic-cardiovascular surgeons: 18.9 percent
3. General surgeons: 15.31 percent
4. Orthopedic surgeons: 14.16 percent
5. Plastic surgeons: 12.7 percent
6. Gastroenterologists: 11.64 percent
7. Obstetrician/Gynecologists: 11.02 percent
8. Urologists: 10.49 percent
9. Pulmonologists: 9.32 percent
10. Oncologists: 9.14 percent[385]

What are Torts?

"In common law jurisdictions, a tort is a civil wrong that unfairly causes someone else to suffer loss or harm resulting in legal liability for the person who commits the tortious act."[386] In case you were curious, the person who commits the act is called a tortfeasor. There are four elements of tort law:

1. Duty
2. Breach of duty
3. Causation
4. Injury

Torts, for the purposes of this discussion, include a much narrower definition. For Medical malpractice, the tort generally defined as something that:

1. Was a civil wrong;
2. Caused an injury; and
3. The victim may seek damages.

A CASE STUDY
In (Alleged) Malpractice

Failure to diagnose

The physician saw the elderly patient on only one occasion. The patient presented complaints of double vision. The patient was found to have a normal exam except for a refractive error. He was instructed regarding these findings and advised to return or to see his family doctor if the headaches persisted. He was also referred to an optometrist for corrective lenses. He subsequently saw his family doctor who diagnosed sinusitis and treated him for that condition. One month later, he developed temporal arteritis and lost the vision in both eyes. Although the ophthalmologist opined there was no deviation from the standard of care, the patient was sympathetic witness because of the patient's age and blindness, and the jury awarded a judgment of millions of dollars.

CHAPTER THIRTEEN *What Have We Learned?*

Quality Management is one process of monitoring, and it is hoped, improving the quality of care provided to the patient and determining Potential Quality Issues (PQI).

Quality actually starts before physicians and healthcare providers are even brought into a Plan's "network." This is the Credentialing Process.

There are also evidence-based guidelines and criteria available to assist in medical decision-making.

In spite of the best credentialing processes, evidence-based guidelines, and Quality Management, deaths from medical errors do occur.

Please remember that medical errors do not equate with medical malpractice. Even in the best of hands, there will be untoward events.

CHAPTER THIRTEEN: Medical Errors and Torts: Death From Medical Care Itself 183

Medical error is defined as a preventable adverse effect of medical care whether or not evident or harmful to the patient. Think of it as human error factor in healthcare. It is highly complex and related to many factors from unavoidable to incompetency and lack of education or experience. It is also important to remember that "(m)edical errors are also associated with extremes of age, new procedures, urgency, and the severity of the medical condition being treated."[387]

Remember that malpractice should be measured against the skill of the provider. That is why we have added the Provider Level when investigating Potential Quality issues (PQIs).

- **P1** Most experienced, competent practitioners would have managed this case in a similar manner

- **P2** Most experienced, competent practitioners might have managed this case differently

- **P3** Most experienced, competent practitioners would have managed this case differently

A 2013 peer-reviewed journal article reported in patient medical error death rate of 1.13 percent, or 400,000 per year.

Physicians get sued under tort law (one of many bases for legal action) for malpractice. Neurosurgeons and thoracic-cardiovascular surgeons have the highest percentage of doctors who face a claim each year, 19.09 percent and 18.9 percent, respectively.

Tectonic plate
Medical errors are probably more common than first thought.

CHAPTER FOURTEEN

When There Is No Consensus

TEACHING POINT

Sometimes there is no obvious evidence-based medical necessity.

It was stated previously that one of the key determinants for how you perceive the actuality of your healthcare coverage has its foundation in where you sit at the healthcare stadium. The case in point being the 'catbird' box seats behind home plate occupied by recipients of Federal Employee healthcare benefits and other "Cadillac" Health plans. But even these seats are not immune from tectonic plates. Now we will introduce the tectonic plate of "no consensus." This earthquake occurs when there is no agreement in the evidence-based literature on the best way to proceed. The patient is definitely on shaky ground.

This is the summation of all that I have been trying to present: how to go from a **victim** to an **informed consumer** of healthcare. This chapter, especially the summary by the patient's husband at the end, is the denouement!* Now, back to the issue at hand. What happens in the scenario where there is no obvious evidence-based medical necessity to support your case?

Sometimes people get better with the use of a placebo. There is no link between cause and effect in the placebo effect.[388.] The placebo effect is quite simply the apparent response to a "dummy" or no treatment.[389] The effect cannot come from the actual treatment itself but occurs when the patient apparently receives an effect.

Why do treatments with no value seem to work? There is a possible explanation. Researchers have used brain scans and other technology, and they think they may

---

*Denouement: the final outcome of the main dramatic complication in a literary work

have found a physiological explanation for the placebo effect. Just like the essence of this chapter, there is no obvious evidence-based reason for the placebo effect. It becomes a confounding variable when you are trying to establish a consensus.[390.]

Here is the hierarchy of proof that the medical world uses to hold data and facts accountable to each other. Look at the added simplified hierarchy as well as the grading system that follows. These grades are based on an independent review of scientific papers and articles that are being presented. This hierarchy can also be utilized to support your case when you disagree with your health plan's coverage decisions.

GRADING THE MEDICAL LITERATURE

The grading scale is the work of the International **Grade** Group. A **strong** (Grade 1) or **weak** (Grade 2) is based on "the balance between benefits, risks, burden, and cost, and the degree of confidence in estimates of benefits, risks, and burden. The system classifies quality of evidence as reflected in *confidence* in estimates of effects."[391] Grade A is **high**. Grade B is **moderate**. Grade C is **low**. The grades are based on factors that include the risk of bias, precision of estimates, the consistency of the results, and the directness of the evidence.

GRADING

1A - Strong recommendation; high-quality evidence; strong recommendation can apply to most patients in most circumstances without reservation

1B - Strong recommendation; moderate-quality evidence; strong recommendation, likely to apply to most patients

1C - Strong recommendation; low-quality evidence; relatively strong recommendation; might change when higher quality evidence becomes available

2A - Weak recommendation; high-quality evidence; weak recommendation, best action may differ depending on circumstances or patients or societal values

2B - Weak recommendation; moderate-quality evidence; weak recommendation, alternative approaches likely to be better for some patients under some circumstances

2C - Weak recommendation; low-quality evidence; very weak recommendation, other alternatives may be equally reasonable

CHAPTER FOURTEEN: When There Is No Consensus

There is an established pecking order or hierarchy of medical data that will allow us to weigh and measure how good the evidence on a particular subject might be.

This grading scale is based on a hierarchy of reliable evidence of proven medical effectiveness:

1. "Well-controlled studies of clinically meaningful endpoints published in refereed medical literature
2. Published formal technology assessments
3. The published reports of national professional medical associations
4. Published national medical policy organization positions, or
5. The published reports of national expert opinion organizations*"

Usually, there is a demonstrable link between cause and effect. How do you judge the validity of that link? How do you rate the evidence?

The best evidence for treatment efficacy is mainly from **meta-analyses** of randomized controlled trials (RCTs). RCTs are "quantitative statistical analysis of several separate but similar experiments or studies in order to test the pooled data for statistical significance."[392]

Here is some background information for the case that follows:

The medical literature will tell us what makes sense — except there are segments of medicine and medical care where there is no consensus as the evidence-based literature is not conclusive, such as the case that follows. Here is another close and personal first-person account of the journey from victim to informed healthcare consumer.

THE HOLE IN THE HEART
There are two kinds of holes in the heart:

1. Atrial septal defect (ASD)

---

*The Code of Federal Regulations (CFR) is the codification of the general and permanent rules and regulations (sometimes called administrative law) published in the Federal Register by the executive departments and agencies of the federal government of the United States. This passage comes from 32 CFR Ch. 1(7-1-07 Edition) Section 199.2

2. Patent foramen ovale (PFO)

PFO BY THE NUMBERS
A-Blood comes from the BODY(low oxygen)
1- Into the RIGHT ATRIUM(B)
2- Into the RIGHT VENTRICLE
C- To the LUNGS (to get oxygen)
➡ Some of the blood (low oxygen) sneaks through the PFO to the LEFT ATRIUM instead
D- Blood comes from the lung (high oxygen)
3-Into the LEFT ATRIUM (E)-mixes with blood from the PFO (lower oxygen)
4-Into the LEFT VENTRICLE (F)
5. Out to the BRAIN & BODY

Although both are holes in the wall of tissue (septum) between the left and right upper chambers of the heart (atria), their causes are quite different. An Atrial Septal Defect, or ASD, is a failure of the septal tissue (the wall between the rooms or chambers) to form between the atria. It is considered a congenital heart defect (something that you are born with).

This case involves a Patient Foramen Ovale, or PFO. It is also a hole between the upper chambers of the heart (atria). More than a quarter of the population has one, and for most, there are no adverse health effects. In fact, the vast majority of those affected don't even know they have it.[393]

When it remains open, it is called a **patent foramen ovale (PFO)**. For the vast majority of the millions of people with a PFO, it is not a problem. Problems can arise when the blood that leaks from the right atrium to the left contains a blood clot.[394] If it goes to the brain, you may have a stroke.[395]

The problem is that medical literature does not agree entirely on the importance and impact of having a PFO. In summary, there was a disconnect in the clinical studies linking PFO to stroke. So, what was the grade level of the evidence in support of addressing the PFO and consequent treatment in the case below? According to the health plan involved, apparently not as a strong recommendation (Grade 1) or quality of evidence as high (Grade A)/moderate (Grade B).

CHAPTER FOURTEEN: When There Is No Consensus

CASE STUDY
The Case In Point

CASE FILE:

1. Active adult female with a congenital hole in her heart; unknown at first

2. Patient had a stroke of unknown cause

3. Work up confirmed a specific "congenital" (left over from fetus) defect

4. She had a leftover hole in her heart (PFO)

5. Medical evidence very unclear as to what to do to prevent another stroke

6. Plan approved blood thinners to prevent second stroke

7. Plan denied surgery to close the hole, because it was experimental

8. Patient and husband became informed consumers

9. Use of the appeal process

10. Continued symptoms led to approval for surgery

The important take away teaching points for all of us are summarized by the patient's husband (at the end of the case). You might consider that summary as the fundamental lesson to be learned for the informed consumer. The following first-person discussion by this patient is riveting. The medical discussion about strokes is important. My overall goal for this case study is to drive home the basic tenant of this book: become an informed consumer of healthcare so you will not become a victim of it.

THE CASE IN POINT
This youngish 40-something-year-old female is a triathlete. She runs marathons, bicycles competitively, and swims. She was training for a Half Ironman. That would be swimming 1.2 miles, bicycling 56 miles, and run-

ning 13.1 miles. We will call her Alice Small, and she was in her usual state of good health.

It was 4:30 pm at her workplace as a dental hygienist. After finishing a patient exam, she had gotten up to tell the Office Manager about the intended treatment. Only she couldn't figure out how to say what she wanted to say. How to tell him about the scaling and root cleaning that was needed. Alice could hear someone talking in the background but when she turned her head to find that person, she could only see out of the right side. There was no vision on the left side.

"I was very confused. All I could say was 'something's wrong.' My office manager thought I was having low blood sugar and suggested that I get something to eat. After about five to 10 minutes, things had improved, but I still had some nausea and a headache.

"I have a history of migraines and thought that it might be that. After about five or 10 minutes I was improved. Other than the nausea and headache. My vision was normal. I could remember, and I could speak. I texted my husband to tell him what had happened. Our mindset was that I am young and healthy. Even though it sounds like a stroke, it couldn't be. Because my answer to his question of: 'How are you feeling now?' was 'I feel fine,' I drove my car home at 5 p.m.

"We were in denial. That night we had supper and over the next five days I biked 50 miles, ran eight miles, and set up a bike ride with a friend. This friend happened to be an eye doctor. As we were biking (four to five days out from the episode in the office), I told him about my sudden and temporary vision loss. He suggested that I see my doctor.

"I called my doctor at Mayo the following Monday, and he asked me to come in that day. He seriously doubted that I had had a migraine variant and thought that it might be a TIA."

CHAPTER FOURTEEN: When There Is No Consensus 191

Author's note: A Transient Ischemic Attack (TIA) is defined as a sudden onset of a focal or localized neurologic symptom and/or sign lasting less than 24 hours and caused by decreased oxygen to the brain (cerebral ischemia) which often returns to normal (reversible). However, there is risk of permanent tissue injury (i.e., infarction or stroke) even when those localize (neurologic) symptoms last less than one hour. About one-half of patients with this "classic" TIA syndrome (<24 hours in duration) have brain findings that match the localized neurological findings on their MRI.[396] They are common (>200,000 US cases per year) and often resolve within days to weeks. They are rare before age 40+. They may be the harbinger of future strokes. Symptoms include weakness on one side of the body, vision problems, and slurred speech. These are transient and often resolve within 24 hours.[397]

Back to Alice:

"As I am doing a Triathlon, I should probably get some brain imagining he suggested. So, off I go and get an MRI under sedation. Afterwards my husband and I go out for breakfast. We get a phone call. 'You had a stroke.'"

Author's note: Alice had the ischemic embolic type of TIA and stroke. Here are the characteristics of this stroke subtype.[398] They have a sudden onset with the symptoms being worse at the onset and improving over time. Hardening of the arteries is usually a risk factor. Men are more commonly affected than women. There is often a history of heart disease. The stroke can be brought on by common things such as getting up at night to urinate or sudden coughing/sneezing.

Alice is waiting to tell us the rest of the story:

"My next stop was the Neurologist. She was very calm and explained everything. The MRI showed a thromboembolic event deep in the left temporal optic tract. An area where brain tumors hide. Next stop. CT of the brain with contrast, Doppler of the carotid artery, CT of lungs, abdominal MRI — all negative. Then they did a 'bubble test' and a transthoracic echocardiogram. The diagnosis was made. PFO with right to left shunt. The source of the blood clot. Next step was the interventional cardiologist."

Author's note: An echocardiogram shows the anatomy, structure, and function of your heart. The standard form of this test is called a bubble test. Why? Because an IV solution of sterile saline (what your blood cells float around in) "is shaken until tiny bubbles form and then is injected into a vein. The bubbles travel to the right side of your heart and appear on the echocardiogram. If there's no hole between the left atrium and right atrium, the bubbles will simply be filtered out in the lungs. If you have a patent foramen ovale (PFO), some bubbles will appear on the left side of the heart.[399]

"This doctor indicated the treatment choices. Anticoagulation (blood thinners) or closure. I wanted to close the hole. The physician sent the prior authorization in and scheduled the surgery. As we were driving to the hospital for the procedure, Cigna denied the surgery as experimental. It appears that I needed to have a second stroke to get the procedure approved.

"My Cardiologist appealed but apparently, the Plan wouldn't talk to the doctor. We asked for a formal appeal with a like specialist. A like specialist talked to my doctor, but he felt that the Plan really didn't want to listen. The procedure was denied again. My husband and I started doing our own research. A good site was the PFO Foundation for Athletes.

"In the meantime, I was cleared to go back to training. After doing a standard 30-miler on the bike I noticed that I was having a more difficult time than usual. I thought that it was because of the lay off and some weight gain. When I came back home, my husband noted that my lips were blue.

"I talked to the cardiologist who was skeptical because it was practically unheard of for patients to desaturate (have a drop in the amount of oxygen in your blood) with a PFO. He did a stress echocardiogram with arterial blood gases and documented an actual difference. The actual desaturation percentage was significant. I had a significant right to left shunt (see the Teddy-Bear diagram from before). Based on this new information, the Plan approved my surgery."

The moral of the story
The moral of the story can be found in this summary from Alice's husband.

"You as a patient had access to the Mayo Clinic (an accredited, teaching hospital famous throughout the world) and also an insurance plan which is backed by the federal government and a benevolent association of detectives. That almost puts you in the VIP box behind the home plate with free beer and hot dogs using the model of a baseball stadium. Yet, despite this, once the diagnosis of cryptogenic stroke was made, you as a patient were left without guidance on best practices. We were cast off and left on our own to advocate for the surgery. The best that the neurology department gave us was that perhaps this was a 40-50 percent risk of future stroke, the cardiologist suggested that perhaps we should sue our insurance company to force their hand in approving the PFO closure. (Suing an insurance company would require years of work and most likely a class action to balance the cost — totally unrealistic advice).

"The reason that you got your surgery approved was that you didn't give up, and you educated yourself. You sought out retired doctors who had worked in the insurance industry, you learned about the RESPECT trial that studies cryptogenic stroke and PFO closure, and you spoke with cardiologists in other states.

"We learned about levels of appeal and that our plan relied on a third party, which, in of itself, was a large corporation to examine appeals even to the extent of having different departments within the same company look at previous denials. This 'having the wolf look after the sheep' approach meant that we were appealing a prior decision to a different group of doctors paid by the same company.

"We got unrealistic advice from another cardiologist who suggested we pay out-of-pocket for the surgery. This would have opened us up to extreme liability for unintended costs arising from the procedure.

"Finally, we learned about meta-analysis in medical research and how revenue recovery strategy of delaying the appeal process benefits the quarter earnings of a company. The most recent meta-analysis of 15-year cryptogenic stroke patients from RESPECT showed a significant decrease in M and M (*Author's note: Morbidity-bad health effects/Mortality-death*) against patients with PFO closure. However, that study was released, yet not published, at the time of the last appeal and thus the company held its earlier position that no statistical benefit for PFO closure.

"All these factors assisted in the final end run. Our hospital did an excellent clinical job with the diagnosis, surgery, and follow-up for Alice. They did absolutely nothing to assist us fight the insurance company despite all the clinical staff agreeing with the decision to perform surgery. What they did do was retain an open mind when we came to them with ideas to appeal. The 'bad gas in the tank' left to right atrial shift was Alice's idea which we researched and presented.

"Once the surgery was performed, the cardiologist informed Alice that he observed the PFO and it was quite large and causing significant shunting of blood."

Teaching points

- learning the motivation and machinations of the insurance industry
- understanding how to read medical research and literature
- seeking expert opinions about how to craft appeals which will be reviewed by the medical and legal community before approval
- thinking creatively about how to transfer liability to the insurance company should they disapprove a procedure
- joining diverse patient discussion groups nationwide

Alice is now asymptomatic and back to training. The moral of the story here is that it pays to be persistent, do your homework, and follow your plan's appeal process. It is also helpful to have physicians who will support your appeal and provide documentation for presentation to the plan. How do you appeal? I never thought that you would ask. We'll discuss that in Part D: What You Need To Know About Protection Against Tectonic Plates. Specifically, Chapter Sixteen.

CHAPTER FOURTEEN *What Have We Learned?*

This is the summation of all that i have been trying to present and is how to go from a **victim** to an **informed consumer** of healthcare.

There is the hierarchy of proof that the medical world uses to hold data and facts accountable to each other. There are times when evidence-based medicine doesn't have all the answers. When this occurs, providers of healthcare, policy-makers, and reviewing organizations such as health plans may not agree with the patient's point of view.

By following a logical approach to the problem, and with the appropriate attitude, the patient will become an informed consumer of healthcare.

Don't forget that you have partners along the way. Your physicians, organizations with expertise in patient advocacy, and last but not least, veteran physician-executives who are always willing to help get to the best results for your care from your healthcare providers and coverage for that care from the payors.

Become familiar with the tools you have at your disposal and don't be afraid to apply them. I quote from Alice's husband:

- learning the motivation and machinations of the insurance industry
- understanding how to read medical research and literature
- seeking expert opinions about how to craft appeals which will be reviewed by the medical and legal community before approval
- thinking creatively about how to transfer liability to the insurance company should they disapprove a procedure
- joining diverse patient discussion groups nationwide

PART D

Food For Thought

CHAPTER FIFTEEN

The Basics Of Healthcare Coverage

TEACHING POINT

HEALTHCARE 101

The Third-Party Payor

Healthcare 101 will be our jumping-off spot. In the United States, health insurance is any program that helps pay for medical expenses, whether through privately purchased insurance, employer-sponsored healthcare coverage, or a health plan funded by the government. Or out of your own pocket.

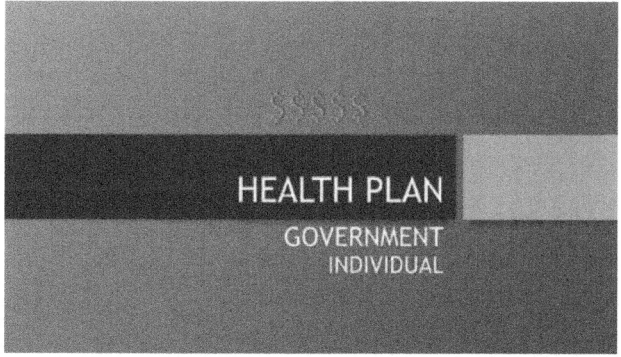

The following definitions will help you better understand what I am trying to depict. You have seen this before in Chapter Twelve and elsewhere. Now I will break it down into the basic components.

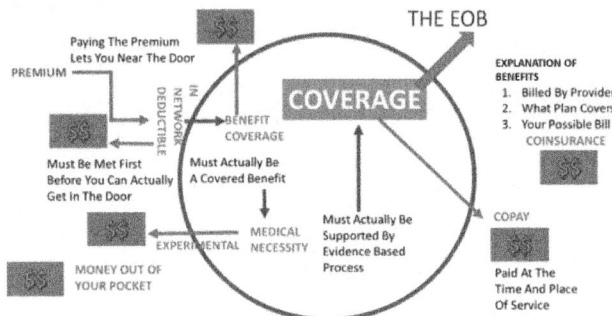

Keep in mind the typical types of health plans that are currently available. Here is a brief snapshot. I will explain each type a little more in a later segment. For now, just familiarize yourself with the alphabet soup taxonomy.*

SOURCE: Kaiser Family Foundation, 2017 Employer Health Benefits Survey.

There is a lot of data available. Allow me to summarize briefly. Overall, the growth of premiums was slowed by a shift toward bigger out-of-pocket costs for employees in the form of high deductibles.

---

*SOURCE: Kaiser Family Foundation, 2017 Employer Health Benefits Survey.

CHAPTER FIFTEEN: The Basics Of Healthcare Coverage

Premiums

"Fifty-six percent of small firms and 98 percent of large firms offer health benefits to at least some of their workers, with an overall offer rate of 57 percent." [400]

1. The average cost of employer-offered health coverage increased 5 percent to $20,000 for a family plan in 2018.

2. Annual 2018 premiums again rose 3 percent (same increase past two years) to $6,896. Employers paid 72 percent of premiums ($4,965.12) and employees paid 18 percent ($1,930.88).

"In August, the National Business Group on Health's (NBGH's) 2019 Large Employers' Healthcare Strategy and Plan Design survey, based on responses from 170 large U.S. employers, projected that the total cost of providing medical and pharmacy benefits will rise 5 percent for the sixth consecutive year in 2019." [401]

- 34 percent of employers with 10 to 499 employees saw their health plan costs increase by more than 10 percent.

- Only 11 percent of employers with 20,000 or more employees experienced similar double-digit increases.

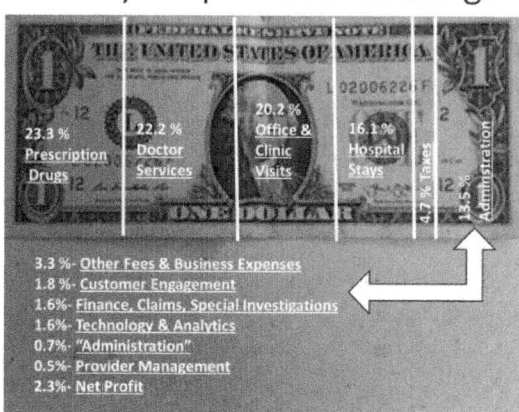

The monthly payment to the insurance company (premium) that lets you near the door (before deductibles are applied) gets spent by the third-party payor. Specifically, here is a 2014-2016 snapshot of inflation-adjusted average annual amounts paid by commercial health insurance plans in 2014-2016 for the medical care of plan members (see above). In other words, how premiums for a typical commercial health insurance plan are "spent."[402] Under the ACA, the net profit is limited.

Deductibles

Deductible are a wide-ranging dollar amount that you must "meet" or pay out of your own pocket before your health insurance begins to pay. "The average deductible among covered workers in a plan with a general annual deductible was $1,573 for single coverage."[403] There has been a shift in employers offering plans with larger deductibles. Enrollment in HDHP (High Deductible Health Plans) is increasing as much as 40 percent over a three-year period. There has been a shift in employers offering plans with larger out-of-pocket costs. **Household income has not kept up.** Out-of-pocket costs have outstripped income increase by as much as 10 percent or more in some places.[404]

The following information comes from Kiplinger.

Some data from 2018. The average deductible for:

- High-deductible plan — $1,600 for employee-only coverage and $3,200 for family coverage
- Average PPO deductible of $500 for employee-only coverage and $1,250 for family coverage

Despite the plans' difference in deductibles, the average maximum out-of-pocket spending limits for the year were similar:

- High-deductible plans were $3,600 for employee-only and $7,200 for family plans (out-of-network care can have higher out-of-pocket spending limits);
- PPOs were $3,500 for in-network care for employee-only and $7,000 for family plans.

Here is what 2019 might bring based on 2018 data:

- Most employers continue to offer high-deductible plans paired with a health savings account (53 percent)
- Most popular insurance option in 2018

- To qualify for a tax-friendly health savings account (HSA) the deductible must be at least $1,350 for single coverage or $2,700 for family coverage

- Typical employer HSA contribution — $500 for workers with single coverage and $1,250 for family coverage

- 41 percent of employees opted for a lower-deductible preferred-provider organization (PPO) plan

- 3 percent of employees opted out for a health maintenance organization (HMO) plan.[405]

If the types of plans are confusing right now, that's understandable. I will go over each of the plan types very soon in this chapter. Your take-away here is that the for-profit healthcare insurance model is creating financial stress. But wait, there are more out-of-pocket expenses yet to be discussed.

Copayment

A copayment is your share of the bill when you enter the door of doctor's office or specialist. It is usually a predefined amount that you pay after your insurance pays "most" of the cost.

"Your copay is a predetermined rate you pay for healthcare services at the time of care. For example, you may have a $25 copay every time you see your primary care physician, a $10 copay for each monthly medication, and a $250 copay for an emergency room visit." [406]

Coinsurance

In general, "Coinsurance is a percentage of a medical charge that you pay, with the rest paid by your health insurance plan, after your deductible has been met. For example, if you have a 20 percent coinsurance, you pay 20 percent of each medical bill, and your health insurance will cover 80 percent."[407] If your plan has a network requirement, this is what you will owe non-network providers after the insurance company pays whatever it will allow. In this case, your out-of-pocket expenses will be greater and sometimes unexpected, especially when you visit the Emergency Department at your local in-network hospital. Explanation? The ED doctor is usually contracted and considered out-of-network. The provider bills you for anything the insurance does not cover.

Summary of Benefits and Coverage

One of the things that may level the playing field a bit is the Summary of Benefits and Coverage.

This is a requirement set forth in the ACA. Any insurance plan, whether offered by your employer or on the Individual marketplace, must provide you with a plain language description of just what exactly your benefits are in a Summary of Benefits and Coverage, or SBC. This must also include a glossary of the terms. Your SBC should be your guidebook.

Here is an example of what a Summary of Benefits and Coverage could do for you. I would recommend that you go to the website in the footnote below and review the template.*

"The Summary of Benefits and Coverage (SBC) document will help you choose a health plan. The SBC shows you how you and the plan would share the cost for covered healthcare services."[408]

NOTE:

1. Information about the cost of your plan (called the premium) would be provided separately.

2. The Benefits and Coverage section is only a summary.

    - For more information about your coverage or to get a copy of the complete terms of coverage, you will need to know your insurance payors' contact information.

    - You will also need to know where you may view a glossary or general definitions of common terms and request a copy.

3. It should answer such questions as:

    - What common medical events are covered (the 10 essential coverage categories including preventive health);

    - Your Rights to Continue Coverage;

---

*https://www.dol.gov/sites/default/files/ebsa/laws-and-regulations/laws/affordable-care-act/for-employers-and-advisers/sbc-template-final.pdf

- Your Grievance and Appeals Rights (remember the case study in Chapter Fourteen?);

- Does this plan provide Minimum Essential Coverage? (Remember the Short-Term and Association Plans?);

- Does this plan meet the Minimum Value Standards? (You may be eligible for a premium tax credit to help you pay for a plan through the ACA marketplace);

- What your plan does not cover (See Covered Benefits below).

Glossary (associated with the Summary of Benefit Coverages):

1. Allowed Amount: This is the maximum payment the plan will pay for a covered healthcare service. May also be called "eligible expense", "payment allowance", or "negotiated rate."

2. Balance Billing: When a provider bills you for the balance remaining on the bill that your plan doesn't cover. This amount is the difference between the actual billed amount and the allowed amount. This happens most often when you see an out-of-network provider. A network provider may not bill you for covered services.

3. Network Provider (Preferred Provider): A provider who has a contract with your health insurer or plan who has agreed to provide services to members of a plan. You will pay less if you see a provider in the network. Also called "preferred provider" or "participating provider."

4. Out-of-pocket Limit: The most you could pay during a coverage period (usually one year) for your share of the costs of covered services. After you meet this limit the plan will usually pay 100 percent of the allowed amount. This limit helps you plan for healthcare costs. This limit never includes your premium, balance-billed charges, or healthcare your plan doesn't cover. Some plans don't count all of your copayments, deductibles, coinsurance payments, out-of-network payments, or other expenses toward this limit.

5. Plan: Health coverage issued to you directly (individual plan) or through an employer, union, or other group sponsor (employer group plan) that provides coverage for certain healthcare costs. Also called "health insurance plan", "policy", "health insurance policy" or "health insurance."

6. Prescription Drug Coverage: Coverage under a plan that helps pay for prescription drugs. If the plan's formulary uses "tiers" (levels), prescription drugs are grouped together by type or cost. The amount you'll pay in cost-sharing will be different for each "tier" of covered prescription drugs.

7. Provider: An individual or facility that provides healthcare services. Some examples of a provider include a doctor, nurse, chiropractor, physician assistant, hospital, surgical center, skilled nursing facility, and rehabilitation center.

8. Referral: A written order from your primary care provider for you to see a specialist or get certain healthcare services. In many health maintenance organizations (HMOs), you need to get a referral before you can get healthcare services from anyone except your primary care provider. If you don't get a referral first, the plan may not pay for the services.

9. Specialist: A provider focusing on a specific area of medicine or a group of patients to diagnose, manage, prevent, or treat certain types of symptoms and conditions.

The Explanation of Benefits, or EOB is a very important piece of information that your insurance plan will send to you. It will usually come after all provider bills have been received, adjudicated (what is to be paid and what you owe), and paid or not. Read it. Check its accuracy on the care you received. Be aware of any potential bill you may be receiving for costs of care not covered by your insurance.

I promised you some clarity on health plan types. Here are some examples of the most commonly offered healthcare plans in our for-profit health insurance model.[409]

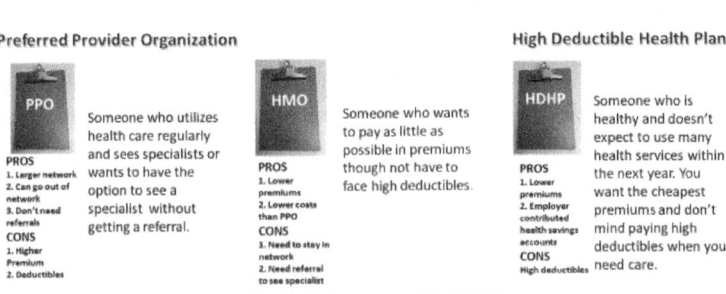

HEALTH CARE PLANS
THE BIG THREE

CHAPTER FIFTEEN: The Basics Of Healthcare Coverage

Point Of Service Plan

Someone who likes being to go out of network for care but wants a PCP coordinating your care.

PROS
1. Can go out of network
2. Don't need referrals

CONS
1. Need to file claims if you go out of network
2. Higher deductibles than PPO/HMO

Exclusive Provider Organization

Someone who doesn't mind having a limited number of doctors/facilities and would rather not have to get a referral to see a specialist.

PROS
Don't need referrals

CONS
1. Need to stay in network for care
2. Limited network

HEALTH CARE PLANS
OTHER CHOICES

First things first: what are the general types of plans, and what type of benefit coverage do they provide? If you are on federally- and/or state-funded Medicare, Medicaid, Tricare, Indian Health Service, or have no insurance, these situations have been addressed in previous chapters. So has coverage by your employer, or a plan in the Individual marketplace. Regardless of the "variation" that describes your situation, you still need to have a handle on the basic definitions of health insurance. Keep reading as this discussion pertains to all of you.

Which type of plan is the best for you? That depends on your specific situation. Here are some variables to consider:

1. Are you sick or well?
2. How is your family's health?
3. If you already have a doctor or doctors, do they accept your plan?
4. What can you afford?
5. Do you want to pay more money upfront before healthcare begins (premiums) or after the care has been received (deductibles, etc.)?
6. How much flexibility do you want when choosing a specialist?

"The two most common health plans have been generally HMOs and PPOs, but High Deductible (HDHPs) have become a lower-cost health insurance option for employers over the past decade. POS and EPO plans are options provided by some employers and health insurers, but they're not nearly as common as HMOs, PPOs, and HDHPs."[410]

TEACHING POINT
BENEFIT COVERAGE

We are feeling the rumbling of a tectonic plate moving under our feet as the employee benefits landscape in the United States has been transformed. Employers are faced with the upward spiraling costs of healthcare and other benefits[411] as there are constant changes in employment and benefits laws.[412] This uncertainty is augmented by the ever-changing healthcare debate, particularly those issues set forth in the Affordable Care Act and attempts to repeal and replace. Not to mention all of the changes brought about by executive order, tax bills, and litigation. The major tectonic plate continues to be cost.[413]

The Cost

The cost of healthcare in the United Sates for 2018 was $3.65 trillion. "That total is about the same size as Spain and Canada's entire economies — combined."[414] What this means is that the 4.4 percent increase in healthcare spending from 2017 has to be paid somehow. Usually it means that the healthcare consumer (us) see more money coming from our pockets to pay for our broken for-profit healthcare insurance model.

BENEFIT COVERAGE DATA[455]

YEAR	2016	2017	2018	FUTURE
National Health Expenditure (NHE)	+4.3% $3.3 trillion $10,348 per person 17.9% of GDP	+4.6 percent $3.5 trillion		Under current law, national health spending is projected to grow at an average rate of 5.5 percent per year for 2017-26 and to reach $5.7 trillion by 2026(α) 2018-4.4% to reach $3.65 trillion(β)
Private Health Insurance	+5.1 percent $1,123.4 billion 34 percent of total NHE	+5.5 percent $1,183.9 billion		+5.6% by 2019. For 2020 through 2025, private health insurance spending growth is projected to be above 5 percent per year, but to generally slow in the final years
Hospital	+4.7 percent $1,082.5 billion	+5.5 percent		Between 2020 and 2027, hospital spending is projected to grow yearly at an average of 5.7% (γ)
Physician & Clinical	+5.4 percent $664.9 billion	+5.0 percent $698 billion		Between 2020 and 2027, physician and clinical spending expected to increase at an average of 5.4%.
Prescription Drugs	+1.3 percent $328 billion		Current trending has leveled off at just under 6 percent and is predicted to stay in that range through 2025.	

455-Kamal, Rabah, et al. "How Much Is Health Spending Expected to Grow?" Peterson-Kaiser Health System Tracker, 12 Dec. 2018, www.healthsystemtracker.org/chart-collection/much-health-spending-expected-grow/
(α)-Centers for Medicare & Medicaid Services, "NHE Fact Sheet," 06 December 2018, www.cms.gov/research-statistics-data-and-systems/statistics-trends-and-reports/nationalhealthexpenddata/nhe-fact-sheet.html
(β) Harmon, Bob, "America's health care economy keeps ballooning," AXIOS, 21 Feb 2019, www.axios.com/health-care-spending-2018-hospitals-doctors-drugs-economy-b522093b-0cd0-4c68-96b1-f31cc08ec264.html
(γ) Piller, Rebecca, "US healthcare spending growth to hit 5.5% by 2027, CMS predicts," HEALTHCAREDIVE, 20 Feb. 2019, www.healthcaredive.com/news/us-healthcare-spending-growth-to-hit-55-by-2027-cms-predicts/548795/

The largest shares of total health spending were sponsored by the federal government (28.3 percent) and households (28.1 percent). The private business share of health spending accounted for 19.9 percent of total healthcare spending, state

CHAPTER FIFTEEN: The Basics Of Healthcare Coverage

and local governments accounted for 16.9 percent, and other private revenues accounted for 6.7 percent.[415]

As a result, employers (and all payors who pay for healthcare) are continuing to research and modify the health plans being offered to employees. In the United States, healthcare insurance has been handled mainly as a benefit of employment. The system has remained in place for decades. There is a long-term trend of rising healthcare costs and variable economic growth, motivating employers, the state and federal government, and other portions of the payor world to reassess and redefine their roles as providers and subsidizers of their constituents' healthcare benefits. For example, many employers, as well as the federal government, are integrating a pay-for-performance philosophy into their health benefits programs, motivating you, the healthcare consumer, to shoulder more responsibility for maintaining and improving their health and for contributing to the costs of your health coverage. Remember the discussion we had in Chapter Seven about healthcare cost and patient compliance?

The Office of the Actuary at the Centers for Medicare and Medicaid Services estimated that "aggregate healthcare spending in the United States will grow at an average annual rate of 5.8 percent from 2015 through 2025, or 1.3 percentage points higher than the expected annual increase in the gross domestic product."[416] That said, let us proceed to what actually determines the coverage currently being paid for. Most insurance plans have three basic guideposts that are utilized to determine coverage: covered benefits, medical necessity, and experimental. This coverage, plus what is charged (and actually paid) for the components of that coverage, leads to the cost of healthcare.

Covered benefits

Covered benefits are health insurance rights and protections that must be listed in each health plan's "Summary of Benefits and Coverage." I would remind you again of the **benefit coverage circle** we saw earlier in this chapter. Now we will begin to look at its various components.

That said, the first piece of the puzzle is usually described under the general heading of covered benefits. According to Healthcare.gov, health insurance rights and protections must be listed in each health plan's "Summary of Benefits and Coverage." Please keep in mind that this overview of the health law refers to the current ACA. Even though it remains unclear, even downright murky, where healthcare law will end up at the end of the day, the general comments still retain relevance.

The ACA is the counterweight, so to speak. It makes the case for "rights and protections" so that the consumer of healthcare coverage will be treated fairly and understand what they are getting into. These "rights and protections" vary as they apply to plans in the various sector of our healthcare "system".

With the caveat that the protections outlined below may not apply to grandfathered health insurance plans, let us begin. We have already discussed the "right to an easy-to-understand summary about a health plan's benefits and coverage."[417] This is the requirement that insurance companies and job-based health plans provide you with the Summary of Benefits and Coverage (SBC) and a uniform glossary of terms used in health coverage and medical care.

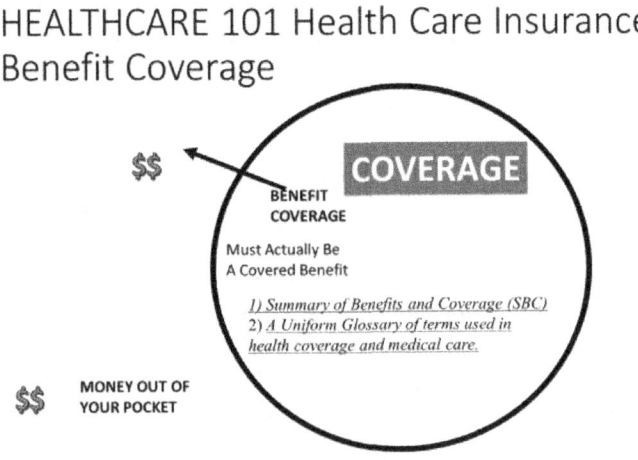

In essence, this document describes what the plan covers and what it costs. At the end of the day, if the benefit is not stated as being covered in the plan, or there is specific verbiage about exclusions, the particular service/procedure/place of service, etc. may not be covered. Plans will often site such coverage, or lack thereof, in their denials. Also, be aware of any "network" criteria. If you must use healthcare providers within the network, there are tectonic plates that will rattle your pocketbook if you decide to go "out-of-network."

Medical Necessity

The second guidepost is that of medical necessity. Doctors have to establish that a medical treatment will "prevent, diagnose, prevent the worsening of, alleviate, correct, or cure conditions" and that "no other medical service or site of service is comparable less costly."[418]

CHAPTER FIFTEEN: The Basics Of Healthcare Coverage

There is a giant conflagration along the tectonic plates of reasonable and necessary. A simple way to view this hurdle to coverage is to see how Medicare defines medical necessity in terms of reasonable and necessary. Yet even that basic definition relies on tectonic plates. The discussion below shows how difficult it has become in today's political and special interest climate to establish basic rules of the road.

WARNING: The definitions below are legal terminology and may not be in terms the English-speaking individual such as yourself might actually be familiar with. I will try to keep that to a minimum and interpret where necessary.

Definition: "No payment may be made for any expenses incurred for items or services, which are not **reasonable and necessary** for the diagnosis or treatment of illness or injury or to improve the functioning of a malformed body member."[419]

Interpretation: Unless it is fair and sensible and required, no payment will be made. But what is reasonable and necessary?

Definition of medical necessity: "**Reasonably** calculated to prevent, diagnose, prevent the worsening of, alleviate, correct, or cure conditions and *no other medical service* or site of service, comparable in effect, available, and suitable or less costly to the health agency."[420]

Interpretation: The service is considered medically necessary and covered when no other viable alternative can be used to prevent an illness, diagnose an illness, stop the illness from getting worse, or cures the condition or makes it better. That actually makes a bit of sense. Let us try this next one on for size and fit.

Definition: **Reasonable** and **necessary** is when a physician or similar provider of healthcare, exercising prudent clinical judgment in accordance with generally accepted standards of medical practice based on credible scientific evidence published in peer-reviewed medical literature.

Interpretation: It has to make sense clinically and not just be for the convenience of those involved (provider and patient), as well as be cost-effective.

Experimental

Definition: If there is scientific evidence to support a healthcare intervention, then you have established that the intervention is not **experimental.** If not, then the medical treatment is not supported by evidence-based medical data.

Interpretation: You have to have rock solid evidence produced under very controlled circumstances to keep that rascal variability from gumming up the works. Remember our discussion in Chapter Fourteen about lack of consensus?

HEALTHCARE 101 Health Care Insurance Medical Necessity

At the end of the day, the hierarchy of medical evidence can be summarized as:

1. Controlled studies of clinically meaningful endpoints, published in established (the term used is 'referred') medical literature;

2. Published formal technology assessment, reports of national medical associations, and/or national policy organizations. Some sort of process which has been reviewed by a well-thought-of medical organization and published; or

3. Published reports of national expert opinion organization. While expert opinion may matter, it does not have the same clout as well controlled studies or published reports of national healthcare organizations.

If a planned service, procedure, therapy, etc. does not meet the criteria of evidence-based medicine, it may be considered experimental. The National Association of Insurance Commissioners (NAIC) is one U.S. standard-setting and regulatory support organization. "Through the NAIC, state insurance regulators establish standards and best practices, conduct peer review, and coordinate their regulatory oversight."[421]

This group has established the hierarchy by which to determine if something is experimental and therefore not medically necessary. Briefly, here is the actual hierarchy of medical and scientific evidence: "Peer-reviewed scientific studies published in or accepted for publication by medical journals that meet nationally recognized requirements for scientific manuscripts."[422]

Plans will use an internal process called a Medical Technology Assessment Committee to review literature and other appropriate sources and determine if there is medical necessity to support coverage. I have served on such committees. They work.

In order to get **benefit coverage** for a service, the science has to be there to establish it as reasonable and necessary. Then the provider of that service has to use his or her best clinical judgment in providing that service. And just like magic, you have established medical necessity and will not be relegated to a procedure or medication not being covered on the grounds that it is experimental.

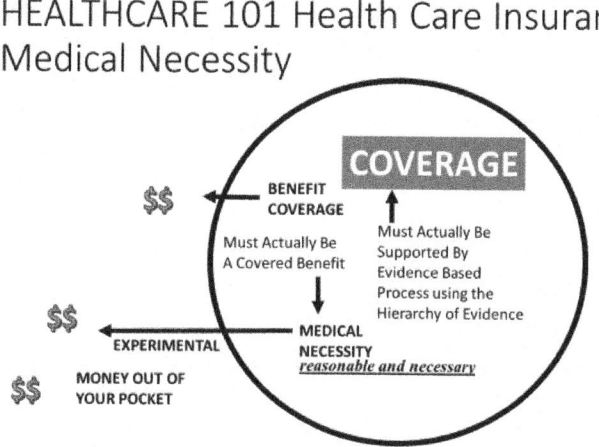

TEACHING POINT

UTILIZATION REVIEW

Timing is everything in managing tectonic plates. Often, healthcare plans will deny claims based on benefit coverage criteria. Remember, we have already discussed benefit coverage. When considering benefit coverage, timing is everything. If your provider does not get the documentation to the plan in the manner prescribed in the Summary of Benefit Coverage (SBC), tectonic plates really get agitated and denials will follow. At the end of the day, the reality is that the job — making sure you are not a victim — is not done until the paperwork is complete.

Review guideposts, as timing is everything in managing tectonic plates.

"Utilization Review is the process of comparing requests for medical services ('utilization') to guidelines or criteria that are deemed appropriate for such services, and making a recommendation based on that comparison."[423]

There are three such reviews based on timeliness:

1. Prospective Review: conducted prior to the delivery of the services requested. Prospective reviews may be for inpatient or outpatient services.

2. Concurrent Review: performed while (for example) the patient is still in the hospital and services are being provided. In a broader sense, it could refer to any review done in real time while the service is being rendered (in patient or outpatient).

3. Retrospective Review: performed after the requested service or procedure has already occurred, and the patient has been discharged (for example). Retrospective reviews may also be inpatient or outpatient.

If the "paperwork" doesn't get to where it needs to be in the timeframe required by the plan, can you spell earthquake?

CHAPTER FIFTEEN *What Have We Learned?*

- Premium: monthly payment to the insurance company that lets you near the door

- Deductible: a wide-ranging dollar amount (depending on your plan) that you must "meet", which means you must pay out of your own pocket before your health insurance begins to pay

- Copayment: Your share of the bill when you enter the door of doctor's office or specialist. It is usually a predefined amount that you pay after your insurance pays "most" of the cost

- Coinsurance: If your plan has a network requirement, this is what you will owe non-network providers after the insurance company pays whatever it will allow. The provider bills. Anything the insurance doesn't cover you may be at risk for.

Covered benefits: According to Healthcare.gov, health insurance rights and protections must be listed in each health plan's "Summary of Benefits and Coverage."

Medical necessity: The service is considered medically necessary and covered when no other viable alternative can be used to prevent an illness, diagnose an illness, stop the illness from getting worse, or cure the condition or make it better.

Reasonable and necessary: when a physician or similar provider of healthcare exercises prudent clinical judgment in accordance with generally accepted standards of medical practice based on credible scientific evidence published in peer-reviewed medical literature.

Experimental: The medical treatment is "not supported by evidence-based medical data" and "usually applied to drugs, procedures, devices." You have to have rock solid evidence produced under very controlled circumstances to keep that rascal variability from gumming up the works.

Utilization review: the process of comparing requests for medical services ("utilization") to guidelines or criteria that are deemed appropriate for such services, and making a recommendation based on that comparison.

Prospective Review: those reviews (inpatient or outpatient services) conducted prior to the delivery of the services requested.

Concurrent Review: performed while the patient is still in the hospital and services are being provided. In a broader sense it could refer to any review done in real time while the service is being rendered.

Retrospective Review: performed after the requested service or procedure has already occurred and the patient has been discharged. Retrospective reviews may be inpatient or outpatient.

CHAPTER SIXTEEN

Protection Against Tectonic Plates

"Diplomacy is the art of saying 'Nice doggie' until you can find a rock."
— Will Rogers, American humorist (1879-1935)[424]

THE APPEAL PROCESS

TEACHING POINT
Appeal process

The impact on the patient (or "the second party") is like a series of tectonic plates sliding along each other in a non-systematic way with many variables that impact healthcare in this country and lead to the documented statistical result of high cost with mixed clinical results. One or more of the tectonic plates will inevitably lead to a denial of healthcare services at least one time in all of our experiences. Maybe more. When that occurs, there are certain steps you can take to stand your ground and espouse your case.

We have discussed case studies and various strategies I utilized over my healthcare career. There is no 'one size fits all.' The U.S. Department of Health and Human Services gives a generic lay of the landscape, at least for as long as the ACA is the law of the land. I try not to bore you with long quotes. In this case, it is important that you understand the right that you have to appeal your case and the steps involved. Appealing is another job that isn't over until the paperwork is complete. I would suggest that if you want the justification for my summary statement that you follow this citation to its source.[425] All of the following section is taken directly from that site, give or take a few interpretations.

Appealing Health Plan Decisions

1. "You have the right to appeal a health insurance company's decision to deny payment for a claim or to terminate your health coverage."[426] You can appeal your insurance company's decision through an internal appeal, which is to ask your insurance company to do a full and fair review of its decision.

2. If your insurance company still denies payment or coverage, the law permits you to have an independent third party decide to uphold or overturn the plan's decision in an external review.

Internal Appeal

1. There are 3 steps in the internal appeals process:

    a) You file a claim, or a request for coverage.

    b) You or a healthcare provider (the first party) will usually file a claim to be reimbursed for the cost of treatment or services;

    c) Your health plan (the third party) denies the claim.[427]

2. The insurer is required to notify the patient, in writing, and explain why the claim was denied

    a) Within 15 days if you're seeking **prior authorization** for a treatment (**prospective**);

    b) Within 30 days for medical services **already received** (**retrospective**);

    c) Within 72 hours for urgent care cases. This is almost **concurrent**, or **at the time of service,** but is technically retrospective as the care has occurred but the bill may not yet have reached the insurance company.[428]

3. In order to file an internal appeal, you, as the patient, must:

    a) Complete all forms required by your health insurer; or

    b) Write to your insurer with your name, claim number, and health insurance ID number; and

    c) Submit any additional information that you want the insurer to consider, such as a letter from the doctor. I will suggest a data format below which might be of use in this process. The Consumer Assistance

Program in your state can file an appeal for you. The problem, or the tectonic plate, is that there may not be such a program available in your state in spite of the ACA. "CAPs that are still in operation are funded exclusively through mechanisms other than federal grant funds."*

4. You have 180 days (6 months) of receiving notice that your claim was denied to complete your appeal. If you have an urgent health situation, you can ask for an external review at the same time as your internal appeal.[429]

External Review

1. If your insurance company denies your request for payment or services after an internal review, you can ask for an independent external review.[430] In an external review,

   a) If your insurance company denies payment for a claim or terminates your health coverage, you can request an appeal;

   b) Your insurance company is required to review and explain its decision;

   c) Insurance company must also let you know how you can disagree with its decision;

   d) Insurance company required to start and complete the process in a timely manner.

2. Some Important Details

   a) Health plans that started on or before March 23, 2010 may be "grandfathered health plans"; appeals and review rights don't apply to grandfathered plans;

   b) Appeal rights depend on the state you live in and the type of health plan you have;

---

*Many states offer help to consumers with health insurance problems through Consumer Assistance Programs (CAPs). Through a federal grant, many states have established CAPs in order to better assist consumers experiencing problems with their health insurance or seeking to learn about health coverage options. State CAPs offer direct assistance by phone, direct mail, email, or walk-in locations to help consumers learn how to obtain or use their insurance effectively. CAPs play a critical role in ensuring that consumers are able to find health insurance and are able to access the benefits to which they are entitled. These programs received funding through Section 1002 of the Affordable Care Act.

c) Some group plans may require more than one level of internal appeal before you can request an external review.

Remember Alice from Chapter Fourteen? She and her husband had many experiences with appeals:

> We learned about levels of appeal and that our plan relied on a third party, which, in of itself, was a large corporation to examine appeals even to the extent of having different departments within the same company look at previous denials. This 'having the wolf look after the sheep' approach meant that we were appealing a prior decision to a different group of doctors paid by the same company.

He was both partially correct and also somewhat pessimistic in his evaluation. The Independent Review Organizations (IROs) who perform at all levels of appeal and who are worth their salt, undergo an accreditation process.

When picking an Independent Review Organization,

1. Make sure Independent Review Organizations have no conflicts of interest;
2. Establish qualifications for physician who actually do the independent medical peer review;
3. Address medical necessity and experimental treatment issues; and
4. Have reasonable time periods for the various types of reviews from standard to expedited peer reviews for the appeals processes.

"Accredited IROs undergo a thorough screening process and standardize their entire operations to provide review for consumers and payer organizations. Health plans and consumers can be assured that appeals receive a comprehensive review and objective decision."[431]

In my professional career, I have hired and worked for IROs. From my own personal experience, there is a professional level of fairness and due process that must be met. But they are not infallible. So, my advice comes by way of Will Rogers. "Diplomacy is the art of saying 'Nice doggie' until you can find a rock." It's important to make sure that your health plan has certain features — features that we will now discuss.

You have to be an informed consumer who is aware of your rights and benefits as you venture forward to joust with your health plan. How these realities can be addressed is called the appeal process. We will go through the usual appeal process available to you, as well as the "scorecard" I use in order to keep the players — and tectonic plates — straight in my mind; not to mention providing the right data for the appeal.

THE APPEAL PROCESS

It is the appeal process that, in effect, removes the gag from the patient and offers you/the patient the ability to move from the sidelines to informed consumer. In other words, it allows you to take an active role in the pursuit of healthcare benefit coverage.

In general, there are three steps in an appeals process. They may be called different things, but essentially the first is actually a **reconsideration** done by the original reviewer at the reviewing plan. In cases of medical necessity review, this will usually be done by a plan equivalent of a healthcare provider. Most often it is a physician. If this review still results in a denial, a second step or a **formal first level appeal** becomes the next move. A second reviewer must review the case. Although the beneficiary may request a peer-to-peer review, (like a specialist) most often a second healthcare professional affiliated with the plan does the review.

The third step or **second level appeal** is the "only step that must occur on an external basis, according to current federal and state laws, although some health plans are now using outside peer reviewers to review cases across all levels of appeals.*" Again, the key here is the request for a same-specialty peer review. Some plans offer a fourth step or **third level appeal** performed by the plan's parent organization or arbitrator.[432] Regardless of how many levels of appeals are gone through and who does them, how you and your physician document the appeals is important.

The scorecard

STEP 1: Documentation of the sentinel event. This would usually be the medical documentation of the initial event that led to the patient's condition. Keep in mind that you are documenting the medical necessity for the denied service, surgery, drug, test, etc.

---

*1) A first level internal appeal or reconsideration. 2) A second level internal appeal or formal first level appeal. (There may be one or two levels of internal appeal, depending on the plan type and design.) 3) A third level external appeal.

a. Initial patient's history and physical, including admission or date of service;

b. Severity of patient's signs and symptoms;

c. Review of systems;

d. Vital signs;

e. Pertinent physical findings, both positive and negative;

f. Level of acuity and risk-potential involved in the patient's evaluation and testing;

g. Pertinent medical evaluation to include laboratory data and radiologic evaluation;

h. Pertinent medical procedures involved in the evaluation;

i. Discharge summary or office notes;

j. All pertinent evaluation results whether they be related to the laboratory, radiology, or procedure;

k. How patient responded to any and all medical, surgical, psychological, and therapy interventions (treatment);

l. Patient's physical evaluation at discharge or end of the treatment.

STEP 2: Follow up with evaluation and testing, including a physical examination, laboratory tests, and any other pertinent data:

a) Medical/surgical;

b) Psychological;

c) Therapy modalities (physical therapy/occupational therapy/speech therapy);

d) Usual and customary interventions with expectations (goals) and documentation of effect/lack of effect.

STEP 3: Establish the need for the treatment you are requesting, especially if it is one that is considered outside of usual and customary treatment.

a) Why are you requesting the treatment?

b) Why did the usual and customary treatment fail?

c) What are your expectations/goals of new technology/treatment/testing?

d) Literature to support

e) Any current criteria for inclusion/exclusion

ACCREDITATION

So, how do you sleep at night wondering if you will get a fair shake from your insurance plan? There is a fairly rigorous process that most healthcare organizations undergo.

Accreditation is the act of granting credit or recognition, especially to a healthcare organization that maintains suitable standards.

Accreditation is also the formal procedure by which an authorized accrediting agency assesses and verifies in writing by issuing a certificate indicating that the healthcare organization's goods or services, procedures or processes, or events or situations meet with established requirements or standards.

Accreditation includes looking at a healthcare organization's:

- attributes
- characteristics
- quality
- qualification
- status

In my experience, the three stalwarts of the accreditation process that I have had the most interface with are as follows.

The Joint Commission

The Joint Commission is a United-States-based nonprofit tax-exempt 501(c) organization that accredits more than 21,000 U.S. healthcare organizations and programs. A majority of state governments recognize Joint Commission accreditation as a condition of licensure for the receipt of Medicaid and Medicare reimbursements. Eighty percent of healthcare organizations in the United States are accredited by this organization.

The Joint Commission's stated mission is, "to continuously improve healthcare for the public, in collaboration with other stakeholders, by evaluating healthcare organizations and inspiring them to excel in providing safe and effective care of the highest quality and value."[433] The accreditation standards are updated, and patient safety goals are expanded on a yearly basis. These changes are posted on the website with the intention of creating process transparency for healthcare organizations, their institutions, practitioners, patients, and advocates.

NCQA

The National Committee for Quality Assurance (NCQA) is an independent 501(c)(3) non-profit organization in the United States. "This organization works to improve healthcare quality through the administration of evidence-based standards, measures, programs, and accreditation. NCQA operates on a formula of measure, analyze, and improve and it aims to build consensus across the industry by working with policymakers, employers, doctors, and patients, as well as health plans."[434]

The NCQA manages three voluntary accreditation programs:

- individual physicians
- health plans
- medical groups

Health plans seek accreditation and measure performance through the administration and submission of the Healthcare Effectiveness Data and Information Set (HEDIS) and Consumer Assessment of Healthcare Providers and Systems (CAHPS) survey. There is also an evidence-based program for case-management accreditation available for uses in all sectors of healthcare organizations.

URAC

The Utilization Review Accreditation Commission (URAC) mission: promote improvement in the quality and efficiency of healthcare management. This is done through a process of accreditation, education, and measurement. URAC's Health Plan Accreditation is considered a nationally recognized symbol of excellence. Accreditation certifies that the healthcare organization meets standards of quality and operational integrity. There is a strong focus consumer protection and empowerment.[435]

CHAPTER SIXTEEN: Protection Against Tectonic Plates

URAC's Health Plan Accreditation focuses on quality improvement and patient safety across the continuum of care, including

- Wellness and health promotion
- Care coordination
- Medication safety and care compliance
- Rewarding quality
- Care delivery through a patient-centered healthcare home network
- Mental health parity
- HIPAA breach requirements
- Measures patient-centeredness, communication and care coordination, patient safety, community, population and public health, efficiency and cost reduction, and effectiveness of clinical care
- Patient experience of care (CAHPS® Survey)

The National Committee for Quality Assurance (NCQA) accredits health plans, provider groups, and various medical businesses. The Joint Commission focuses on hospitals, laboratories, and many types of medical institutions. The Joint Commission and NCQA certify their clients in different ways. I would remind you of the discussion we had in Chapter Thirteen about some apparent issues with the accreditation process.

It should be noted that a British Medical Journal observational study indicated that hospital accreditation by independent organizations in the United States, such as The Joint Commission, is not associated with lower mortality and is "only slightly associated with reduced readmission rates for the 15 common medical conditions selected in this study."[436] Another take away message was that being accredited by The Joint Commission was not superior to another independent accrediting organization.

In fact, there might be issues with the Joint Commission as far as psychiatric hospitals are concerned: "More than 100 psychiatric hospitals have remained fully accredited by the nation's major hospital watchdog despite serious safety violations that include lapses linked to the death, abuse, or sexual assault of patients."[437] Less than 1 percent of such facilities did not pass accreditation. Yet, follow-up visits by state inspectors resulted in 16 percent of these facilities having "severe safety" violations.

The Center for Medicare and Medicaid Services (CMS) even upped the ante of oversight of the 10 federally approved healthcare accreditation organizations. This was in response to an earlier Wall Street Journal report that found that the Joint Commission (which accredits almost 80 percent of hospitals in the United States) took no action to revoke or modify their accreditation even when other agencies found problems after the fact.

"Hospitals kept their full accreditation even in cases where they had been ousted from the Medicaid program for safety violations."[438] CMS will begin posting performance data on the accreditation organizations to include issues that may have been missed and found by other agencies such as Medicaid.

So, there you have it. You do not have to go quietly into the night if your health plan denies a service. By doing your research and being an informed consumer like Alice and her husband, you can level the playing field and even perhaps tip it in your favor.

CHAPTER SIXTEEN What Have We Learned?

As a general rule, you have a right to appeal decisions by your health plan or payor. You have the right to question your plan's denial of a service at three different levels along the way:

1. Reconsideration: informal second look by the initial reviewer (usually a physician)
2. Formal first level appeal: review by a second reviewer (usually a physician), usually in the employ of your payor
3. Formal second level review: review by a third-party reviewer (usually a physician), usually in the employ of an independent review organization (IRO).

You have the right to request a same specialty reviewer.

There is an **accreditation process** that assures the impartiality and validity of the reviewers. Recent data has brought the accreditation process under scrutiny. Please keep in mind the positives and the negatives.

CHAPTER SEVENTEEN

Accountable Care Organizations

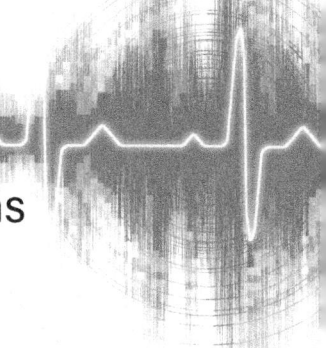

TEACHING POINT

ACCOUNTABLE CARE ORGANIZATIONS

Enlightened Health plans will incorporate a myriad of "tools" in an attempt to integrate the evidence-based medicine review into the interface of tectonic plates with the patient. This approach is part of the concept of an "Accountable Care Organization" (ACO) anchored by the "Patient Centered Medical Home (PCMH)."

I have mentioned how disorganized and variable the American healthcare "system" is in doing business as the so-called for-profit healthcare insurance model. This model may excel at developing life-saving innovative and evidence-based treatments, but our healthcare delivery system has ignored or been slow to give due attention to population health and the other essentially non-healthcare related factors that drive health outcomes (Chapter Two).

To address our tectonic plates of better health (**quality**), better availability of care (**access**), and lower costs (**cost**), positive changes must occur in our American Healthcare in transition. Enter the Accountable Care Organization. It is vital that the providers of healthcare shape it. Appropriately directing medical and other resources and avoiding unintended harm to well-functioning systems of care is absolutely essential as well. If real sustainable improvement in-patient care is to occur, the providers of healthcare must become engaged and partner with policy-makers.

Accountable Care Organizations (ACOs)

Elliott S. Fisher is the director of the Dartmouth Institute and the John E. Wennberg Distinguished Professor of Health Policy, Medicine and Community and

Family Medicine at the Geisel School of Medicine at Dartmouth. This discussion of the ACO is gleaned from articles he has published.[439]

"Accountable care organizations (ACOs) are part of a new payment and delivery model that aims to improve quality of care while controlling costs for populations of patients. ACOs took conceptual shape about 10 years ago as an approach to achieve these goals in a manner that fosters flexibility."[440] "Unlike the managed care movement in the 1990s, capitated payments have not been a foundational element of the ACO movement, although components of capitation will likely prove important. ACOs were therefore less disruptive to the status quo and with inclusion in the Affordable Care Act of 2010 they gained considerable momentum."[441]

According to the Council Of Accountable Physician Practices, here is the scoop on ACOs. The Council of Accountable Physician Practices (CAPP) is a coalition of organized multi-specialty medical groups and health systems.[442] As the business structures that support patient-centered care are often not apparent to the patient, you might find it difficult to know if a doctor's practice is part of an Accountable Care Organization. If the care looks coordinated between primary care and specialists, then you have ACO physician groups whose mission is to provide quality coordinated care. Here are the clues:

1. Doctors of many specialties are working together, and you have a good choice of doctors in the group so that you can find one that works best for you.

2. You have easy access to specialists because they work within the medical group or are effectively linked to the group; this reduces delays in receiving care and facilitates easier care coordination.

3. All doctors — primary care and specialists — have access to your electronic medical records and can share information through a confidential electronic computer system. In the most integrated systems, the electronic medical record is also available at the hospital.

4. You receive supportive services and preventive care (health educators, nurses, nutrition counseling, etc.) easily and directly from your doctor's office.

5. The group uses medical teams to allow for 24-hour access to medical services and this team also has access to your full medical record.

6. It is easy to get labs, X-rays, physical therapy, and other services because many of these services are located within or near your doctor's office and may also share information and computer systems.

7. The group regularly conducts surveys rating the care patients receive from the medical group or doctor. This indicates that the medical group is assessing the quality of care patients receive so that the group and its doctors perform their best and are held accountable for delivering high quality care.

Does this sound like the doctors you usually receive your care from? If so, then you may already be part of an ACO. The Patient Centered Medical Home (PCMH) is a care delivery model where your treatment is coordinated through your primary care physician to ensure that you receive the necessary care when and where you need it, in a manner you can understand.[443]

RETURN ON INVESTMENT

Remember our discussion about how providers get paid in Chapter Four, from whatever the market will bear to the very controlled? These two extremes are revisited below.

We will begin with the most traditional and cost-provoking model, "**fee-for-service.**" It is a production model and "requires patients or payers to reimburse the healthcare provider for each service performed." While **access** is encouraged, there is no incentive to improve **quality** or contain **cost**.[444]

In the **capitation** healthcare payment model, patients are assigned a per member per month (PMPM) payment based on their age, race, sex, lifestyle, medical history, and benefit design. The compensation is based on expected utilization.[445]

Again, we will visit the Medicare space to discuss how they pay ACOs. The Medicare Shared Savings Program (MSSP) is a voluntary program open to health systems and physician groups. It has become the most popular ACO contract in the U.S. with over 404 participating organizations. MSSP offers two tracks: upside-only with smaller share of savings, or two-sided risk with more favorable sharing rate. Patients are assigned retrospectively based on primary care billings.

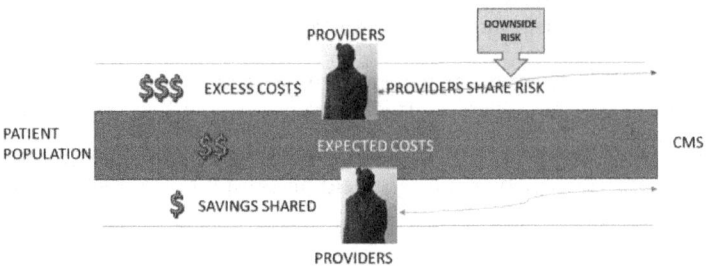

ACOs are eligible to share in portion of savings resulting from reduced utilization. Bonuses are contingent upon meeting quality targets. The Centers for Medicare and Medicaid Services (CMS) released the 2015 financial and quality performance data for its accountable care organization (ACO) programs for the fourth performance year (PY4) of the Pioneer ACO Program and third performance year (PY3) of the Medicare Shared Savings Program (MSSP)[446]:

1. Produced **cost** savings of $466 million in 2015 for Medicare (small increase of about $55 million over savings generated in 2014)

2. Average **quality** scores continued to increase in both programs

On January 18, 2017, CMS announced the selection of 99 new Accountable Care Organizations (ACOs) and 79 renewing ACOs that are joining or continuing their participation in the Medicare Shared Savings Program for the 2017 performance year. This seventh application cycle would increase the Shared Savings Program to 480 participating ACOs. This information was updated in December 2018.[447]

And where are we today? Evaluations of the accountable care organization payment models — including the Medicare Shared Savings Program, Colorado's Accountable Care Collaborative, and Oregon's Coordinated Care Organizations — revealed successes in overall performance (**access**) and spending (**cost**), but further assessment was required to address their effect on patients' health and quality of life (**quality**), according to two studies and an editorial published in JAMA Internal Medicine.[448] Here are the findings:

1. Post-acute care spending dropped by 9 percent (**cost**)— or about $106 per beneficiary ($3.07 three years into the program, $115.15 fours years into the program, and $74.57 five years into the program);

2. No drop in **quality**;

3. ACOs that joined the program in the first year (2012) showed the best reductions in costs[449] and ACOs in the MSSP for at least four years were behind almost all of the $314 million saved in 2017;

4. Decrease in spending was primarily driven by fewer patients being discharged into skilled nursing facilities and shorter lengths of stay for those who were admitted.

*Please keep in mind that CMS changed how it calculated ACO benchmarks that may have contributed to the positive financial results. Specifically, in 2017, CMS began to incorporate regional spending into benchmark calculations for ACOs that participated in MSSP for a second agreement period.

TECTONIC PLATE ALERTS

Alert #1

There is an assumption that downside risk isn't a reliable predictor of an ACO's success. In fact, assuming risk has become a possible deal-breaker moving forward. CMS is pushing for MSSP participants to assume "downside risk" sooner. This is not an idea that providers (the first party) are wild about. A National Association of ACOs survey seemed to indicate that as many as three out of four Accountable Care organizations may leave the MMSP based on that push.[450]

The Center for Medicaid and Medicare Innovation Director, Adam Boehler, stresses that the move to value-based care would be slow and deliberate — and implied it would remain voluntary when it comes to physician-assumed risk. "Despite (CMS head) Verma's statements, Center for Medicaid and Medicare Innovation Director Adam Boehler later said CMS won't force providers into risk-based contracting."[451]

Alert #2

Just because a healthcare provider organization — and this can be the first party providers as well as the third-party healthcare insurance organizations — has gotten bigger or merged either horizontally (in the same field) or vertically (across other fields), this does not necessarily mean that they have become an Accountable Care Organization. It may just be a business strategy to gather market share and the ability to charge more. Here is the three-party (beware the fourth) healthcare insurance model in case you forgot.

THREE PARTY (Beware the 4th) SYSTEM

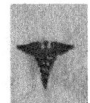

There's **one party** — **the provider** who provides the service
1. has its own master list of charges for different services.
2. different from provider to provider

There's a **second party** — the **patient**, who receives the service.

And there's a **fourth party** — the **decision makers** driven by "for-profit" motivation

And there's a **third party** — the **insurance company**, who pays for the service.
1. don't pay those listed charges
2. negotiates for lower prices with **each** hospital and doctor on every plan.
3. negotiated prices even can vary within an insurance company depending on which plan a patient has.

CHAPTER SEVENTEEN *What Have We Learned?*

A major step in removing yourself from the ranks of healthcare victims is to understand the following:

- Doctors of many specialties work together
- Easy access to specialists linked to the group
- All doctors have access to your electronic medical records and can share information
- You receive supportive services and preventive care
- The group uses medical teams to allow for 24-hour access to medical services
- It is easy to get labs, X-rays, physical therapy, and other services
- The group regularly conducts surveys rating the care patients receive
- Some ACOs even incorporate hospitals and other places of service

Return On Investment
Post-acute care spending dropped by 9 percent (**cost**) — or about $106 per beneficiary with no drop in **quality**. ACOs that joined the program in the first year (2012) showed the best reductions in costs. The decrease in spending was primarily driven by fewer patients being discharged into skilled nursing facilities and shorter lengths of stay for those who were admitted.

Tectonic Plate Alerts
Downside risk is still a bone of contention.

Just because a healthcare providing organization has gotten bigger or merged either horizontally (in the same field) or vertically (across other fields), this does not necessarily mean that they have become an Accountable Care Organization. It may just be a business strategy to gather market share and the ability to charge more.

CHAPTER EIGHTEEN

A Case Study In Health Plan Engineering

In this final chapter, I would like to address a way forward being espoused in different quarters of the debate about what to do to fix American healthcare in transition. As to what would be best for you given all the tectonic plates and evolving seats at the healthcare ballpark, I must admit that I am not absolutely sure.

Here is one example of health plan engineering based on my trip to Abu Dhabi, one of seven Emirates in the United Arab Emirates (UAE). They share many of the healthcare issues that we have discussed. They also have gone to universal healthcare sponsored by the government, a model shared throughout the globe but not in the United States.

Why is this relevant to our discussion? The American voter is nearing 50 percent when it comes to approving the passing a national health plan in the United States.

The concept of one-party payor or Medicare for all is based on the healthcare systems in other countries. Most are well-known, like England or Canada. The United Arab Emirates (UAE) is also a one-payor system but not as well know. It also happens to be one place where I have some experience and first-hand knowledge.

With that background in mind, many of the same topics we have discussed in the previous chapters were also germane for the UAE. So how has a **one-party payor** worked out for the Emirati? Let us say that there were many opportunities for growth (improvements). The next two slides will give you an overview without (I hope) losing you in the weeds.

A CASE STUDY IN HEALTH PLAN ENGINEERING: ABU DHABI

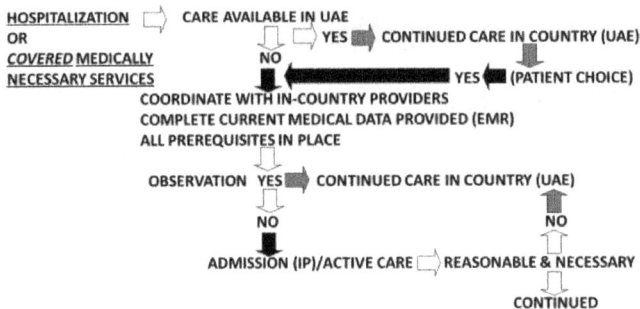

A CASE STUDY IN HEALTH PLAN ENGINEERING: UNITED STATES

I have gone through this introductory process to introduce the topic of a single-party payor system.

I am not an expert on this subject, so for this discussion I have asked a colleague of mine to take up this final topic. Ed Weisbart, MD chairs the Missouri chapter of

CHAPTER EIGHTEEN: A Case Study In Health Plan Engineering

Physicians for a National Health Program, part of the 26-year-old 18,000-member non-profit organization that advocates for improving Medicare and providing it to all Americans. He also volunteers as a physician in a variety of safety net clinics and other non-profits across the St. Louis area.

The remainder of this chapter is an op-ed provided by Dr. Weisbart specifically for this book. My purpose is to give you his compassionate and caring physician/physician-executive's discussion of a potential solution to the tectonic plates of American healthcare in transition based on the healthcare insurance for-profit model. I will meet you on the other side and pontificate my summary of all of this and what direction I believe we need to be headed in when it comes to American healthcare in transition.

Dr. Weisbart, the stage is yours.

> I recently saw a patient with an acute flare of his gouty arthritis. He's been treated for this problem for many years and can completely avoid these disabling attacks when he takes his prescribed medication. For the last two decades, he's worked as a floor-polisher at a local corporate office. They recently outsourced his job to an independent contractor, who immediately hired him to do the same work at the same wage. But because he was a new employee for this contractor, he had to wait three months until they would provide him with insurance. During this gap he was unable to afford his medication, tried to live without it, and had the predictably painful attack of an entirely preventable problem. He missed work for a week and now his job is in jeopardy.
>
> Physicians like me see these stories over and over again.
>
> For those who have access to it, the American healthcare system provides some of the world's best results. Despite the fact that life expectancy for Americans is several years shorter than it is for those in any other modern nation,[452] the most senior of Americans surprisingly have lower mortality rates than people the same age in many peer nations. Once we turn 65, our nation's health gradually improves, year by year, surpassing coun-

try by country. The most senior among us have some of the world's best health outcomes.[453]

Only in America does turning age 65 mean that you're guaranteed health insurance.

Before age 65, Americans have a bewildering array of insurance providers. Insurance varies by copays, coinsurance, deductibles, out-of-pocket maximums, prior authorizations, and even by what's included as a covered benefit. Among those with insurance, many have very limited (if any) coverage for physical therapy, palliative care, mental health, nutrition counseling, eyeglasses, hearing aids, and a long list of other important components of a comprehensive healthcare system. One of the most frustrating aspects of American insurance is the restrictions it places on patient control over their own selections for specific physicians, pharmacies, and hospitals. This Byzantine complexity is a uniquely American problem, described in words that most Americans don't fully understand and baffle those in other countries.

The variations in type of American insurance are not randomly spread across the country. Your insurance — and therefore your access to healthcare and your life expectancy — varies widely by zip code, income, gender, vocation,[454] and even by race.[455,456]

It turns out that the variation in insurance offerings are among the most powerful drivers of the life-expectancy variations among races. Although African-Americans live several years less than whites, on average, this gap nearly closes when the differences in insurance are removed.

There are at least three examples that demonstrate this:

- Every American on dialysis is provided Medicare. African-Americans on dialysis — and therefore on Medicare — live longer than white Americans on dialysis.[457]

CHAPTER EIGHTEEN: A Case Study In Health Plan Engineering

- Within the Veterans Administration, where everyone has the same insurance regardless of racial heritage, African-American live to be older than whites.[458]

- Life expectancy differences between races nearly disappear once we reach the age of Medicare.[459]

These and other data points convince me that the United States has much of the world's best healthcare delivery system. It's far from perfect, but our larger problem is that we just don't let every American use it. The tragic irony is that universal healthcare would be less expensive for our nation.

How can we spend less by covering more people?
As of the writing of this chapter, there have been at least 28 different studies done by different economists in different institutions with different models, each of which concluded that a solution such as single-payor "Improved Medicare for All" would either be cost-neutral or would save tremendous expenses for the nation.[460]

The most recent of these studies, from the Political Economic Research Institute of the University of Massachusetts-Amherst, anticipates that households and private businesses overall would pay 9.6 percent less on healthcare than they do today. They acknowledge that the use of healthcare would increase as people would see their physicians and dentists more frequently for example and that this would drive up expense by 12 percent. They also estimate that the nation's expenses would fall by 9 percent due to less need for system administration, by 5.9 percent due to lower prices on pharmaceuticals (a 40 percent drop in the 14.7 percent of spending on pharmacy), 2.8 percent drop from uniform rates on the delivery side, and a 1 percent drop due to fraud and waste programs. Overall, that 12 percent increase in cost from utilization would be balanced by a 19 percent saving. Rolling this together, that means that the $3.24 trillion our nation spent on healthcare in 2017 would have been reduced by $310 billion to $2.93 trillion.[461]

$2.93 trillion sounds like a lot of money, but as economist Gerald Friedman stated, "If we can pay for the status quo, we can pay for a program that is less expensive."[462]

How would we build a system of universal health insurance?
The United States has an imperfect but highly successful program to build upon. Since Medicare was enacted in 1965, it has rescued countless seniors from poverty, provided them nearly unfettered control over their own healthcare decisions, and is probably the key reason our seniors achieve the world's best remaining life expectancies. The most sensible solution is to build on its decades of success, improve a few critical issues, and provide that to all Americans.

The overwhelming majority of American physicians and hospitals accept Medicare, which enables seniors to see virtually any physician, anywhere in the country, whether home or traveling out of their area.[463] Few Americans with employment-based insurance enjoy that level of freedom and autonomy.

There are two main aspects of Medicare that need to be improved: the financial barriers and the benefit design.

Medicare today has significant copays and deductibles and no limit on how much those items can add up to. For that reason, most seniors today purchase a "supplemental policy" (also known as a Medigap, wrap, Plan F, Plan G, or a variety of other subtypes) or join a Medicare Advantage program. These options greatly reduce or even eliminate those financial burdens and help seniors avoid the medical bankruptcies that still happen to those on traditional Medicare.

So the first thing that needs to be improved in Medicare is the elimination of copays, coinsurance, and deductibles. Improved Medicare will include first-dollar coverage for prescription drugs, outpatient care, hospitalization, and a long list of other medically necessary items.

The second major improvement needed in Medicare is to correct the gaps in coverage. Most Americans agree that Medicare should cover things like dentistry, hearing aids, eyeglasses, and other similar items. 70-80 percent of us are even willing to fund that with a modest payroll tax increase.[464]

In addition to improving Medicare, the United States needs to expand it to cover everyone in the United States.

- Cover the president, Congress, school teachers, unions, fast food workers — everybody who lives here. My neighbor's health impacts my own.

- Cover the wealthy alongside those of low income. This eliminates the expensive, humbling, and intrusive process of assessing individual finances. It also means an end to the acrimony over state decisions about Medicaid expansion.

- The very concept of insurance is to spread the risk of an unexpected problem across a broad pool of people without that problem. Everyone is vulnerable to the problem, so everyone needs a defense for the day their unlucky number is called. The more people in that pool, the easier it is for the pool to absorb a problem when the inevitable happens. Small businesses, with 100 employees, can be overwhelmed by one employee with cancer or hepatitis, the treatment for which can easily cost more than that employee's entire annual salary. The larger the pool, the more predictable the costs and the easier it is to absorb the cost of expensive care. Having all 330,000,000 Americans in the same risk pool is the most stable strategy.

- Having 330,000,000 people in the same plan also enables the most powerful price negotiations for prescription drugs and other services. Pharmaceutical manufacturers, for example, need to be reimbursed well enough to want to continue producing medications, but not at the current level that quickly leaps out of the reach of far too many of us.

In short, improving and expanding Medicare to every American isn't just a nice thing to do — it makes compelling business sense for the nation.

This strategy eliminates almost any role for the health insurance industry. Insurers could still sell insurance for things that are not included in Medicare (mandatory private rooms, medically unnecessary cosmetic surgery, some dental procedures, etc.), but they would be barred from selling insurance that duplicates what every American would be provided. That by itself comes with dramatic savings. Insurance companies today report 15 to 20 percent overhead[465] while traditional Medicare (parts A and B) report overhead levels of 2.2 percent.[466] The only way to close that gap is to provide all Americans with Medicare.

There are other solutions
No two countries organize their healthcare in the same manner, but there are some common patterns, recently reviewed by the American Academy of Family Physicians.[467] There are important differences within each of the categories below, but this high-level summary is a good introduction (BHC author's note: I have added the per capita cost of healthcare for each of these models to underscore the ROI):

- **National Health Insurance:** Canada ($4,826), Ireland ($5,528), Spain ($3,300)[468], and Australia ($4,543) rely upon a "National Health Insurance" model. The government's role is focused on a fair finance model but without a direct role in the delivery of care. Physician practices and hospitals are typically independently owned and operated. This is very similar to our own Medicare system with a federal role in finance but not in actual healthcare delivery. On average, countries with this form of universal National Health Insurance spend 50 percent of what the United States spends per person on healthcare ($10,224-$11,121).[469, 470]

- **National Health Service:** The United Kingdom ($4,246),[471] New Zealand ($3,683), and Italy ($3,542)[472] organize the payment into a socialized system, with their government largely employing physicians and owning hospitals. These countries spend roughly 70 percent less than what we spend here. These systems are similar to how the Veterans Administration is organized within the United States.

- **All Payer "Bismarck" Model:** Switzerland ($8,009), the Netherlands ($5,386), Germany ($5,728), France ($4,902), Belgium($4,774), and Austria ($5,440)[473] use the "Bismarck" model with mixed funding streams, private delivery, and highly regulated non-profit insurers. They spend roughly 60 percent of what we spend on healthcare. This could be considered an extension of the changes introduced by the Affordable Care Act.

Compared to the "Multi-Payer" model in the United States, each of these international models rely upon far higher numbers of primary care physicians, enjoy virtually 100 percent coverage of their population, and have life expectancies several years longer than our own.

None of these strategies directly solves every healthcare problem, but by including their entire population within the same single system, whatever that system is, they have created something powerful that is desperately missing from the United States: a business case to improve the health of the nation.

In the United States, an insurer that promoted itself as delivering the best care for cancer would quickly be deluged with expensive cancer patients and need to price itself out of the insurance market. An insurer that invested heavily in promoting the long-term health of its members would find that the typical 20-25 percent annual turnover of its members means that they were actually improving the health of their competition's members. Many insurers in the United States resisted and delayed covering the newer curative treatments for Hepatitis C because they knew that the long-term costs of untreated disease were eventually going to be borne elsewhere.

The easiest way to establish a business case for improving the nation's health is to have everyone in the nation covered under the same risk pool for their entire life. Suddenly, less expensive early treatments reduce the long-term higher costs borne by the same system. Until we have a system that makes sense economically for the nation, and financially for individuals, we will continue to see people pushed into the gaps. They don't just fall into the gaps; they are actively pushed there.[474] This is unconscionable.

In summary,

> Single payer does not represent a magical panacea that would cure all of the ills with our nation's healthcare system. It does, however, establish an alignment between health outcomes and economic performance. In doing so, it would be the first step in a series of innovations and reforms that would help the United States recover its role as a global leader.[475]

"Medicare Public Option"
Some people are concerned that single payer Medicare for All is too large a step to take in a single leap. Instead, they advise placing Medicare on the market as another option people could purchase when shopping for insurance. If Medicare is such a great insurer, the reasoning goes, then let it compete head-to-head with other insurers. Those who want it could purchase it, and the rest don't need to be involved. That's the way a free market determines winners and losers.

The problem is, the basic principles of a free market do not and cannot apply to health insurance. Far too many of us have the illusion that illnesses happen only to other people, whereas all of the available evidence demonstrates that illness eventually visits us all. It's one thing to decide you don't need a new cellular phone; it's another to decide that you won't be in a car accident or have a heart attack in the coming year.

Adding a "public option" to the already crowded insurance market will do nothing about one of our nation's most serious problems: the high cost of healthcare. The remarkable shift from more than 15 percent overhead down to 2 percent overhead described above would simply not happen by adding a "public option" to the market.

The United States has roughly 20 million uninsured Americans today, most of whom simply can't afford to pay market-based premiums. It is unlikely that more than 1 million of those people would opt into the public option, and it's very likely that those who do would be the ones most in need of care. That means that a public option would quickly become the equivalent of a high-risk pool, further increasing its price and limiting its appeal. Millions of Americans would remain uninsured, and millions more would remain underinsured as this does nothing to improve insurance for people outside of the public option.

It would take years for the country to adopt legislation creating a public option, and then several more years to assess its success. That would reasonably delay by five to 10 years the fundamental reforms Medicare for All will bring.

It's not about economics or medicine — it's about political will.
Survey after survey has shown that Americans across the political spectrum now agree that Medicare for All is the best road forward for our nation. This represents a dramatic shift in a short period of time. In 2013, only 42 percent of Americans thought it was the government's responsibility to ensure that all Americans have health coverage. By 2017, that ratio had reversed and 60 percent saw it as an appropriate responsibility.[476] In 2018, support for Medicare for All had reached 86 percent among Democrats, 68 percent among independents, and 52 percent among Republicans.[477] Support among physicians increased from 42 percent in 2008 to 56 percent in 2017.[478] There is widespread bipartisan national support for Medicare for All everywhere except in Congress. Although none of the issues discussed should be considered partisan, and indeed most Americans agree across political boundaries, not a single Republican in the House or Senate have cosponsored the legislation to accomplish this. It has remained entirely within the camp of the Democratic party.

The Medicare for All bill (HR 676) was first introduced in the House of Representatives in 2003 with 38 cosponsors. By 2008, it had grown to a record high of 93 cosponsors. After passage of the Affordable Care Act, support gradually reduced as many of the advocates shifted towards defending and enhancing the ACA. By 2016, the Medicare for All bill had only 62 cosponsors.

This shifted after the general election. The 2017-2018 Congress saw 123 cosponsors to the same bill. And the similar bill in the Senate was cosponsored by every one of the Democratic senators considered likely to run for president in 2020.

In this short five-year stretch, the United States shifted from a strong majority who felt the government shouldn't even be involved in healthcare to becoming a required stance for a presidential run from one of the major political parties.

There are many choices before us. The least acceptable strategy is staying the course.

POSTSCRIPT

Are You Listening?

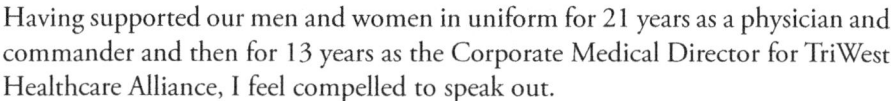

Having supported our men and women in uniform for 21 years as a physician and commander and then for 13 years as the Corporate Medical Director for TriWest Healthcare Alliance, I feel compelled to speak out.

What I wish to share with you is very pertinent to the subject of American healthcare in transition. In fact, I feel so strongly about the issue of providing affordable healthcare to many of our vulnerable fellow Americans that I am publishing a discussion of healthcare in America. I was nudged "into the fray", so to speak, by a comment from a sitting congressman who stated that no one ever died from lack of healthcare. Although he walked back this statement, the fact that vulnerable Americans might be at risk of the ultimate negative healthcare result (death) continued to trouble me. There is much about healthcare that hasn't been discussed that is eminently germane to any discussion of the subject. What I have tried to do is go beyond partisan bickering and ideology and concentrate on the confounding variables that our decision-makers are dealing with. I have even become so bold as to offer some advice.

Like you and many other Americans, what motivates me is to do what is right, not just what is politically expedient. Our providers of healthcare, decision-makers from both sides of the aisle, patient advocates, and you, the ultimate consumer of healthcare, have the opportunity to do this!

CONSUMERS OF HEALTHCARE

There's a second party, the consumer of healthcare, who receives the service. Now we have come full cycle to the place where I, as a Physician Executive, will ask some questions. This set of questions and statements is only for you, the "second party" of our for-profit healthcare insurance model.

- As the generally disenfranchised participant of our healthcare insurance model, do you know where you sit in our healthcare ballpark?
- Are you aware of the **tectonic plates** at your feet?
- How does the **cost** of the for-profit healthcare insurance model impact you?
- Remember, the third party, the payer, is actually the for-profit health insurance model with multiple payers from private (insurance companies) to public (Medicare, Medicaid, VA, TRICARE, Indian Health Service) to individual (ACA marketplace).
- Many are underserved (underinsured) or have no healthcare insurance at all (uninsured). There is also a group of you who just don't use your healthcare insurance (non-compliant).
- Become familiar with the tools you have at your disposal and don't be afraid to apply them.

Teaching points:

- Learn the motivation and machinations of the insurance industry
- Understand how to read medical research and literature
- Seek expert opinions about how to craft appeals that will be reviewed by the medical and legal community before approval
- Think creatively about how to transfer liability to the insurance company should they disapprove a procedure
- Join diverse patient discussion groups nationwide

You know where you sit in the Healthcare Ballpark. You have taken a step toward becoming an informed healthcare consumer. Step up to the plate. Swing away.

PROVIDERS OF HEALTHCARE

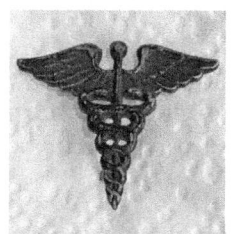

There's the 'first' party, the **provider** who provides the service. As I said in the first postscript for the Consumer of Healthcare, we have come full cycle to the place where I, as a Physician Executive, will ask some questions. This set of information is only for you, the "first party" of our for-profit healthcare insurance model.

Physicians could recapture the moral high ground and advocate for equitable access to patient-centric care. A career in medicine makes physicians uniquely able to see how tragically easy it would be to better treat hypertension and prevent the high-cost strokes, heart attacks, and renal failure.

"So, Doctor, how long can I live without taking my blood pressure medicines?" Although we physicians hear these stories every day, our legislators seldom have direct access to them.

Society grants physicians the privilege to hear these stories; it is therefore incumbent upon us to help our legislators understand how policy decisions that undermine universal access place American citizens — our grandmothers, friends, and neighbors — into untenable dilemmas.

The voice of physicians is uniquely able to impact the dialogue. See Moving Forward below.

There are those who exhort physician leadership and consideration of a one-party payor system. The broadest division among the one-party payor system advocates is in how the delivery of care is organized. Many have chosen to preserve the private delivery of healthcare, where physicians and hospitals are free to organize themselves, much as happens today in Canada. Those single-payor systems are classified as "National Health Insurance," as the nationalization is focused on the insurance functions, not the delivery services.

I have talked about the Accountable Care Organization and other things to help the consumer of healthcare avoid the tectonic plates and the earthquakes that lurk below based on our current "system" of variability.

1. Doctors of many specialties are working together, and you have a good choice of doctors in the group so that you can find one that works best for you.

2. You have easy access to specialists because they work within the medical group or are effectively linked to the group; this reduces delays in receiving care and facilitates easier care coordination.

3. All doctors — primary care and specialists — have access to your electronic medical records and can share information through a confidential electronic computer system. In the most integrated systems, the electronic medical record is also available at the hospital.

4. You receive supportive services and preventive care (health educators, nurses, nutrition counseling, etc.) easily and directly from your doctor's office.

5. The group uses medical teams to allow for 24-hour access to medical services and this team also has access to your full medical record.

6. It is easy to get labs, X-rays, physical therapy, and other services because many of these services are located within or near your doctor's office, and office may also share information and computer systems.

7. The group regularly conducts surveys rating the care patients receive from the medical group or doctor. This indicates that the medical group is assessing the quality of care patients receive so that the group and its doctors perform their best and are held accountable for delivering high-quality care.

Regardless of the format we select for American healthcare, rewards should be based on performance. One model has been the MACRP, or Medicare Access and CHIP Reauthorization Act.

DECISION-MAKERS

Previously in my postscripts for the Consumers and Providers, I mentioned that we have come full cycle to the place where I, as a Physician Executive, will ask some questions. But this time my comments will be directed to the decision-makers in our for-profit healthcare insurance model.

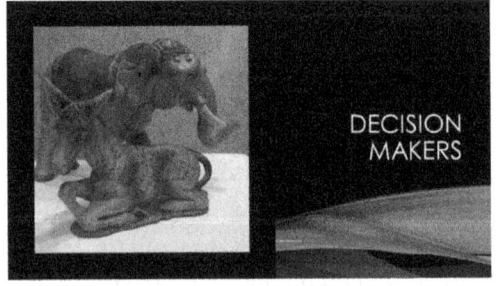

Do not consider American Healthcare in transition in the current vacuum in which previous tectonic plates were conceived. In other words, remember the Prime Directive!

The Prime Directive

No decision-maker in the room should knowingly interfere with the natural progression of American healthcare in transition. Don't be the victim of hearsay and evidence of that ilk. It is like the placebo effect in medical research; these data results are false. There is an actual hierarchy of proof, and you should use it in your deliberations.

Bring the recognized experts from all sides of American healthcare in transition to the table. Get consensus from those involved in the process. Include the first party, or the healthcare providers from physicians (primary care and specialists) to NP/PAs, nurses, therapists, pharmacists, ancillary providers, hospitals, long-term acute care, rehabilitation hospitals, SNFS, nursing homes, medical technology, and even the pharmaceutical industry. They all "provide" for the consumers of healthcare. All should get an equal chair at the table, even the Public Sector, including the VA/TRICARE and the Indian Health Service.

Keep in mind that any model without an evidence-based approach to **access**, **cost**, and **quality** will always be at risk for overpayment to the first party or providers of healthcare. Especially when it involves the **confounding variables**.[479] Just because we have government (the proposed one-party payor) programs, it does not necessarily mean that there will not be "disagreement" between **payor** and **provider** that will require interaction.[480]

Use of an evidence-based grading system (or one that makes sense to those gathered around the table) and applying it to every argument and document brought to support the pathways being discussed is paramount in importance. And yes, looking at what the rest of the civilized world is doing as far as healthcare should be included with appropriate representation. Well-respected healthcare organizations such as the Kaiser Family Foundation, the OECD, Commonwealth Fund should also have a seat at the table, even Medicare for All advocates and the Medicaid buy-in folks. You get my drift. If it makes sense to include first-party, second-party, and third-party representatives, do so.

Follow the rules of evidence!

Grading:

1A - Strong recommendation; high-quality evidence; strong recommendation, can apply to most patients in most circumstances without reservation

1B - Strong recommendation; moderate-quality evidence.; strong recommendation, likely to apply to most patients

1C - Strong recommendation; low-quality evidence; relatively strong recommendation, might change when higher quality evidence becomes available

2A - Weak recommendation; high-quality evidence; weak recommendation, best action may differ depending on circumstances or patients or societal values

2B - Weak recommendation; moderate-quality evidence; weak recommendation, alternative approaches likely to be better for some patients under some circumstances

2C - Weak recommendation; low-quality evidence; very weak recommendation, other alternatives may be equally reasonable

Remember the confounding variables of healthcare costs, or variability:

1) Medical devices and technology

2) Pharmaceuticals

3) Healthcare services

4) Patient compliance

5) Administrative

6) The costs involved with **not** being able to afford healthcare coverage

Healthcare reform is not deficit reduction!

The health insurance plan for profit model for American healthcare in transition should be changed!

MOVING FORWARD

Find the return on investment

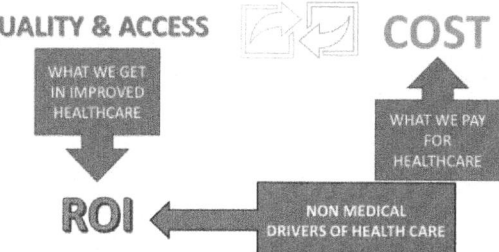

We have discussed the need for consideration of some other sort of model for American healthcare in transition other than the for-profit administrative healthcare insurance "system" currently in effect. The healthcare consumer fears loss of access to their physician and the costs associated with this model. The purpose of the Affordable Care Act was to improve affordability and accessibility, oversee, coordinate, and govern the many pieces in play. It did, and it didn't. What it did do was stretch across both the private and public payor structure and add more Americans to the roles of the insured. It also brought controversy and the immediate call for repeal and replacement.

Consider keeping the things about the ACA that make sense:

- Preexisting condition coverage
- Mandates for insurance coverage
- Coverage for 10 essential health benefits:
    1. Ambulatory care
    2. Inpatient care
    3. Pharmacy
    4. Preventive services

5. Rehabilitation

6. Laboratory and x-ray

7. Maternity

8. Emergency care

9. Mental health services

10. Pediatric care

- Quality Assurance
- Accountable care organizations
- An appeal process

HOW I WOULD APPROACH HEALTHCARE

Please review the payment model I discussed in the Provider section above. I support physician leadership, even when considering a one-party payor system. The broadest division among one-party payor system advocates is how the delivery of care is organized.

The Democrats have revealed their "Medicare for All" proposal. According to the Wall Street Journal, the Medicare for All Act of 2019, the federal government would pay for the following:

1. Health coverage for all Americans to include items we have discussed previously such as premiums, copays, and deductibles;

2. Expansion of Medicare to younger Americans essentially replacing both Medicaid (low income/disabled) and employer-paid (workers) healthcare coverage;

3. The current for-profit healthcare insurance model would be reduced to supplying supplemental coverage only, which will not go unnoticed by the **forth-party** decision-makers whose job it is to maintain profit for the current **third-party payors**;

4. Benefits seem to be along the line of current ACA coverage and also include prescription-drug coverage, long-term care, and full mental health coverage (including addiction);

5. The VA and Indian Health Service would continue, but there was no discussion of the Tricare Program.[481]

I have always supported the private delivery of healthcare, augmenting whatever system is in place. Under this proposal, it seems that hospital and other **first-party** providers of healthcare appear to be ticketed for lower reimbursement. The payment plan?

"The legislative text won't include a financing plan. Opponents of a single-payer system say it would require major tax increases and cost more than $30 trillion in its first decade. Supporters say it would save money by reducing the expected pace of U.S. healthcare spending. Funding options include a so-called wealth tax and increasing the marginal tax rate."[482]

I would remind you of Dr. Weisbart's discussion of the 28 evidence-based articles available to support the ROI (return on investment) when it comes to the net impact on deficit reduction and the viability of the plan in terms of dollars and cents. The Political Economic Research Institute of the University of Massachusetts-Amherst anticipates that households and private businesses overall would pay 9.6 percent less on healthcare than they do today.[483] How would that come about?

The use of healthcare would increase as people would see their physicians and dentists more frequently, for example, and that this would drive up expense by 12 percent. This would be balanced by a 9 percent decrease due to less need for system administration, 5.9 percent decrease due to lower prices on pharmaceuticals, 2.8 percent drop from uniform rates on the delivery side, and a 1 percent drop due to fraud and waste programs. Overall, the 12 percent increase in cost from utilization would be balanced by a 19 percent saving. If we apply that to the $3.5 trillion dollars which healthcare cost in 2018, there would be a reduction of over $310 billion.[484]

And what are our "system" choices? The **Beveridge Model**, the **Bismarck model**, the **National Health Insurance model**, and the **out-of-pocket model**.[485]

The Beveridge Model: single-payer national health service that was first developed by Sir William Beveridge in 1948

Examples: United Kingdom, Spain, New Zealand, Cuba

Relevance to the U.S.: similar to the Veterans Health Administration

This form of single-payer is most similar to the **National Health Service** of the United Kingdom and typically has physicians directly employed by the national government. Most primary care physicians in Great Britain remain privately organized but carry national contracts while the government employs specialists (first-party). The funding for healthcare comes through income taxes, meaning that healthcare is free at the point of service (the third-party payor is the government). The closest version of this in the United States would be the way care is organized within our Veterans Administration, where both primary and specialty care physicians are employed directly by the VA system (government). But even this format has been modified in the United States with a "choice" program where the private sector fills in the appointment (**access**) gap. The central tenant of the Beveridge Model is that healthcare is a right.

The Bismarck Model: social health insurance model

Examples: Germany, Belgium, Japan, Switzerland

Relevance to the U.S.: similar to employer-based healthcare plans and some aspects of Medicaid

Germany has a universal multi-payer healthcare system paid for by a combination of statutory health insurance officially called "sickness funds" and private health insurance, colloquially also called "private sickness funds."[486]

This is the world's oldest national social health insurance system, with origins dating back to Otto von Bismarck's social legislation in the 19th century. The healthcare system is regulated by the Federal Joint Committee, a public health organization authorized to make binding regulations growing out of health reform bills passed by lawmakers, along with routine decisions regarding healthcare in Germany. The National Mandate is that health insurance is compulsory for the whole population. Remember the mandate to buy insurance in the ACA (Chapters Eight and Nine)?

Providers (the first party) are paid via capitation (Chapter Four).

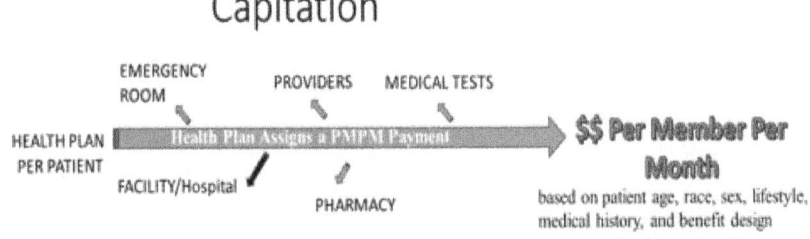

There are three mandatory health benefits, which are co-financed by employer and employee. There are health insurance, accident insurance, and long-term care insurance. Germany has a universal multi-payer system (third-party payors) with two main types of health insurance: statutory health insurance "sickness funds" and private sickness funds.

Statutory health insurance "sickness funds"	"Private sickness funds"
Government Funds: 77% of total	Private Funds: 23% of total
Salaried workers/employees who earn less than 60,750 Euros a year are automatically enrolled into one of 130 public non-profit "sickness funds"	Salaried workers and employees who make over 60,750 Euros can opt for private health insurance. This is used in addition to the government-funded healthcare.
Public health insurance contributions are based on the worker's salary	Self-employed workers must pay the entire contribution themselves. Common rates for all members Private insurers charge risk-related contributions

The National Health Insurance Model: single-payer national health insurance

Examples: Canada, Taiwan, South Korea

Relevance to the U.S.: similar to Medicare

This system incorporates aspects of the two systems above. Like in the Beveridge Model, the government acts as the single-party payor. As with the Bismarck Model, providers are providers of healthcare are from the private sector. Unlike our For-Profit-Healthcare Insurance Model, the National Health Insurance Model does not make a profit or deny claims. "The balance between public insurance and private practice allows hospitals to maintain independence while also reducing internal complications with insurance policies."[487]

The Out-of-Pocket Model: market-driven healthcare

Examples: rural areas in India, China, Africa, South America

Relevance to the U.S.: similar to treatment for uninsured or underinsured (Chapter Three)

We have discussed in great detail the **American for-profit healthcare insurance model.**

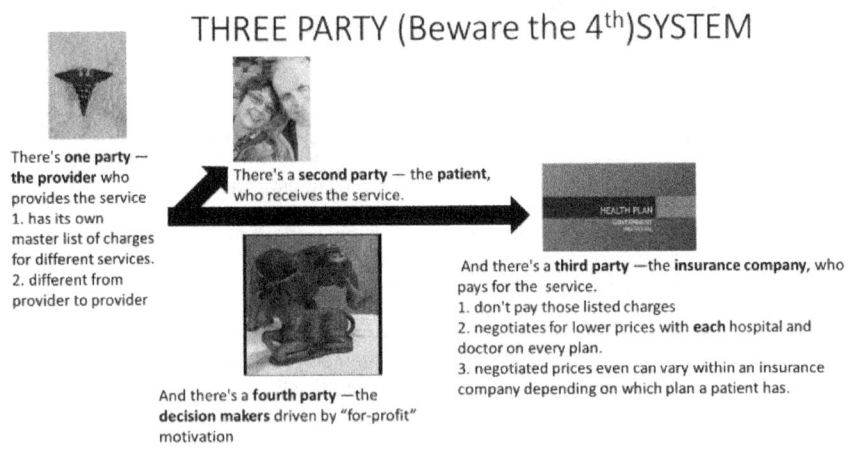

And the large out-of-pocket costs in a fee-for-service environment.

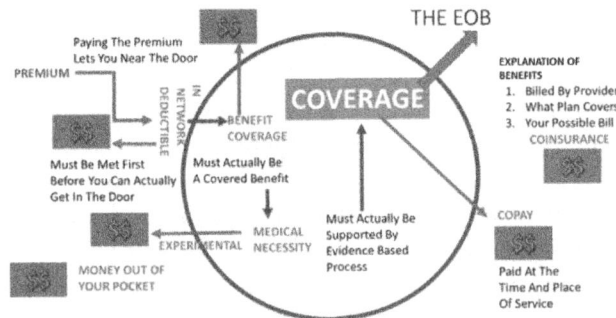

What current American model would be the basis for the government-sponsored healthcare portion? And the envelope, please. The winner is the Bismarck model.

In my mind, we might look at the TRICARE program currently in place for our active-duty military and dependents and retirees under the age of 65. This is the model that I advocate. It is a workable single-payor system merged effectively with the private sector. And when the private sector (as well as the government) applied evidence-based medicine to how care is covered, the system worked. The end game was excellent universal **access** with improved **quality** of care at a lower **cost**. This would be classified as a "National Health Insurance," as the nationalization is focused on the insurance functions, not the delivery services.

The DoD has made some changes since I exited the role of Corporate Medical Director for a TRICARE contractor. And why? Cost! To pay for healthcare for our soldiers, sailors, and airmen, and their dependents as well as retirees under 65 years old; the U.S. Department of Defense (DoD) uses the same pot of money from which it buys guns, tanks, and ships. As cost raises for medical care, there is less available for the items of war.

As a result, the DoD has taken local control away from each Service and lodged it in the Defense Health Agency or DHA. "The Defense Health Agency (DHA) is a joint, integrated Combat Support Agency that enables the Army, Navy, and Air Force medical services to provide a medically ready force and ready medical force to Combatant Commands in both peacetime and wartime. The DHA supports the delivery of integrated, affordable, and high-quality health services to Military Health System (MHS) beneficiaries and is responsible for driving greater integration of clinical and business processes across the MHS."[488]

At the end of the day, the mission becomes **readiness** and **health** "to deliver the Quadruple Aim: increased readiness, better health, better care, and lower cost." The Agency Goals:

"1. Empower and care for our people

2. Optimize operations across the Military Health System

3. Co-create optimal outcomes for health, well-being, and readiness

4. Deliver solutions to combatant commands" [489]

"What you're hearing is, this is a Military Health System and not an Air Force or an Army or Navy or even a Defense Health Agency system," said Lt. Gen. Dorothy Hogg, the Air Force Surgeon General. "All the parts are required in order for MHS to be the best it can be. That's why we're all committed" to making sure transformation is successful.[490]

As I mentioned above, when a payor system is considered, my preference would be the Bismarck model based on a current one-party payor model. The way the DHA/MHS is approaching this needed change could be a lesson to our forth-party decision-makers as a way forward. Some of the more popular and better-known models being discussed are Medicare-for-all and Medicaid buy-in programs. All options should be on the table during the discussion. The final product should be aligned with the private sector to provide the care in a form of an Accountable Care Organization.

So where do we go from here? Remember the **four healthcare models** as you listen to the political debate that will rage around healthcare leading up to the 2020 election. We still have to help the second party — you, the healthcare consumer — and the first party — the provider of healthcare — find the best way forward while influencing the decision-makers. As our current for-profit health insurance model is broken, and the ACA is under constant attack, there will be a big change for the healthcare insurance industry. Let us work together to make the changes count. Whatever we come up with needs to be a patient-centered medical home*. One in which the **return-on-investment** is measured in human terms and not capital gains.

THREE THINGS ARE CLEAR

So, there you have it: American healthcare in transition from the perspective of a Physician/Physician-Executive with almost 50 years of experience in this system. I certainly don't have all the answers; I probably have more questions than answers, actually. But three things are clear.

No. 1: You, the healthcare consumer (and by extension, the provider of healthcare) must become informed about what is right and wrong with the system we currently have. In that way, we can let our thoughts be known and apply those lessons we have learned toward influencing the decision-makers. One way to do this is at the ballot box. You have concerns. You have your opinions about the ACA, the current law of the land. You have spoken as recently as the midterm elections in 2018. You know where you sit in the Healthcare Ballpark. You have taken a step toward becoming an informed healthcare consumer. Step up to the plate. Swing away.

No. 2: "Sixteen states appealed a Texas judge's ruling that invalidated the Affordable Care Act, opening the next phase of legal proceedings over the fate of the Obama-era healthcare law."[491] The ACA that we have discussed in detail has been

---

*A patient-centered philosophy that drives primary care excellence. The medical home is best described as a model or philosophy of primary care that is patient-centered, comprehensive, team-based, coordinated, accessible, and focused on quality and safety.

around since 2010. It currently remains in effect during the appeals process. This process will take a long time. We can be sure that this tectonic plate will continue to be a major bone of political contention into 2020 and the presidential election.

No. 3: There will be some interesting discussion around the "Medicare for All" proposal being espoused by certain politicians of the Democrat persuasion in Washington, D.C.

About the Author

For this part of the discussion, please allow me to utilize the experience I have garnered in over 40 years in the healthcare industry. Who is this brash character asking you to essentially "Trust me, I'm a doctor?" Well, here we will go into my bona fides.

There is one caveat, however, that you should be keeping in mind. Please allow me to use a short vignette before I briefly lay out my career for you to determine how much credibility you will bestow upon me.

In the early 1920s, a silent movie western star Tom Mix was making a movie about the life and times of Wyatt Earp. He invited the old marshal to visit the set as a technical advisor. After doing a scene in which Mr. Mix shot four bad guys and rescued three damsels in distress, without losing his 40-gallon hat or mussing a single strand of hair, he asked Wyatt if that was the way it happened back in Tombstone during his tenure as marshal.

Wyatt paused for a moment and then said: "Yup that's the way it happened all right, give or take a lie or two." Keeping Wyatt's salient comment in mind, here is my brief resume.

As a Physician and Physician Executive with almost 50 years in service supporting the patient, the author shares passion and concern about the current healthcare law of the land the ACA. After spending the first 21 years of his career in the United States Army, the author went on to a varied and successful career in Medicine. He is board certified in Pediatrics with a Public Administration Masters Degree. The lessons he learned while commanding at Ft. Sheridan, Illinois during his last two years in the military set the stage.

The essence was that as a physician you can make a difference in people's lives one person at a time — a very limited reach in actuality. Even from his position as Chief of Pediatrics at various assignments — which still included seeing patients pretty much full-time — the ability to help large segments of the population that he served remained limited. As a "Physician Executive" (read "Commander" of the medical resources at Ft. Sheridan, Illinois), the opportunity to help large groups of people became a reality.

The author then had a varied career in the private sector with stops as the Chief of Staff at the Cigna Staff Model in Long Beach, California and the Medical Director post for The Traveler's Insurance Company. After the merging of the Metropolitan Life and Traveler's Medical Plans when they were divested to form Metra-Health, the author served as the United Healthcare (UHC) Medical Director for the greater Los Angeles area.

Moving to Arizona, the author became an assistant vice-president for the Pharmacy Benefit Manager PCS. In that role, he developed utilization review and quality improvement processes to facilitate the prescription drug care being provided to a national patient base.

While at PCS, the opportunity presented itself for him to again serve the military community, both active duty and retired. The author became the corporate medical director for a healthcare contractor. In that role, he was able to apply all the lessons learned from his various experiences in the healthcare industry to this very deserving group of beneficiaries.

After 13 years in that role, the author formed his own Professional Limited Liability Healthcare Consulting Company, where he continues to bring his years of experience in the medical field to his customers and healthcare beneficiaries.

"I know a thing or two because I've seen a thing or two." (My apologies to a well-known insurance company).

Acknowledgments

This book was conceived during a discussion with Maj. (Retired) John Duffy, a decorated war hero turned poet and has been nominated for a Pulitzer Prize in Poetry. The concept was that someone with some actual experience at the Physician Executive level might just be the person to turn the complicated American healthcare in transition industry into a written and easy-to-follow guide.

Other sources of material included in this book come from real first-hand actual people I have known, and they augment the case studies. Alice Small, a real person (kept anonymous) who, along with her husband, are the definition of informed consumers of healthcare. You know who you are. A special thanks to Gail Daubert RN, JD and her law firm of Reed Smith for the work they do pro bono for those on the outside of our healthcare ballpark looking in.

Justin Cain, Scott Cain, and Marcus Reeder of CainHealth. These healthcare experts create informed participants. My thanks also to Ronald Taylor who helped me understand other ballpark visitors beyond those who seemed obvious. Also, my thanks to the healthcare administrator Kathy Fliehler and psychologist Dr. Blake Chafee for being my second set of eyes on content; Kendra Fuller Lindley who has observed the healthcare process for a long time and has definite opinions about the way ahead; and last but not least, Dr. Joel Brill for applying his special knack for knowing when you are skating to where the puck will be and not where it last was.

My teachers have been numerous, including Dr. David Bee, a colleague, wounded Viet Nam physician and supplier of words of encouragement; Dr. David Cook, MD, MPH, FACP Chief Medical Officer, The Key Family of Companies who provided insights into the concept of ROI; Dr. Ed Weisbart, who made me think long and hard about what I was trying to accomplish; Joseph P. McMenamin, who has both an MD and a legal degree that made him a key voice in my ear; and Mike Temenski, a fellow model railroad enthusiast who helps "sophomore" companies (firms that have made it past start-up, but who are encountering unexpected problems) understand the challenges that they face. And, finally, Andrew Rowe. You know why you are here.

I must also thank the team of Ron and Peg Williams. Ron is a retired colonel United States Army Medical Corps and is still a practicing pediatrician and his wife is a pediatric NP. They and Ron's son, Kurt Williams, an actual educator who has taught in the UAE, have my thanks. Edi Shannon, an entrepreneur and business women and director of a magical choral group, Joyful Sounds, knows how to get people involved with a project. Two 'retired' educators who currently teach incoming freshmen with athletic scholarships how to become adults at Rutgers University, George and Donna Sher and my "big brother" Uncle Raymond Casulli, with companion Marlene Captain, all deserve my thanks for providing life's lessons and insight into who I want to be when I grow up.

My son-in-law, Adrian Baker, was concerned that most people will not read a book such as this at home. Adrian is the reason why we designed the content approach and format. He suggested that people will use a "fast food" bulleted format if given the opportunity, something like you can get on Facebook or YouTube or the like. He is the brother in the story described in our Case Study the Wake-Up Call. I also give thanks to John Baker, the actual patient who has graciously allowed his story to be told and to Adrian's wife and my daughter, Nancy Marie Baker, and her PhD in Physical Therapy.

And while we are at it, my other children deserve mention: Thomas, Lisa, and Marie and my seven grandsons and one granddaughter. As I mature, they have become one major reason to continue to do what I do so that I may have the benefit of life's lessons they teach. By the way, my son Tom (at a much younger age) adorns my business card.

Have at it!
Brian

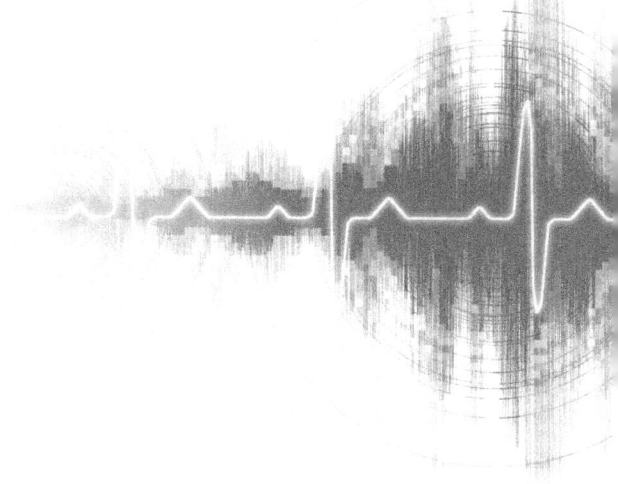

Endnotes

Introduction

1. "Yogi Berra Quotes." *BrainyQuote*, Xplore, www.brainyquote.com/quotes/yogi_berra_447752.

2. Bloom, Ester. "Here's How Much Members of Congress Pay for Their Health Insurance." *CNBC*, CNBC, 25 July 2017, www.cnbc.com/2017/07/25/heres-how-much-members-of-congress-pay-for-their-health-insnce.html.

Part A Summary

3. Edwards-Levy, Ariel. "Voters Say Healthcare Is Their Top Issue In The 2018 Election. That's A Good Sign For Democrats." *The Huffington Post*, TheHuffingtonPost.com, 6 Apr. 2018, www.huffingtonpost.com/entry/voters-say-health-care-is-their-top-issue-in-the-2018-election-thats-a-good-sign-for-democrats_us_5ac642e2e4b09d0a119103c4.

4. Bryan, Bob. "Americans Hate Republicans' Idea to Cut Medicare, Medicaid, and Social Security to Bring down the Soaring Deficit. And They Have Another Idea the GOP Won't like." *Business Insider*, Business Insider, 29 Oct. 2018, www.businessinsider.com/poll-medicare-medicaid-social-security-cuts-vs-gop-tax-law-hike-2018-10.

Chapter One

5. "Press Release CMS Office of the Actuary Releases 2016 National Health Expenditures." *CMS.gov Centers for Medicare & Medicaid Services*, 6 Dec. 2017, www.cms.gov/newsroom/press-releases/cms-office-actuary-releases-2016-national-health-expenditures.

6. "NHE-Fact-Sheet." *CMS.gov Centers for Medicare & Medicaid Services*, 6 Dec. 2018, www.cms.gov/research-statistics-data-and-systems/statistics-trends-and-reports/nationalhealthexpenddata/nhe-fact-sheet.html.

7. Matthews, Dylan. "The Gigantic Cuts in Donald Trump's Latest Budget Proposal, Explained." *Vox.com*, Vox Media, 12 Feb. 2018, www.vox.com/policy-and-politics/2018/2/12/16996832/trump-budget-2019-release-explained.

8. "Three Big Differences Between SSI and SSDI." *SpecialNeedsAnswers*, 21 Nov. 2014, specialneedsanswers.com/three-big-differences-between-ssi-and-ssdi-14866.

9. "What's Medicare?" *Medicare.gov - the Official U.S. Government Site for Medicare*, 27 Dec. 2018, www.medicare.gov/sign-up-change-plans/decide-how-to-get-medicare/whats-medicare/what-is-medicare.html.

10. "Press Release CMS Office of the Actuary Releases 2017 National Health Expenditures." *CMS.gov Centers for Medicare & Medicaid Services*, 6 Dec. 2018, www.cms.gov/newsroom/press-releases/cms-office-actuary-releases-2017-national-health-expenditures.

11. Cubanski, Juliette, and Tricia Neuman. "The Facts on Medicare Spending and Financing." *The Henry J. Kaiser Family Foundation*, The Henry J. Kaiser Family Foundation, 22 June 2018, www.kff.org/medicare/issue-brief/the-facts-on-medicare-spending-and-financing/.

12. Op Cit. "NHE-Fact-Sheet." *CMS.gov Centers for Medicare & Medicaid Services*, 6 Dec. 2018

13. Op cit. Cubanski, Juliette, and Tricia Neuman. "The Facts on Medicare Spending and Financing." *The Henry J. Kaiser Family Foundation*, The Henry J. Kaiser Family Foundation, 22 June 2018

14. "What Is the Difference between ICD and CPT Coding?" *Quora-Ask New Questions*, 27 June 2018, www.quora.com/What-is-the-difference-between-ICD-and-CPT-coding.

15. Heidelbaugh, Joel J. J Fam Pract, "10 Billing & Coding Tips to Boost Your Reimbursement." *MDedge* , 7 Apr. 2017, www.mdedge.com/jfponline/article/63368/practice-management/10-billing-coding-tips-boost-your-reimbursement.

16. Jorge, Margarida, and Ethan Rome. "Seniors Will Pay the Price for Trump's Medicare Cuts." *MarketWatch*, MarketWatch, 18 Feb. 2018, www.marketwatch.com/story/seniors-will-pay-the-price-for-trumps-medicare-cuts-2018-02-14.

17. Pear, Robert. "Sniffles? Cancer? Under Medicare Plan, Payments for Office Visits Would Be Same for Both." *The New York Times*, The New York Times, 22 July 2018, www.nytimes.com/2018/07/22/us/politics/medicare-payments-trump.html.

18. Masterson, Les. "Hundreds of Groups Raise Concerns about E/M Payment Proposal." *Healthcare Dive*, 29 Aug. 2018, www.healthcaredive.com/news/hundreds-of-groups-raise-concerns-about-em-payment-proposal/531195/.

19. "170 Groups Send Letter on Proposed Changes to Physician Payment Rule." *Selecting & Using a Health Information Exchange | AMA*, 27 Aug. 2018, www.ama-assn.org/170-groups-send-letter-proposed-changes-physician-payment-rule.

20. American College of Rheumatology. "Press Releases." *Rheumatology.org*, 28 Aug. 2018, www.rheumatology.org/About-Us/Newsroom/Press-Releases/ID/943/126-Patient-and-Provider-Groups-to-CMS-Proposed-EM-Service-Cuts-Will-Hurt-Sickest-Medicare-Patients.

21. Abraham, Tony. "After Provider Uproar, CMS Steps Back from Major E/M Revamp." *Healthcare Dive*, 2 Nov. 2018, www.healthcaredive.com/news/after-provider-uproar-cms-steps-back-from-major-em-revamp/541221/.

22. O'Brien, Sarah. "Trump Is Targeting Medicare Drug Prices. Here's What Part D Coverage Costs." *CNBC*, CNBC, 11 May 2018, www.cnbc.com/2018/05/11/trump-is-targeting-medicare-drug-prices-heres-what-part-d-coverage-costs.html.

23. Op Cit. "NHE-Fact-Sheet." *CMS.gov Centers for Medicare & Medicaid Services*, 6 Dec. 2018

24. Op cit. Cubanski, Juliette and Tricia Neuman, "The Facts on Medicare Spending and Financing," *The Henry J. Kaiser Family Foundation*, The Henry J. Kaiser Family Foundation, 2 June 2018.

25. Cubanski, Juliette, et al. "Medicare Part D: A First Look at Prescription Drug Plans in 2018 - Findings." *The Henry J. Kaiser Family Foundation*, The Henry J. Kaiser Family Foundation, 13

Oct. 2017, www.kff.org/report-section/medicare-part-d-a-first-look-at-prescription-drug-plans-in-2018-findings/.

26. Walker, Joseph. "High-Price Drugs Raise Costs for Seniors in Medicare Part D." *The Wall Street Journal*, Dow Jones & Company, 29 May 2017, www.wsj.com/articles/high-priced-drugs-raise-costs-for-seniors-in-medicare-part-d-1496055603.

27. Williams, Sean. "The Average American Spends This Much on Prescription Drugs Each Year." *The Motley Fool*, The Motley Fool, 12 Dec. 2015, www.fool.com/investing/general/2015/12/12/the-average-american-spends-this-much-on-prescript.aspx.

28. "Financial Management-Federal Medical Assistance Percentage (FMAP)." *Medicaid.gov*, 2016, www.medicaid.gov/medicaid/finance/index.html.

29. "FY2017 Federal Medical Assistance Percentages." *ASPE*, 16 July 2016, aspe.hhs.gov/basic-report/fy2017-federal-medical-assistance-percentages.

30. "Enhanced Federal Medical Assistance Percentage (FMAP) for CHIP." *The Henry J. Kaiser Family Foundation*, The Henry J. Kaiser Family Foundation, 7 June 2018, www.kff.org/other/state-indicator/enhanced-federal-matching-rate-chip/.

31. Op Cit. "NHE-Fact-Sheet." *CMS.gov Centers for Medicare & Medicaid Services*, 6 Dec. 2018

32. "Federal and State Share of Medicaid Spending." *The Henry J. Kaiser Family Foundation*, The Henry J. Kaiser Family Foundation, 11 Oct. 2018, www.kff.org/medicaid/state-indicator/federalstate-share-of-spending/?currentTimeframe=0&sortModel=%7B%22colId%22%3A%22Location%22%2C%22sort%22%3A%22asc%22%7D.

33. "The Value of Medicaid: Providing Access to Care and Preventive Health Services." *AHIP*, 17 Dec. 2018, www.ahip.org/value-of-medicaid-access-to-care-report/.

34. Masterson, Les. "Most Medicaid Managed Care Programs Consider Social Determinants of Health." *Healthcare Dive*, 17 Dec. 2018, www.healthcaredive.com/news/most-medicaid-managed-care-programs-consider-social-determinants-of-health/544488/.

35. "New Report Explores How Managed Care Contracts and § 1115 Demonstrations Address Social Determinants of Health." *Center for Healthcare Strategies*, 13 Dec. 2018, www.chcs.org/news/new-report-explores-how-managed-care-contracts-and-%C2%A7-1115-demonstrations-address-social-determinants-of-health/.

36. "Most Americans — Across Parties — Say 2018 Candidates' Position on Pre-Existing Condition Protections Will Matter to Their Vote; Do Not Want Supreme Court to Overturn These ACA Protections." *The Henry J. Kaiser Family Foundation*, The Henry J. Kaiser Family Foundation, 25 July 2018, www.kff.org/health-reform/press-release/poll-july-2018-changes-to-affordable-care-act-health-care-in-midterms-and-the-supreme-court/.

37. "The Cost and Coverage Implications of the ACA Medicaid Expansion: National and State-by-State Analysis." *The Henry J. Kaiser Family Foundation*, The Henry J. Kaiser Family Foundation, 15 May 2013, www.kff.org/health-reform/report/the-cost-and-coverage-implications-of-the/.

Chapter Two

38. Manning, Hadley Heath, and Edwin Park. "Should Medicaid Be Converted to a Block-Grant Program?" *The Wall Street Journal*, Dow Jones & Company, 12 Apr. 2017, www.wsj.com/articles/should-medicaid-be-converted-to-a-block-grant-program-1491962400

39. Veterans Health Administration. "Veterans Health Administration." *Learn to Communicate Assertively at Work*, 10 June 2009, www.va.gov/health/aboutvha.asp.

40. Landen, Rachel. "Pattern of Problems with VA Healthcare System." *Modern Healthcare*, 7 May 2014, www.modernhealthcare.com/article/20140507/NEWS/305079939.

41. "U.S. GAO - About GAO - Overview." *U.S. Government Accountability Office (U.S. GAO)*, 27 Dec. 2018, www.gao.gov/about/index.html.

42. Hayes, Tara O'Neill. "TRICARE: The Military's Healthcare System." *AAF*, 27 Aug. 2015, www.americanactionforum.org/insight/tricare-the-militarys-health-care-system/.

43. "Annual Evaluation of the TRICARE Program." *Military Health System*, 9 May 2018, www.health.mil/Military-Health-Topics/Access-Cost-Quality-and-Safety/Health-Care-Program-Evaluation/Annual-Evaluation-of-the-TRICARE-Program.

44. "Indian Health Service (IHS)." *Phoenix Area*, 27 Dec. 2018, www.ihs.gov/aboutihs/.

45. Op cit. Edwards-Levy, Ariel, "Voters Say Health Care Is A Top Issue In The 2018 Election — A Good Sign For Democrats," HuffPost Politics, 06 April 2018.

46. "Health Insurance Coverage of the Total Population." *The Henry J. Kaiser Family Foundation*, The Henry J. Kaiser Family Foundation, 29 Nov. 2018, www.kff.org/other/state-indicator/total-population/.

47. "Access to Health Services." *Healthcare-Associated Infections | Healthy People 2020*, 29 Dec. 2018, www.healthypeople.gov/2020/topics-objectives/topic/Access-to-Health-Services.

48. Ibid.

49. Op cit. "Key Facts about the Uninsured Population," The Henry J. Kaiser Family Foundation, The Henry J. Kaiser Family Foundation, 07 Dec. 2018.

50. Early release of selected estimates based on data from the 2016 National Health Interview Survey, tables 1.1a, 1.1b- "National Center for Health Statistics." *Centers for Disease Control and Prevention*, Centers for Disease Control and Prevention, 31 Mar. 2017, www.cdc.gov/nchs/fastats/health-insurance.htm.

51. Caldwell, Patrick, et al. "Here's Exactly How Many People Will Be Uninsured under Each Republican Healthcare Bill." *Mother Jones*, 21 July 2017, www.motherjones.com/politics/2017/07/heres-exactly-how-many-people-will-be-uninsured-under-each-republican-health-care-bill/

52. "Impact of Trump's Proposed Reforms on the Number of People with Insurance Coverage, 2018." *Commonwealth Fund*, 21 Sept. 2016, www.commonwealthfund.org/chart/2016/impact-trumps-proposed-reforms-number-people-insurance-coverage-2018.

53. Op Cit. "Key Facts about the Uninsured Population," *The Henry J. Kaiser Family Foundation*, The Henry J. Kaiser Family Foundation, 07 Dec. 2018.

54. Ibid.

55. Robertson, Lori. "Medicaid's Doctor Participation Rates." *FactCheck.org*, 5 May 2017, www.factcheck.org/2017/03/medicaids-doctor-participation-rates/.

56. Op cit. "Preventive Services Covered by Private Health Plans under the Affordable Care Act," *The Henry J. Kaiser Family Foundation*, The Henry J. Kaiser Family Foundation, 04 Aug. 2015.

57. Ibid.

Chapter Three

58. Op Cit. Edwards-Levy, Ariel, "Voters Say Health Care Is A Top Issue In The 2018 Election — A Good Sign For Democrats," HuffPost Politics, 06 April 2018.

59. Casprini, M., "Soaring costs, loss of benefits top Americans' healthcare worries: Reuters/Ipsos poll." Reuters, 15 June 2018, www.businessinsider.com/r-soaring-costs-loss-of-benefits-top-americans-healthcare-worries-reuters-ipsos-poll-2018-6

60. "U.S. Health Expenditure as GDP Share 1960-2018 | Statistic." *Statista*, 2018, www.statista.com/statistics/184968/us-health-expenditure-as-percent-of-gdp-since-1960/.

61. "National Healthcare Spending In 2016: Spending And Enrollment Growth Slow After Initial Coverage Expansions." *Health Affairs*, 6 Dec. 2017, www.healthaffairs.org/doi/abs/10.1377/hlthaff.2017.1299.

62. "How Much Is Health Spending Expected to Grow?" *Peterson-Kaiser Health System Tracker*, 12 Dec. 2018, www.healthsystemtracker.org/chart-collection/much-health-spending-expected-grow/#item-annual-percentage-point-difference-growth-rates-makes-large-difference-spending-time_2016.

63. "Underinsured and Uninsured Adults at High Risk of Going Without Needed Care and of Financial Stress." *Commonwealth Fund*, www.commonwealthfund.org/chart/underinsured-and-uninsured-adults-high-risk-going-without-needed-care-and-financial-stress.

64. Papanicolas, Irene. "Healthcare Spending in the United States and Other High-Income Countries." *JAMA*, American Medical Association, 13 Mar. 2018, jamanetwork.com/journals/jama/article-abstract/2674671.Healthcare

65. Torrey, Trisha. "What Does Fraudulent Medical Upcoding Cost Me?" *Verywell Health*, Verywellhealth, 22 Dec. 2018, www.verywellhealth.com/what-is-upcoding-2615214.

66. "Visitors Insurance." *Visitors Coverage Blog - Visitor Insurance, Travel Insurance for USA*, blog.visitorscoverage.com/infographics-average-cost-of-medical-services-in-the-usa/.

67. Morra, Dante, et al. "US Physician Practices Versus Canadians: Spending Nearly Four Times As Much Money Interacting With Payers." *Health Affairs*, Aug. 2011, www.healthaffairs.org/doi/abs/10.1377/hlthaff.2010.0893.

68. Laporte, John. "Topic: Physicians." *Statista*, 2018, www.statista.com/topics/1244/physicians/.

69. Ibid.

70. "Reducing Waste in Healthcare." *Health Affairs*, 13 Dec. 2012, www.healthaffairs.org/do/10.1377/hpb20121213.959735/full/.

71. Merlis, Mark. "Simplifying Administration of Health Insurance." *National Academy of Social Insurance*, Robert Wood Johnson Foundation, Jan. 2009, www.nasi.org/usr_doc/Simplifying_Administration_of_Health_Insurance.pdf.

72. Jiwani, A, et al. "Billing and Insurance-Related Administrative Costs in United States' Healthcare: Synthesis of Micro-Costing Evidence." *Current Neurology and Neuroscience Reports.*, U.S. National Library of Medicine, 13 Nov. 2014, www.ncbi.nlm.nih.gov/pubmed/25540104.

73. Himmelstein, David, et al. "A Comparison Of Hospital Administrative Costs In Eight Nations: US Costs Exceed All Others By Far." *Health Affairs*, Sept. 2014, www.healthaffairs.org/doi/abs/10.1377/hlthaff.2013.1327.

74. Sakowski, Julie Ann, et al. "Peering Into The Black Box: Billing And Insurance Activities In A Medical Group." *Health Affairs*, 2009, www.healthaffairs.org/doi/abs/10.1377/hlthaff.28.4.w544.

75. Casalino, Lawrence P., et al. "What Does It Cost Physician Practices To Interact With Health Insurance Plans?" *Health Affairs*, 2009, www.healthaffairs.org/doi/abs/10.1377/hlthaff.28.4.w533.

76. Iuga, Aurel. "Employed Physicians More Dissatisfied than Independent Doctors." *Healthcare Dive*, 3 Dec. 2018, www.healthcaredive.com/news/employed-physicians-more-dissatisfied-than-independent-doctors/543082/.

77. Enthoven, Alain. "Opinion | A Better Choice for Employee Healthcare." *The Wall Street Journal*, Dow Jones & Company, 22 Nov. 2018, www.wsj.com/articles/a-better-choice-for-employee-health-care-1542922699.

78. Ibid.

79. "Reducing Waste in Healthcare." *Health Affairs*, 13 Dec. 2012, www.healthaffairs.org/do/10.1377/hpb20121213.959735/full/.

80. Thompson, Derek. "Why Is American Healthcare So Ridiculously Expensive?" *The Atlantic*, Atlantic Media Company, 28 Mar. 2013, www.theatlantic.com/business/archive/2013/03/why-is-american-health-care-so-ridiculously-expensive/274425/.

81. Etehad, Melissa and Kim, Kyle. "The U.S. Spends More on Healthcare than Any Other Country - but Not with Better Health Outcomes." *Los Angeles Times*, Los Angeles Times, 18 July 2017, www.latimes.com/nation/la-na-healthcare-comparison-20170715-htmlstory.html.

82. From an idea discussed with David Cook, MD, MPH, FACP, Chief Medical Officer, The Key Family of Companies. Used with permission.

83. Squires, David. "U.S. Healthcare from a Global Perspective | Commonwealth Fund." *Commonwealth Fund*, 8 Oct. 2015, www.commonwealthfund.org/publications/issue-briefs/2015/oct/us-health-care-global-perspective.

84. "Spending on Health: Latest Trends." *OECD-Focus On:* June 2018, www.oecd.org/health/health-systems/Health-Spending-Latest-Trends-Brief.pdf.

85. "Achievements in Public Health, 1900-1999: Control of Infectious Diseases." *Centers for Disease Control and Prevention*, Centers for Disease Control and Prevention, 30 July 1999, www.cdc.gov/mmwr/preview/mmwrhtml/mm4829a1.htm.

86. Luhbe, Tammy. "Millions More Americans Were Uninsured in 2017." *CNNMoney*, Cable News Network, 16 Jan. 2018, money.cnn.com/2018/01/16/news/economy/uninsured-americans/index.html.

87. "Health Policies and Data." *Estadísticas - OECD*, 2012, www.oecd.org/els/health-systems/characteristics-2012-results.htm.

88. Berchick, Edward. "Who Are the Uninsured?" *Census Bureau QuickFacts*, United States Census Bureau, 12 Sept. 2018, www.census.gov/library/stories/2018/09/who-are-the-uninsured.html.

89. Collins, Sara R, et al. "The Problem of Underinsurance and How Rising Deductibles Will Make It Worse." *Commonwealth Fund*, 20 May 2015, www.commonwealthfund.org/publications/issue-briefs/2015/may/problem-of-underinsurance.

90. "Underinsured Rate Increased Sharply In 2016; More Than Two Of Five Marketplace Enrollees And A Quarter Of People With Employer Health Insurance Plans Are Now Underinsured." *Commonwealth Fund*, 18 Oct. 2017, www.commonwealthfund.org/press-release/2017/underinsured-rate-increased-sharply-2016-more-two-five-marketplace-enrollees-and-.

Chapter Four

91. Mack, Sammy. "They Paid How Much? How Negotiated Deals Hide Healthcare's Cost." *NPR*, NPR, 15 Nov. 2014, www.npr.org/sections/health-shots/2014/11/15/364064088/they-paid-how-much-how-negotiated-deals-hide-health-cares-cost.

92. "What the Heck Is a DRG? And Why Should I Care About Case Mix?" *Coder Coach*, 6 Jan. 2011, codercoach.blogspot.com/2011/01/what-heck-is-drg-and-why-should-i-care.html.

93. Klein, Ezra, "21 Graphs that Show Americas' Health-care Prices are Ludicrous," The Washington Post, March 26, 2013.

Chapter Five

94. Renzulli, Kerri Anne. "The Highest-Paying Jobs in 2016 | Money." *Time*, Time, 9 Mar. 2016, time.com/money/4251274/highest-paying-jobs-glassdoor-2016/.

95. Lorenzetti, Laura. "Here's How Much Different Types of Doctors Are Paid." *Fortune*, Fortune, 4 Apr. 2016, fortune.com/2016/04/04/doctor-salaries/.

96. Peckham, Carol. "Medscape Physician Compensation Report 2016." *Medscape Log In*, 1 Apr. 2016, www.medscape.com/features/slideshow/compensation/2016/public/overview.

97. LaPointe, Jacqueline, "Less Than a Third of Docs Owned Independent Practices in 2018," REVCYCLE INTELLIGENCE, Practice Management News, 20 Sep. 2018, revcycleintelligence.com/news/less-than-a-third-of-docs-owned-independent-practices-in-2018

98. Merritt Hawkins, "Survey: Physicians Generate an Average $2.4 Million a Year Per Hospital," 25 Feb. 2019, www.merritthawkins.com/uploadedFiles/MerrittHawkins_PressRelease_2019.pdf

99. Masterson, Les, "Physicians make their hospitals $2.4M yearly, report finds," HEALTHCARE-DIVE, 26 Feb. 2019, www.healthcaredive.com/news/physicians-make-their-hospitals-24m-yearly-report-finds/549142/

100. Skinner, Jonathan, et al. "Making Sense Of Price And Quantity Variations In U.S. Healthcare." *Health Affairs*, 30 Dec. 2015, www.healthaffairs.org/do/10.1377/hblog20151230.052473/full/.

101. "Home." *The Dartmouth Atlas of Healthcare*, 2018, www.dartmouthatlas.org/.

102. Op cit. Klein, Ezra, "21 graphs that show America's health-care prices are ludicrous," The Washington Post, 26 Mar. 2013.

103. Op Cit. "Home." The Dartmouth Atlas of Healthcare, 2018

104. Richards, Edward P. "Food and Drug Cosmetic Act (FD&C) Chapter V Drugs and Devices." *The Climate Change and Public Health Law Site*, 13 Dec. 2018, biotech.law.lsu.edu/blaw/fda/fdcact5a.htm.

105. Shaw, Gina. "Artificial Joints: Knee and Hip Replacement Rates Rising." *WebMD*, WebMD, 27 Nov. 2007, www.webmd.com/arthritis/features/hip-knee-replacements-rise#1.

106. Op Cit. Klein, Ezra, "21 graphs that show America's health-care prices are ludicrous," The Washington Post, 26 Mar. 2013.

107. Center for Devices and Radiological Health. "Device Advice: Comprehensive Regulatory Assistance." *U S Food and Drug Administration Home Page*, Center for Drug Evaluation and Research, 2018, www.fda.gov/MedicalDevices/DeviceRegulationandGuidance.

108. Ibid.

109. Burton, Thomas M. "FDA Is Revamping Clearance Procedures for Medical Devices." *The Wall Street Journal*, Dow Jones & Company, 26 Nov. 2018, www.wsj.com/articles/fda-is-revamping-clearance-procedures-for-medical-devices-1543234015

110. "COMPLETE PUBLIC VERSION OF THE 2016 ANNUAL STATISTICAL REPORT for the SPINAL CORD INJURY MODEL SYSTEMS ." *THE NATIONAL SPINAL CORD INJURY STATISTICAL CENTER*, https://Www.nscisc.uab.edu/Public/2016%20Annual%20Report%20-%20Complete%20Public%20Version.Pdf, 2016.

111. "Spinal Cord Injury Facts & Statistics." *Functional Goals per Level of Complete Spinal Cord Injury*, 2015, www.sci-info-pages.com/facts.html.

112. Hansebout, Robert R, et al. "Acute Traumatic Spinal Cord Injury." *UpToDate*, 18 July 2018, www.uptodate.com/contents/acute-traumatic-spinal-cord-injury.

113. "Nontraumatic Spinal Cord Injury Information." *MyVMC*, 26 May 2018, www.myvmc.com/diseases/nontraumatic-spinal-cord-injury/.

114. Cardenas, D D, et al. "Etiology and Incidence of Rehospitalization after Traumatic Spinal Cord Injury: a Multicenter Analysis." *Current Neurology and Neuroscience Reports.*, U.S. National Library of Medicine, Nov. 2004, www.ncbi.nlm.nih.gov/pubmed/15520970.

115. Op Cit. Edwards-Levy, Ariel, "Voters Say Health Care Is A Top Issue In The 2018 Election — A Good Sign For Democrats," HuffPost Politics, 06 April 2018.

116. Op Cit. Caspani, Maria, "Soaring costs, loss of benefits top Americans' healthcare worries: Reuters/Ipsos poll," *Reuters*, Busines Insider, 15 Jun. 2018.

117. Op Cit. Klein, Ezra, "21 graphs that show America's health-care prices are ludicrous," *The Washington Post* Economic Policy 26 Mar. 2013.

118. Williams, Sean. "Prescription Drug Prices Have Doubled in Just 7 Years for Older Americans, Study Shows." *The Motley Fool*, The Motley Fool, 26 Mar. 2016, www.fool.com/investing/general/2016/03/26/prescription-drug-prices-have-doubled-in-just-7-ye.aspx.

119. Kamal, Rabah, et al. "How Much Is Health Spending Expected to Grow?" *Peterson-Kaiser Health System Tracker*, 12 Dec. 2018, www.healthsystemtracker.org/chart-collection/much-health-spending-expected-grow/.

120. "Press Release CMS Office of the Actuary Releases 2017-2026 Projections of National Health Expenditures." *CMS.gov Centers for Medicare & Medicaid Services*, 14 Feb. 2018, www.cms.gov/newsroom/press-releases/cms-office-actuary-releases-2017-2026-projections-national-health-expenditures.

121. "Big Majorities Say Government Should Work to Curb Prescription Drug Price Hikes." *Nightly Business Report*, 29 Sept. 2016, nbr.com/2016/09/29/big-majorities-say-government-should-work-to-curb-prescription-drug-price-hikes/.

122. Kodjak, Alison. "Tighter Patent Rules Could Help Lower Drug Prices, Study Shows." *NPR*, NPR, 23 Aug. 2016, www.npr.org/sections/health-shots/2016/08/23/491053523/tighter-patent-rules-could-help-lower-drug-prices-study-shows.

123. Office of the Commissioner. "FDA In Brief - FDA in Brief: FDA Works to Encourage and Optimize Drug Competition with Transparency." *U S Food and Drug Administration Home Page*, Center for Drug Evaluation and Research, 15 Dec. 2017, www.fda.gov/NewsEvents/Newsroom/FDAInBrief/ucm589275.htm.

124. Herper, Matthew. "How To Charge $1.6 Million For a New Drug And Get Away With It." *Forbes*, Forbes Magazine, 8 Aug. 2012, www.forbes.com/sites/matthewherper/2012/03/19/how-to-charge-1-6-million-for-a-new-drug-and-get-away-with-it/#2e89a5906468.

125. "10 Essential Facts About Medicare and Prescription Drug Spending." *The Henry J. Kaiser Family Foundation*, The Henry J. Kaiser Family Foundation, 20 Nov. 2017, www.kff.org/infographic/10-essential-facts-about-medicare-and-prescription-drug-spending/.

126. Office of the Commissioner. "Developing Products for Rare Diseases & Conditions." *U S Food and Drug Administration Home Page*, Center for Drug Evaluation and Research, 2018, www.fda.gov/forindustry/developingproductsforrarediseasesconditions/default.htm.

127. Hopkins, James S, and Andrew Martin. "These New Pharma Bros Are Wreaking Havoc on Prescription Drug Prices." *Bloomberg.com*, Bloomberg, 6 Apr. 2018, www.bloomberg.com/news/features/2018-04-06/when-these-new-pharma-bros-show-up-drug-prices-tend-to-go-monumentally-higher.

128. Kesselheim, Aaron S, et al. "JAMA: Answer to High Cost of Prescription Drugs?" *Why the US Needs a Single Payer Health System | Physicians for a National Health Program*, 30 Aug. 2016, www.pnhp.org/news/2016/august/jama-answer-to-high-cost-of-prescription-drugs.

129. "An Overview of Medicare." *The Henry J. Kaiser Family Foundation*, The Henry J. Kaiser Family Foundation, 18 Apr. 2018, www.kff.org/medicare/issue-brief/an-overview-of-medicare/.

130. "An Overview of the Medicare Part D Prescription Drug Benefit." *The Henry J. Kaiser Family Foundation*, The Henry J. Kaiser Family Foundation, 15 Oct. 2018, www.kff.org/medicare/fact-sheet/an-overview-of-the-medicare-part-d-prescription-drug-benefit/.

131. Op Cit. Kesselheim, Aaron S. et al. "The High Cost of Prescription Drugs in the United States: Origins and Prospects for Reform," *JAMA*, 23/30 Aug. 2016

132. "Generic Drugs: Information, Cost, and Types." *WebMD*, WebMD, 2018, www.webmd.com/a-to-z-guides/questions-about-generic-drugs-answered#1

133. Lupkin, Sydney. "FDA Fees On Industry Haven't Fixed Delays In Generic Drug Approvals." *NPR*, NPR, 1 Sept. 2016, www.npr.org/sections/health-shots/2016/09/01/492235796/fda-fees-on-industry-havent-fixed-delays-in-generic-drug-approvals.

134. Mezher, Michael. "FDA on Pace for Record Generic Approvals in 2018." *Regulatory Affairs Professionals Society (RAPS)*, 4 Sept. 2018, www.raps.org/news-and-articles/news-articles/2018/9/fda-on-pace-for-record-generic-approvals-in-2018.

135. Wazana, A. "Physicians and the Pharmaceutical Industry: Is a Gift Ever Just a Gift?" *Current Neurology and Neuroscience Reports.*, U.S. National Library of Medicine, 19 Jan. 2000, www.ncbi.nlm.nih.gov/pubmed/10647801.

136. Pew Prescription Project. "Persuading the Prescribers: Pharmaceutical Industry Marketing and Its Influence on Physicians and Patients." *The Pew Charitable Trusts*, 11 Nov. 2013, www.pewtrusts.org/en/research-and-analysis/fact-sheets/2013/11/11/persuading-the-prescribers-pharmaceutical-industry-marketing-and-its-influence-on-physicians-and-patients.

137. Ibid.

138. Ibid.

139. "Senate Finance Committee Releases Report on Drug Industry CME Grants." *FDA Law Blog*, 8 May 2007, www.fdalawblog.net/2007/05/senate_finance_/.

140. Mullin, Rick. "Cost to Develop New Pharmaceutical Drug Now Exceeds $2.5B." *Scientific American*, 24 Nov. 2014, www.scientificamerican.com/article/cost-to-develop-new-pharmaceutical-drug-now-exceeds-2-5b/.

141. Agorist, Matt. "Harvard Study Finally Admits Drug Prices Are High Because Govt Grants Big Pharma a Monopoly." *The Free Thought Project*, 27 Aug. 2017, thefreethoughtproject.com/harvard-study-govt-pharma-monopoly/.

142. Prasad, Vinay. "Cost of Developing a Single Cancer Drug." *JAMA*, American Medical Association, 1 Nov. 2017, jamanetwork.com/journals/jamainternalmedicine/fullarticle/2653012.

143. Wieczner, Jen. "The Real Reasons for the Pharma Merger Boom." *Fortune*, Fortune, 28 July 2015, fortune.com/2015/07/28/why-pharma-mergers-are-booming/.

144. Harding, David, et al. "The Renaissance in Mergers and Acquisitions: The Surprising Lessons of the 2000s." *Bain Brief - Bain & Company*, 2 Aug. 2018, www.bain.com/insights/the-renaissance-in-mergers-and-acquisitions/.

145. Op cit. Kesselheim, Aaron S. et al. "The High Cost of Prescription Drugs in the United States: Origins and Prospects for Reform," JAMA, 23/30 Aug. 2016

146. Jacobson, S G, and A V Cideciyan. "Treatment Possibilities for Retinitis Pigmentosa." *Current Neurology and Neuroscience Reports.*, U.S. National Library of Medicine, 21 Oct. 2010, www.ncbi.nlm.nih.gov/pubmed/20961252.

147. Office of the Commissioner. "Press Announcements - FDA Approves Novel Gene Therapy to Treat Patients with a Rare Form of Inherited Vision Loss." *U S Food and Drug Administration Home Page*, Center for Drug Evaluation and Research, 19 Dec. 2017, www.fda.gov/NewsEvents/Newsroom/PressAnnouncements/ucm589467.htm.

148. Loftus, Peter. "Drug Firm Spark Therapeutics Will Charge $850,000 for Vision-Loss Gene Therapy." *The Wall Street Journal*, Dow Jones & Company, 3 Jan. 2018, www.wsj.com/articles/drug-firm-spark-therapeutics-will-charge-850-000-for-vision-loss-gene-therapy-1514986201.

149. Wapner, Jessica. "How Prescription Drugs Get Their Prices, Explained." *Newsweek*, 28 July 2017, www.newsweek.com/prescription-drug-pricing-569444.

150. Biologics Evaluation and Research. "About the Center for Biologics Evaluation and Research (CBER)." *U S Food and Drug Administration Home Page*, Center for Drug Evaluation and Research, 2 Mar. 2017, www.fda.gov/AboutFDA/CentersOffices/OfficeofMedicalProductsandTobacco/CBER/.ucm133077.htm

151. "In a Landscape of 'Me Too' Drug Development, What Spurs Radical Innovation?" *HBS Working Knowledge*, 12 June 2018, hbswk.hbs.edu/item/in-a-landscape-of-me-too-drug-development-what-spurs-radical-innovation?cid=wk-rss.

152. Walker, Joseph, "Trump Policy Change Is a Win for Drugmakers," The Wall Street Journal March 22, 2018, www.wsj.com/articles/trump-policy-change-is-a-win-for-drugmakers-1521716400

153. "Ten Challenges in the Prescription Drug Market-and Ten Solutions." *Brookings.edu*, The Brookings Institution, 2 May 2017, www.brookings.edu/research/ten-challenges-in-the-prescription-drug-market-and-ten-solutions/.

154. Mathews, Anna Wilde, and Joseph Walker. "UnitedHealth Will Pass Drug Rebates Directly to Some Consumers." *The Wall Street Journal*, Dow Jones & Company, 6 Mar. 2018, www.wsj.

com/articles/unitedhealth-will-pass-drug-rebates-directly-to-some-consumers-1520337601

155. Hopkins, Jared S. and Peter Loftus, "Drug Firms Blame Middlemen For Prices," *The Wall Street Journal* Business/Healthcare/Health, 5 Feb 2019, www.wsj.com/articles/flip-the-script-drugmakers-blame-middlemen-for-price-hikes-11549364401

156. Loftus, Peter. "A Billionaire Pledges to Fight High Drug Prices, and the Industry Is Rattled." *The Wall Street Journal*, Dow Jones & Company, 21 Oct. 2018, www.wsj.com/articles/a-billionaire-decided-to-fight-high-drug-prices-and-the-industry-is-rattled-1540145686.

157. "ICER Value Assessment Framework." *ICER*, 28 Dec. 2018, icer-review.org/methodology/icers-methods/icer-value-assessment-framework/.

Chapter Seven

158. Op Cit. Klein, Ezra, "21 graphs that show America's health-care prices are ludicrous," *The Washington Post* Economic Policy 26 Mar. 2013.

159. Op Cit. Caspani, Maria, "Soaring costs, loss of benefits top Americans' healthcare worries: Reuters/Ipsos poll," *Reuters*, Business Insider, 15 Jun. 2018.

160. Epstein, Randi Hutter. "Major Medical Mystery: Why People Avoid Doctors." *The New York Times*, The New York Times, 31 Oct. 2000, www.nytimes.com/2000/10/31/health/major-medical-mystery-why-people-avoid-doctors.html.

161. "HEALTHCARE COSTS AND PATIENT COMPLIANCE." *American Healthcare in Transition*, 15 Oct. 2018, americanhealthcareintransition.com/health-care-costs-and-patient-compliance/.

162. Ault, Alicia. "Kaiser survey: Many women skipping preventive care," MD Edge Family Medicine, Family Practice News, 28 May 2014, www.mdedge.com/familymedicine/article/82661/health-policy/kaiser-survey-many-women-skipping-preventive-care

163. Ranji, Usha, et al. "Overview: 2017 Kaiser Women's Health Survey - Executive Summary." The Henry J. Kaiser Family Foundation, The Henry J. Kaiser Family Foundation, 14 March 2018, www.kff.org/report-section/executive-summary-2017-kaiser-womens-health-survey/.

164. Ibid.

165. "Home - US Preventive Services Task Force." *Home - US Preventive Services Task Force*, 2018, www.uspreventiveservicestaskforce.org/.

166. Hillstead, Richard, et al. "Can Electronic Medical Record Systems Transform Healthcare? Potential Health Benefits, Savings, And Costs." *Health Affairs*, 2005, www.healthaffairs.org/doi/full/10.1377/hlthaff.24.5.1103.

167. National Centers for Disease Control and prevention, "Health and Economic Costs of Chronic Diseases," National Center for Chronic Disease Prevention and Health Promotion (NCCDPHP), 23Oct. 2018, www.cdc.gov/chronicdisease/about/costs/index.htm#refl

168. "ADHERENCE TO LONG-TERM THERAPIES: EVIDENCE FOR ACTION." *World Health Organization*, World Health Organization, 21 Dec. 2015, www.who.int/chp/knowledge/publications/adherence_report/en/.

169. Herrick, Devon M, and Amanda Frost. "Can Consumers Be Smart Health-Care Shoppers?" *The Wall Street Journal*, Dow Jones & Company, 12 Apr. 2017, www.wsj.com/articles/can-consumers-be-smart-health-care-shoppers-1491962640.

Chapter Eight

170. "Affordable Healthcare." *Obamacare Facts*, 31 Oct. 2016, obamacarefacts.com/affordable-healthcare.

171. Roland, James. "The Pros and Cons of Obamacare." *Healthline*, Healthline Media, 15 June 2015, www.healthline.com/health/consumer-healthcare-guide/pros-and-cons-obamacare.

172. "Health Insurance Coverage For Children and Young Adults Under 26." *HealthCare.gov*, 31 Dec. 2018, www.healthcare.gov/young-adults/children-under-26/.

173. Norris, Louise. "Billions in ACA Rebates Show 80/20 Rule's Impact." *Healthinsurance.org*, 31 Dec. 2018, www.healthinsurance.org/obamacare/billions-in-aca-rebates-show-80-20-rules-impact/.

174. Page, Leigh. "What's At Risk in Repealing the ACA? How Will It Affect You?" *Medscape Family Medicine*, 23 Feb. 2017, www.medscape.com/features/slideshow/aca-repeal.

175. Op cit. Roland, James. "The Pros and Cons of Obamacare." Healthline, Healthline Media, 15 June 2015

176. "What Tax Changes Did the Affordable Care Act Make?" *Tax Policy Center*, 2018, www.taxpolicycenter.org/briefing-book/what-tax-changes-did-affordable-care-act-make.

177. Manville, George. "Groups Urge Halt to ACA Employer Mandate Penalties." *United States*, 31 May 2018, www.mercer.us/our-thinking/healthcare/groups-urge-halt-to-aca-employer-mandate-penalties.html.

178. Sheen, Robert. "New CMS Rule Keeps ACA Employer Mandate Intact." *The ACA Times*, First Capitol Consulting, Inc, 6 June 2018, acatimes.com/new-cms-rule-keeps-aca-employer-mandate-intact/.

179. Casselman, Ben. "Yes, Some Companies Are Cutting Hours In Response To 'Obamacare'." *FiveThirtyEight*, FiveThirtyEight, 13 Jan. 2015, fivethirtyeight.com/features/yes-some-companies-are-cutting-hours-in-response-to-obamacare/.

180. Brandt, Caitlin, et al. "Enrollment Challenges for the Affordable Care Act (ACA)." *Brookings.edu*, The Brookings Institution, 29 July 2016, www.brookings.edu/blog/usc-brookings-schaeffer-on-health-policy/2015/11/20/enrollment-challenges-for-the-affordable-care-act-aca-2/.

181. Page, Leigh, "Repealing the ACA: A Close Look at What Could Happen," Medscape Family Medicine, 23 February 2017, www.medscape.com/viewarticle/875959

182. Glied, Sherry A, and Adlan Jackson. "Access to Coverage and Care for People with Preexisting Conditions: How Has It Changed Under the ACA? | Commonwealth Fund." *Commonwealth Fund*, 22 June 2017, www.commonwealthfund.org/publications/issue-briefs/2017/jun/coverage-care-preexisting-conditions-aca.

183. HHS Office Public Affairs. "Pre-Existing Conditions." *HHS.gov*, US Department of Health and Human Services, 31 Jan. 2017, www.hhs.gov/healthcare/about-the-aca/pre-existing-conditions/index.html.

184. "Pre-Existing Condition Definition." *Healthinsurance.org*, 27 July 2018, www.healthinsurance.org/glossary/pre-existing-condition/.

185. "An Estimated 52 Million Adults Have Pre-Existing Conditions That Would Make Them Uninsurable Pre-Obamacare." *The Henry J. Kaiser Family Foundation*, The Henry J. Kaiser Family

Foundation, 1 May 2017, www.kff.org/health-reform/press-release/an-estimated-52-million-adults-have-pre-existing-conditions-that-would-make-them-uninsurable-pre-obamacare/.

186. Gee, Emily. "Number of Americans with Pre-Existing Conditions by Congressional District." *Center for American Progress*, 7 Dec. 2018, www.americanprogress.org/issues/healthcare/news/2017/04/05/430059/number-americans-pre-existing-conditions-congressional-district/.

187. Bilhari, Michael, "Understanding Health Insurance Exclusions & Creditable Coverage: Your Guide to Pre-Existing Conditions and the Rules That Protect You," verywellhealth, Health Insurance, 05 December 2018, www.verywellhealth.com/pre-existing-conditions-exclusions-1738633

188. Adapted from: Adelberg, Michael et al. "The American Healthcare Act vs. The Better Care Reconciliation Act vs. The Affordable Care Act: A Side-by-Side Comparison." *Publications | Insights | Faegre Baker Daniels*, 14 July 2017, www.faegrebd.com/en/insights/publications/2017/3/the-american-health-care-act-vs-the-better-care-reconciliation-act-vs-the-affordable-care-act-a-side.

189. Op Cit. Gee, Emily, "Number of Americans with Pre-Existing Conditions by Congressional District," *Centers For American Progress* Health Care, 05 Apr. 2017.

190. Williams, Roberton. "What's Happened To The ACA Penalty Tax?" *Forbes*, Forbes Magazine, 11 Apr. 2017, www.forbes.com/sites/beltway/2017/04/10/whats-happened-to-the-aca-penalty-tax/#c4ec71898e45.

191. Lei, Rebecca K.K. and Alicia Parlapiano, "Millions Pay the Obamacare Penalty Instead of Buying Insurance. Who Are They?" The New York Times, 28 Nov. 2017, www.nytimes.com/interactive/2017/11/28/us/politics/obamacare-individual-mandate-penalty-maps.html

192. Galewitz, Phil. "How Many Americans Paid the Obamacare Tax Penalty in 2016." *The Daily Signal*, The Daily Signal, 11 Jan. 2017, www.dailysignal.com/2017/01/11/how-many-americans-paid-the-obamacare-tax-penalty-in-2016/.

193. Mach, Annie L., "The Individual Mandate for Health Insurance Coverage: In Brief," Congressional Research Service, 19 Mar. 2018, fas.org/sgp/crs/misc/R44438.pdf

194. HHS Office & Public Affairs. "Lifetime & Annual Limits." *HHS.gov*, US Department of Health and Human Services, 31 Jan. 2017, www.hhs.gov/healthcare/about-the-aca/benefit-limits/index.html.

195. Op Cit. www.medscape.com/viewarticle/875959

196. "Age Band Rating (ACA)." *Life Insurance Awareness Month*, NAIFA, 2018, www.naifa.org/practice-resources/prp/age-band-rating-aca.

197. US Preventive Services Task Force. "Browse Information for Consumers." Home , Dec. 2018, www.uspreventiveservicestaskforce.org/Tools/ConsumerInfo/Index/information-for-consumers.

198. Ibid.

199. "How Medicaid Healthcare Expansion Affects You." *HealthCare.gov*, 31 Dec. 2018, www.healthcare.gov/medicaid-chip/medicaid-expansion-and-you/.

200. "A 50-State Look at Medicaid Expansion." *Families USA*, 4 Dec. 2018, familiesusa.org/product/50-state-look-medicaid-expansion.

201. Rosenbaum, Sara, and Timothy M Westmoreland. "The Supreme Court's Surprising Decision On The Medicaid Expansion: How Will The Federal Government And States Proceed?" *Health Affairs*, Aug. 2012, www.healthaffairs.org/doi/full/10.1377/hlthaff.2012.0766.

202. Armour, Stephanie. "Medicaid Expansion Gains Popularity in Red States." *The Wall Street Journal*, Dow Jones & Company, 14 June 2018, www.wsj.com/articles/medicaid-expansion-gains-popularity-in-red-states-1528974001.

203. Armour, Stephanie. "Virginia Is Poised to Expand Medicaid." *The Wall Street Journal*, Dow Jones & Company, 31 May 2018, www.wsj.com/articles/virginia-is-poised-to-expand-medicaid-1527727529.

204. Norris, Louise. "Maine and the ACA's Medicaid Expansion: Eligibility, Enrollment and Benefits." *Healthinsurance.org*, 24 Dec. 2018, www.healthinsurance.org/maine-medicaid/.

205. "How Repealing Portions of the Affordable Care Act Would Affect Health Insurance Coverage and Premiums." *Congressional Budget Office*, 17 Jan. 2017, www.cbo.gov/publication/52371.

206. "Understanding Obamacare Subsidies." *EHealth Insurance Resource Center*, EHealth Insurance Resource Center, 26 Sept. 2018, resources.ehealthinsurance.com/affordable-care-act/aca-obamacare-subsidies.

207. "Summary of the 2018 CHIP Funding Extension." *The Henry J. Kaiser Family Foundation*, The Henry J. Kaiser Family Foundation, 24 Jan. 2018, www.kff.org/medicaid/fact-sheet/summary-of-the-2018-chip-funding-extension/.

208. "Health Insurance Marketplace Calculator." *The Henry J. Kaiser Family Foundation*, The Henry J. Kaiser Family Foundation, 30 Nov. 2018, www.kff.org/interactive/subsidy-calculator/.

209. "Repealing the Individual Health Insurance Mandate: An Updated Estimate." *Congressional Budget Office*, Nov. 2017, www.cbo.gov/system/files/115th-congress-2017-2018/reports/53300-individualmandate.pdf

210. Armour, Stephanie. "Pressure Grows to Fund Children's Health Program." *The Wall Street Journal*, Dow Jones & Company, 29 Aug. 2017, www.wsj.com/articles/pressure-grows-to-fund-childrens-health-program-1504034320.

211. Kamal, Rabah, et al. "How the Loss of Cost-Sharing Subsidy Payments Is Affecting 2018 Premiums." *The Henry J. Kaiser Family Foundation*, The Henry J. Kaiser Family Foundation, 15 Nov. 2017, www.kff.org/health-reform/issue-brief/how-the-loss-of-cost-sharing-subsidy-payments-is-affecting-2018-premiums/.

212. (231) HHS Office of the Secretary,Office of Budget, and OB. "FY2015 Budget in Brief - CMS CMMI." *HHS.gov*, US Department of Health and Human Services, 4 June 2014, www.hhs.gov/about/budget/fy2015/budget-in-brief/cms/innovation-programs/index.html.

213. Cubanski, Juliette, et al. "What Are the Implications of Repealing the Affordable Care Act for Medicare Spending and Beneficiaries?" *Filling the Need for Trusted Information on National Health...*, 9 Jan. 2017, kff.org/medicare/issue-brief/what-are-the-implications-of-repealing-the-affordable-care-act-for-medicare-spending-and-beneficiaries/.

214. "Costs in the Coverage Gap." *Medicare.gov - the Official U.S. Government Site for Medicare*, 31 Dec. 2018, www.medicare.gov/drug-coverage-part-d/costs-for-medicare-drug-coverage/costs-in-the-coverage-gap.

215. "Medicaid Disproportionate Share Hospital (DSH) Payments." *Medicaid.gov*, 30 Dec. 2018, www.medicaid.gov/medicaid/financing-and-reimbursement/dsh/.

216. Mitchell, Allison. "Medicaid Disproportionate Share Hospital Payments." *Congressional Research Service*, 17 June 2016, fas.org/sgp/crs/misc/R42865.pdf.

217. "Cadillac Tax." *Cigna, a Global Health Insurance and Health Service Company*, 2018, www.cigna.com/health-care-reform/cadillac-tax.

218. Vaida, Bara. "The IPAB: The Center Of A Political Clash Over How To Change Medicare." *Kaiser Health News*, Kaiser Health News, 22 Mar. 2012, khn.org/news/ipab-faq/.

219. Dinerstein, Chuck. "Is Independent Payment Advisory Board the First Skirmish in Repealing Obamacare?" *Millennials, the Deaf Generation?* | *American Council on Science and Health*, 16 Feb. 2017, www.acsh.org/news/2017/02/16/independent-payment-advisory-board-first-skirmish-repealing-obamacare-10867.

220. Norris, Louise. "10 Ways the GOP Sabotaged Obamacare." *Healthinsurance.org*, 7 Oct. 2018, www.healthinsurance.org/blog/2017/05/17/10-ways-the-gop-sabotaged-obamacare/.

221. Jost, Timothy. "Judge Rules Against Administration In Cost-Sharing Reduction Payment Case." *Health Affairs*, 12 May 2016, www.healthaffairs.org/do/10.1377/hblog20160512.054852/full/.

222. Jost, Timothy. "Status Reports In DC Cost-Sharing Reduction Case Highlight Stakes Going Forward." *Health Affairs*, 30 Oct. 2017, www.healthaffairs.org/do/10.1377/hblog20171030.550661/full/.

223. Chang, Alvin. "Who Trump Actually Hurts by Stopping Payments to Insurance Companies, Explained with a Cartoon." *Vox.com*, Vox Media, 20 Oct. 2017, www.vox.com/health-care/2017/10/20/16507786/trump-obamacare-executive-order-csr-cartoon.

Chapter Nine

224. Op cit. Edwards-Levy, Ariel, "Voters Say Health Care Is A Top Issue In The 2018 Election — A Good Sign For Democrats," *HuffPost* Politics, 06 April 2018.

225. Op cit. Caspani, Maria, "Soaring costs, loss of benefits top Americans' healthcare worries: Reuters/Ipsos poll," *Reuters*, Business Insider, 15 Jun. 2018.

226. Baker, Sam, "Exclusive poll: Democrats have an edge on healthcare," AXIOS, 31 July 2018, www.axios.com/democrats-have-an-edge-on-health-care-65bf3a70-67ce-4374-ae8f-7393ab8c641c.html

227. Duehren, Andrew. "Voters Focus on Economy, Healthcare and Immigration in Midterms." *The Wall Street Journal*, Dow Jones & Company, 3 Sept. 2018, www.wsj.com/articles/voters-focus-on-economy-health-care-and-immigration-in-midterms-1535979600.

228. Armour, Stephanie, and Louise Radnofsky. "Trump Administration Pushes Conservative Goals in Health-Care Market Changes." *The Wall Street Journal*, Dow Jones & Company, 6 Mar. 2018, www.wsj.com/articles/trump-administration-pushes-conservative-goals-in-health-care-market-changes-1520377333?mod=searchresults&page=1&pos=1.

229. Collins, Sar R., "The ACA Protects People with Preexisting Conditions; Proposed Replacements Would Not," The Commonwealth Fund, To The Point, 1 November 2018, www.commonwealthfund.org/blog/2018/aca-protects-people-preexisting-conditions-proposed-replacements-would-not

230. Luhby, Tami. "Trump Administration Unveils Short-Term Health Plans as Alternative to Obamacare." *CNNMoney*, Cable News Network, 20 Feb. 2018, money.cnn.com/2018/02/20/news/economy/trump-obamacare-short-term-health-insurance/index.html.

231. Norris, Louise. "The Problem with Association Health Plans." *Healthinsurance.org*, 19 Sept. 2018, www.healthinsurance.org/blog/2018/06/01/the-problem-with-association-health-plans/.

232. Armour, Stephanie. "Get Health Coverage at Work? Lawsuit Against ACA Could Affect You, Too." *The Wall Street Journal*, Dow Jones & Company, 13 June 2018, www.wsj.com/articles/get-health-coverage-at-work-lawsuit-against-aca-could-affect-you-too-1528924250.

233. Glied, Sherry A., and Adlan Jackson, "Access to Coverage and Care for People with Preexisting Conditions: How Has It Changed Under the ACA?," The Commonwealth Fund, 22 June 2017, www.commonwealthfund.org/publications/issue-briefs/2017/jun/access-coverage-and-care-people-preexisting-conditions-how-has

234. Op cit. Mach, Annie L., "The Individual Mandate for Health Insurance Coverage: In Brief," 19 Mar. 2018

235. Scott, Dylan. "CBO: 13 Million More Uninsured If You Repeal Obamacare's Individual Mandate." *Vox.com*, Vox Media, 8 Nov. 2017, www.vox.com/policy-and-politics/2017/11/8/16623154/cbo-obamacare-individual-mandate-new-baseline.

236. Kamal, Rabah, et al. "How Repeal of the Individual Mandate and Expansion of Loosely Regulated Plans Are Affecting 2019 Premiums." *The Henry J. Kaiser Family Foundation*, The Henry J. Kaiser Family Foundation, 30 Oct. 2018, www.kff.org/health-reform/issue-brief/how-repeal-of-the-individual-mandate-and-expansion-of-loosely-regulated-plans-are-affecting-2019-premiums/.

237. Weixel, Nathaniel, et al. "Overnight Healthcare: CBO Finds Bill Delaying Parts of ObamaCare Costs $50B | Drug CEO Defends 400 Percent Price Hike | HHS Declares Health Emergency Ahead of Hurricane." *TheHill*, The Hill, 11 Sept. 2018, thehill.com/policy/healthcare/overnights/406157-overnight-health-care-cbo-house-gop-bill-delaying-key-parts-of.

238. Ibid.

239. Armour, Stephanie, and Brent Kendall. "Federal Judge Rules Affordable Care Act Is Unconstitutional Without Insurance-Coverage Penalty." *The Wall Street Journal*, Dow Jones & Company, 15 Dec. 2018, www.wsj.com/articles/federal-judge-rules-affordable-care-act-is-unconstitutional-11544838743.

240. "The ACA Remains Critical for Insurance Coverage and Health Funding, Even Without the Individual Mandate." *Consumer Health First*, 15 June 2018, www.consumerhealthfirst.org/home/2018/6/15/the-aca-remains-critical-for-insurance-coverage-and-health-funding-even-without-the-individual-mandate

241. "10 Essential Health Benefits Insurance Plans Must Cover Under the Affordable Care Act." *Families USA*, 27 Apr. 2018, familiesusa.org/blog/10-essential-health-benefits-insurance-plans-must-cover-starting-in-2014.

242. "The Affordable Care Act Is Improving Access to Preventive Services for Millions of Americans." *ASPE*, 5 Nov. 2016, aspe.hhs.gov/pdf-report/affordable-care-act-improving-access-preventive-services-millions-americans.

243. Sung, Jane. "Protecting Affordable Health Insurance for Older Adults: The Affordable Care Act's Limit on Age Rating ." *AARP Public Policy Institute*, Jan. 2017, www.aarp.org/content/dam/aarp/ppi/2017-01/Protecting-Affordable-Health-Insurance-for-Older.pdf.

244. "Preventive Services Covered by Private Health Plans under the Affordable Care Act." *The Henry J. Kaiser Family Foundation*, The Henry J. Kaiser Family Foundation, 4 Aug. 2015, www.kff.org/health-reform/fact-sheet/preventive-services-covered-by-private-health-plans/.

245. "What Short-Term Health Insurance Covers." *EHealth Insurance Resource Center*, EHealth Insurance, 19 Apr. 2018, www.ehealthinsurance.com/resources/short-term/short-term-health-insurance-plans-cover.

246. Dawson, Lindsey, and Jennifer Kates. "Short-Term Limited Duration Plans and HIV." *The Henry J. Kaiser Family Foundation*, The Henry J. Kaiser Family Foundation, 21 June 2018, www.kff.org/hivaids/issue-brief/short-term-limited-duration-plans-and-hiv/.

247. Gallegos, Alicia. "Trump Administration Rule Erodes ACA Contraceptive Mandate." *MDedge Psychiatry*, 8 Dec. 2018, www.mdedge.com/obgyn/article/184087/contraception/trump-administration-rule-erodes-aca-contraceptive-mandate?utm_source=News_MDedge_eNL_110818_F&utm_medium=email&utm_content=Breaking%3A%2BTrump%2Badmin%2Brules%2Berode%2BACA%2Bcontraceptive%2Bmandate.

248. Scott, Dylan. "How Medicaid Became the Most Important Battleground in American Healthcare." *Vox.com*, Vox Media, 10 Nov. 2017, www.vox.com/policy-and-politics/2017/11/10/16118644/medicaid-future.

249. Rudowitz, Robin and Rachel Garfield, "10 Things to Know about Medicaid: Setting the Facts Straight," Henry j Kaiser Family Foundation, Medicaid, 12 April 2018, www.kff.org/medicaid/issue-brief/10-things-to-know-about-medicaid-setting-the-facts-straight/?gclid=CjwKCAiAyrXiBRAjEiwATI95mZ483mcoO1BkG5iQP6U0XPQgNR8UhCWO_kzEfq1025EwKbgYJs0MwRoCWqcQAvD_BwE

250. Kominski, Gerald F, et al. "The Affordable Care Act's Impacts on Access to Insurance and Healthcare for Low-Income Populations." *Annual Reviews*, Mar. 2017, www.annualreviews.org/doi/full/10.1146/annurev-publhealth-031816-044555?url_ver=Z39.88-2003&rfr_id=ori%3Arid%3Acrossref.org&rfr_dat=cr_pub%3Dpubmed.

251. Garfield, Rachel, et al. "The Coverage Gap: Uninsured Poor Adults in States That Do Not Expand Medicaid." *The Henry J. Kaiser Family Foundation*, The Henry J. Kaiser Family Foundation, 13 June 2018, www.kff.org/uninsured/issue-brief/the-coverage-gap-uninsured-poor-adults-in-states-that-do-not-expand-medicaid/.

252. "Explaining Healthcare Reform: Questions About Health Insurance Subsidies," Henry J. Kaiser Family Foundation, Health Reform, 20 November 2018, www.kff.org/health-reform/issue-brief/explaining-health-care-reform-questions-about-health/

253. Op Cit. Garfield, Rachel et al. "The Coverage Gap: Uninsured Poor Adults in States that Do Not Expand Medicaid," Henry j Kaiser Family Foundation, Medicaid, 12 Jun. 2018.

254. Morgan, Dan, "Obamacare bombshell: Trump kills key payments to health insurers," CNBC, Health and Science, 12 October 2017, www.cnbc.com/2017/10/12/obamacare-bombshell-trump-kills-key-payments-to-health-insurers.html

255. Mathews, Anna Wilde, and Melanie Evans. "Insurers' Policy Warnings Raise Stakes in Health Fight." *The Wall Street Journal*, Dow Jones & Company, 30 June 2017, www.wsj.com/articles/insurers-policy-warnings-raise-stakes-in-health-fight-1498865398.

256. Norris, Louise. "'Bare Counties' Just Got Covered. Here's Why." *Healthinsurance.org*, 19 Sept. 2018, www.healthinsurance.org/blog/2017/08/25/latest-update-on-bare-counties/

257. Lee, Chris, "More Insurers Are Participating in the ACA Marketplaces in 2019," Henry J. Kaiser Family Foundation, 14 Nov 2018, www.kff.org/health-reform/press-release/more-insurers-are-participating-in-the-aca-marketplaces-in-2019/

258. Armour, Stephanie. "Health Exchange Premiums Would Rise 20% in 2018 If Subsidies Ended, CBO Estimates." *The Wall Street Journal*, Dow Jones & Company, 16 Aug. 2017, www.wsj.com/articles/health-exchange-premiums-would-rise-20-in-2018-if-subsidies-ended-cbo-estimates-1502821843.

259. Kamal, Rabah, et al. "How Repeal of the Individual Mandate and Expansion of Loosely Regulated Plans Are Affecting 2019 Premiums." *The Henry J. Kaiser Family Foundation*, The

Henry J. Kaiser Family Foundation, 30 Oct. 2018, www.kff.org/health-reform/issue-brief/how-repeal-of-the-individual-mandate-and-expansion-of-loosely-regulated-plans-are-affecting-2019-premiums/.

260. Armour, Stephanie, and Brent Kendall. "Federal Government Doesn't Have to Pay Billions to Health Insurers, Court Rules." *The Wall Street Journal*, Dow Jones & Company, 14 June 2018, www.wsj.com/articles/appeals-court-rules-against-insurer-moda-health-over-aca-payments-1528989913.

261. Mathews, Anna Wilde. "Trump Administration to Resume 'Risk Adjustment' Payments to Insurers." *The Wall Street Journal*, Dow Jones & Company, 25 July 2018, www.wsj.com/articles/trump-administration-to-resume-risk-adjustment-payments-to-insurers-1532484221.

262. Semanskee, Ashley, et al. "Data Note: Changes in Enrollment in the Individual Health Insurance Market." *The Henry J. Kaiser Family Foundation*, The Henry J. Kaiser Family Foundation, 31 July 2018, www.kff.org/health-reform/issue-brief/data-note-changes-in-enrollment-in-the-individual-health-insurance-market/.

263. Ibid.

264. Scott, Dylan, "Obamacare sign-ups surge in final tally," Vox, 21 Dec 2018, https://www.vox.com/2018/12/7/18130519/obamacare-health-insurance-enrollment-2019-data

265. "Number of ACA (Obamacare) sign-ups during 2018 open enrollment, by U.S. state," Statistics, The Statistics Portal, www.statista.com/statistics/453371/signup-numbers-during-open-enrollment-us-obamacare-by-state/ accessed 27 January 2019

266. "Out-of-Pocket Maximum/Limit - HealthCare.gov Glossary." *HealthCare.gov*, 31 Dec. 2018, www.healthcare.gov/glossary/out-of-pocket-maximum-limit/.

267. "Aging Consumers without Subsidies Hit Hardest by 2017 Obamacare Premium & Deductible Spikes." *HealthPocket*, 26 Oct. 2016, www.healthpocket.com/healthcare-research/infostat/2017-obamacare-premiums-deductibles#.WU2iwWjytPY.

268. Holahan, John, et al. "Changes in Marketplace Premiums, 2017-2018." *Urban Institute-Robert Wood Johnson Foundation*, Mar. 2018, www.urban.org/sites/default/files/publication/97371/changes_in_marketplace_premiums_2017_to_2018_0.pdf.

269. Livingston, Shelby. "Where the ACA Health Insurance Exchanges Stand in 2018." *Modern Healthcare*, 11 Apr. 2017, www.modernhealthcare.com/reports/180411where-aca-exchanges-stand/.

270. Semanskee, Ashley et al. "How Premiums Are Changing In 2018," Henry J. Kaiser Family Foundation, Healthcare Costs, 29 Nov 2017, www.kff.org/health-costs/issue-brief/how-premiums-are-changing-in-2018/

271. Op cit. Livingston, Shelby and graphics by Fan Fei, "Where the ACA health insurance exchangs stand in 2018," *Modern Healthcare*, 11 Apr. 2017.

272. "Average Market Premiums Spike Across Obamacare Plans in 2018." *HealthPocket*, 27 Oct. 2017, www.healthpocket.com/healthcare-research/infostat/2018-obamacare-premiums-deductibles#.XB09-FxKhPa.

273. Sloan, Chris et al., "2019 Premium Increases Lowest on Average Since 2015," Avalere, Press Releases, Federal & State Policy, 13 September 2018, avalere.com/press-releases/2019-premium-increases-lowest-on-average-since-2015

274. Bryan, Bob. "Here's How Much Obamacare Premiums Will Increase in Every State." *Business Insider*, Business Insider, 2 Nov. 2018, www.businessinsider.com/obamacare-premium-increases-by-state-trump-effect-2018-11.

275. Kamal, Rabah, et al. "2019 Premium Changes on ACA Exchanges." *The Henry J. Kaiser Family Foundation*, The Henry J. Kaiser Family Foundation, 20 Nov. 2018, www.kff.org/health-costs/issue-brief/tracking-2019-premium-changes-on-aca-exchanges/.

276. "Out-of-Pocket Maximum/Limit - HealthCare.gov Glossary." *HealthCare.gov*, 1 Jan. 2019, www.healthcare.gov/glossary/out-of-pocket-maximum-limit.

277. "2019 ACA Payment Notice Items for Employer Plans." *The Impact of Smart Home Technology | HUB International*, HUB International, 24 May 2018, www.hubinternational.com/products/employee-benefits/compliance-bulletins/2018/05/2019-out-of-pocket-maximum/.

278. Armour, Stephanie, "Trump's Proposed ACA Rules Could Boost Costs for Millions of People Republicans say subsidies for consumers are inflated; Democrats see another effort to sabotage the health law," The Wall Street Journal, 17 January 2019, www.wsj.com/articles/trumps-proposed-aca-rules-could-lift-costs-for-millions-of-people-11547775475

279. Ibid

280. Armour, Stephanie. "Republicans Bet Health-Care Funds Shuffle Will Help Get Spending Bill Passed." *The Wall Street Journal*, Dow Jones & Company, 17 Jan. 2018, www.wsj.com/articles/republicans-bet-health-care-funds-shuffle-will-help-get-spending-bill-passed-1516226255.

281. Blumenthal, David. "How the New U.S. Tax Plan Will Affect Healthcare." *Harvard Business Review*, 19 Dec. 2017, hbr.org/2017/12/how-the-new-u-s-tax-plan-will-affect-health-care.

282. Ibid.

283. Rubin, Richard, and Natalie Andrews. "House Votes to Repeal Tax on Medical Devices." *The Wall Street Journal*, Dow Jones & Company, 24 July 2018, www.wsj.com/articles/house-votes-to-repeal-tax-on-medical-devices-1532467519.

284. Vestal, Christine, "Health Insurance and Death Rates," PEW, Stateline, 12 May 2014, www.pewtrusts.org/en/research-and-analysis/blogs/stateline/2014/05/12/health-insurance-and-death-rates

285. Dalrymple II, Jim. "A GOP Congressman Said 'Nobody Dies' Because They Don't Have Healthcare, And People Are Freaking Out." *BuzzFeed*, BuzzFeed, 7 May 2017, www.buzzfeed.com/jimdalrympleii/republican-congressman-nobody-dies-because-they-dont-have?utm_term=.mp8m9lKld#.buAnaAgAD.

286. "CARE WITHOUT COVERAGE: Too Little Too Late." *Institute of Medicine (National Academy of Medicine)*, 2 May 2002, www.nationalacademies.org/hmd/~/media/Files/Report%20Files/2003/Care-Without-Coverage-Too-Little-Too-Late/Uninsured2FINAL.pdf.

287. Dorn, Stan. "Updating the Institute of Medicines Analysis on the Impact of Uninsurance on Mortality." *Urban Institute*, Jan. 2008, www.urban.org/sites/default/files/publication/31386/411588-Uninsured-and-Dying-Because-of-It.PDF.

288. Kronick, Richard. "Health Insurance Coverage and Mortality Revisited." *Health Services Research*, 2009 Aug; 44(4): 1211–1231, 21 Apr. 2009, www.ncbi.nlm.nih.gov/pmc/articles/PMC2739025/

289. Ibid.

290. VAN DER WEES, PHILIP J., et al. "Improvements in Health Status after Massachusetts Healthcare Reform," The Milbank Quarterly, 2013 Dec; 91(4): 663–689, 10 December 2013, www.ncbi.nlm.nih.gov/pmc/articles/PMC3876186/

291. Sommers, Benjamin D., et al. "Changes in Mortality After Massachusetts Healthcare Reform: A Quasi-Experimental Study." *Annals of Internal Medicine*, American College of Physicians, 6 May 2014, annals.org/aim/article-abstract/1867050/changes-mortality-after-massachusetts-health-care-reform-quasi-experimental-study.

292. "'People Are Dying Here': Federal Hospitals Fail Native Americans." *PressFrom - US*, 9 July 2017, us.pressfrom.com/news/us/-66559-people-are-dying-here-federal-hospitals-fail-native-americans/.

293. Kaplan, Thomas, and Robert Pear. "Senate Health Bill in Peril as C.B.O. Predicts 22 Million More Uninsured." *The New York Times*, The New York Times, 26 June 2017, www.nytimes.com/2017/06/26/us/politics/senate-health-care-bill-republican.html.

294. "H.R. 1628, Better Care Reconciliation Act of 2017." *Congressional Budget Office*, 26 June 2017, www.cbo.gov/publication/52849.

295. Mathes, Tim, et al. "50% Adherence of Patients Suffering Chronic Conditions — Where Is the Evidence?" GMS | GMS Journal for Medical Education | Medical Doctors' Job Specification Analysis: A Qualitative Inquiry, 13 Nov. 2012, www.egms.de/static/en/journals/gms/2012-10/000167.shtml.

296. Sommers, Benjamin D, et al. "Mortality and Access to Care among Adults after State Medicaid Expansions | NEJM." *New England Journal of Medicine*, 13 Sept. 2012, www.nejm.org/doi/10.1056/NEJMsa1202099.

297. Calsyn, Maura, and Lindsay Rosenthal. "Access to Medicaid Reduces Mortality Rates." *Center for American Progress*, 1 Apr. 2013, www.americanprogress.org/issues/healthcare/news/2013/04/01/57839/access-to-medicaid-reduces-mortality-rates/.

298. Casull, Brian H. "This Can Kill You: American Healthcare in Transition." *Amazon*, Amazon, 6 June 2017, www.amazon.com/This-Can-Kill-You-Transition/dp/1547175249.

299. Kochaneck, Kenneth D, et al. "Deaths: Final Data for 2014." *National Vital Statistics Report*, 3 Apr. 2017, www.cdc.gov/nchs/data/nvsr/nvsr65/nvsr65_04.pdf.

300. Armour, Stephanie, and Siobhan Hughes. "New Push to Topple Affordable Care Act Looms." *The Wall Street Journal*, Dow Jones & Company, 25 May 2018, www.wsj.com/articles/new-push-to-topple-affordable-care-act-looms-1527240601.

301. Woolhandler, Steffie, and David U. Himmelstein. "The Relationship of Health Insurance and Mortality: Is Lack of Insurance Deadly?" *Annals of Internal Medicine*, American College of Physicians, 19 Sept. 2017, annals.org/aim/fullarticle/2635326/relationship-health-insurance-mortality-lack-insurance-deadly.

302. Hellmann, Jessie. "McConnell: GOP Could Try to Repeal ObamaCare Again after Midterms." *TheHill*, The Hill, 17 Oct. 2018, thehill.com/homenews/senate/411896-mcconnell-gop-could-try-to-repeal-obamacare-again-after-midterms.

303. Armour, Stephanie, and Reid J. Epstein. "Health Law Is Back as Campaign Issue-This Time for Democrats." *The Wall Street Journal*, Dow Jones & Company, 11 May 2018, www.wsj.com/articles/democrats-campaign-on-health-care-expansion-in-wake-of-gops-failed-aca-repeal-1526040001.

Chapter Ten

304. Davis, Elizabeth. "Why You Pay More If You're Hospitalized for 'Observation'." *Verywell Health*, Verywellhealth, 1 Dec. 2018, www.verywellhealth.com/an-explanation-of-inpatient-v-observation-status-1738455.

305. Medicare Benefit Policy Manual (Chapter 6, Section 20.6A and B) at CMS012673." *CMS.gov Centers for Medicare & Medicaid Services*, 14 May 2018, www.cms.gov/Regulations-and-Guidance/Guidance/Manuals/Internet-Only-Manuals-Ioms-Items/Cms012673.html.

306. "2 Midnight Inpatient Admission Guidance &Patient Status Reviews for Admissions on or after October 1, 2013," CMS FREQUENTLY ASKED QUESTIONS , www.cms.gov/Research-Statistics-Data-and-Systems/Monitoring-Programs/Medical-Review/Downloads/QAsforWebsitePosting_110413-v2-CLEAN.pdf

307. Ibid.

308. Ibid.

309. Ibid.

310. Ibid.

311. Landi, Heather. "122 Short-Term Acute Care Hospitals File Lawsuit Against HHS Over Two-Midnight Rule." *Healthcare Informatics Magazine*, 1 Aug. 2016, www.healthcare-informatics.com/news-item/payment/122-short-term-acute-care-hospitals-file-lawsuit-against-hhs-over-two-midnight.

312. Mathews, Anna Wilde, and Melanie Evans. "Flurry of Health-Care Deals Reflects Shift Away From Hospitals." *The Wall Street Journal*, Dow Jones & Company, 20 Dec. 2017, www.wsj.com/articles/as-medical-care-shifts-out-of-hospitals-companies-plan-deals-1513716507.

313. Bryant, Meg. "Hospital Bankruptcies Soar, with 20 since 2016." *Healthcare Dive*, 1 Nov. 2018, www.healthcaredive.com/news/hospital-bankruptcies-soar-with-20-since-2016/541097/.

314. Conyers, Julie. "Small Hospital Closures Mean Loss of Access to Care." *The Bulletin*, 4 Jan. 2018, bulletin.facs.org/2018/01/small-hospital-closures-mean-loss-of-access-to-care/#.WpW-SiqinFPZ.

315. Mathews, Anna Wilde. "Behind Your Rising Health-Care Bills: Secret Hospital Deals That Squelch Competition." *The Wall Street Journal*, Dow Jones & Company, 18 Sept. 2018, www.wsj.com/articles/behind-your-rising-health-care-bills-secret-hospital-deals-that-squelch-competition-1537281963

316. "Prospective Payment Systems - General Information." *CMS.gov Centers for Medicare & Medicaid Services*, 15 Nov. 2018, www.cms.gov/medicare/medicare-fee-for-service-payment/prospmedicarefeesvcpmtgen/index.html.

317. "Hospital Readmissions Reduction Program (HRRP)." *CMS.gov Centers for Medicare & Medicaid Services*, 28 Nov. 2018, www.cms.gov/Medicare/Medicare-Fee-for-Service-Payment/AcuteInpatientPPS/Readmissions-Reduction-Program.html.

318. Ibid.

319. Jencks, Stephen F, et al. "Rehospitalizations among Patients in the Medicare Fee-for-Service Program | NEJM." *New England Journal of Medicine*, 2 Apr. 2009, www.nejm.org/doi/full/10.1056/NEJMsa0803563.

320. Ibid.

321. Boccuti, Cristina, and Giselle Casillas. "Aiming for Fewer Hospital U-Turns: The Medicare Hospital Readmission Reduction Program." *The Henry J. Kaiser Family Foundation*, The Henry J. Kaiser Family Foundation, 16 Feb. 2018, www.kff.org/medicare/issue-brief/aiming-for-fewer-hospital-u-turns-the-medicare-hospital-readmission-reduction-program/.

322. Zuckerman, Rachel B, et al. "Readmissions, Observation, and the Hospital Readmissions Reduction Program | NEJM." *New England Journal of Medicine*, 21 Apr. 2016, www.nejm.org/doi/full/10.1056/NEJMsa1513024.

323. Wadhera, Rishi K, et al. "Association of the Hospital Readmissions Reduction Program With Heart Failure, AMI, and Pneumonia Mortality." *JAMA*, American Medical Association, 25 Dec. 2018, jamanetwork.com/journals/jama/fullarticle/2719307.

324. Bryant, Meg. "JAMA Findings Suggest 'Unintended Harm' from Hospital Readmissions Reduction Program." *Healthcare Dive*, 21 Dec. 2018, www.healthcaredive.com/news/jama-findings-suggest-unintended-harm-from-hospital-readmissions-reductio/544950/.

325. "HOW DO I HANDLE NON-COVERED SERVICE REQUESTS?" *Healthnet Federal Services-Tricare*, www.tricare-west.com/content/hnfs/home/tw/prov/res/prov_faq/provider/claims/non-covered_services.html.

326. "Increases in Part B Premiums and the Hold Harmless Provision." *Medicare Interactive*, 2018, www.medicareinteractive.org/get-answers/medicare-health-coverage-options/original-medicare-costs/increases-in-part-b-premiums-and-the-hold-harmless-provision.

Chapter Eleven

327. Horvitz-Lennon, Marcella, et al. "From Silos To Bridges: Meeting The General Healthcare Needs Of Adults With Severe Mental Illnesses." *Health Affairs*, 2006, www.healthaffairs.org/doi/10.1377/hlthaff.25.3.659.

328. "Book Review | NEJM." *New England Journal of Medicine*, 30 Aug. 2001, www.nejm.org/doi/full/10.1056/NEJM200108303450917#t=article.

329. Gabel, Jon R. "More Than Half Of Individual Health Plans Offer Coverage That Falls Short Of What Can Be Sold Through Exchanges As Of 2014." *Health Affairs*, June 2012, www.healthaffairs.org/doi/full/10.1377/hlthaff.2011.1082.

330. Satcher, David. "A Report of the Surgeon General–Executive Summary." *The International Journal of Psychosocial Rehabilitation*, Feb. 2000, www.psychosocial.com/policy/satcher.html.

331. Op cit. McNeil, Barbara J., "Hidden Barriers to Improvement in the Quality of Care," The New England Journal of Medicine, 29 Nov. 2001.

332. "Alcohol Safety Information." Alcohol Safety, 2011, rageonthesamepage.uconn.edu/celeron/alcoholsafety.html.

333. "DUI & DWI Legal Limit, Laws, & Enforcement." *DMV.ORG*, 1 Jan. 2019, www.dmv.org/automotive-law/dui.php.

334. The US Burden of Disease Collaborators. "US Burden of Diseases, Injuries, and Disease Risk Factors, 1990-2016." *JAMA*, American Medical Association, 10 Apr. 2018, jamanetwork.com/journals/jama/fullarticle/2678018.

335. "CDC - Fact Sheets - Alcohol." *Centers for Disease Control and Prevention*, Centers for Disease Control and Prevention, 5 May 2017, www.cdc.gov/alcohol/fact-sheets.htm.

336. National Institute on Drug Abuse, "The Science of Drug Use and Addiction: The Basics," NIH, Media Guide, July 2018, www.drugabuse.gov/publications/media-guide/science-drug-use-addiction-basics.

337. Ibid.

338. Ibid.

339. "America's Opioid Epidemic and Its Effect on the Nation's Commercially-Insured Population." *Blue Cross Blue Shield*, 2018, www.bcbs.com/the-health-of-america/reports/americas-opioid-epidemic-and-its-effect-on-the-nations-commercially-insured.

340. Goodwin, James S, et al. "Association of Chronic Opioid Use With US County Presidential Voting Patterns in 2016." *JAMA*, American Medical Association, 22 June 2018, jamanetwork.com/journals/jamanetworkopen/fullarticle/2685627.

341. Florence, C S, et al. "The Economic Burden of Prescription Opioid Overdose, Abuse, and Dependence in the United States, 2013." *Current Neurology and Neuroscience Reports.*, U.S. National Library of Medicine, Oct. 2016, www.ncbi.nlm.nih.gov/pubmed/27623005.

342. National Institute on Drug Abuse. "Opioid Overdose Crisis." *NIDA*, 6 Mar. 2018, www.drugabuse.gov/drugs-abuse/opioids/opioid-overdose-crisis #seven.

343. Ibid.

344. Muhri, Pradip K, et al. "Associations of Nonmedical Pain Reliever Use and Initiation of Heroin Use in the United States." *Center For Behavioral Health Statistics And Quality*, Aug. 2013, www.samhsa.gov/data/sites/default/files/DR006/DR006/nonmedical-pain-reliever-use-2013.htm.

345. Cicero, T J, et al. "The Changing Face of Heroin Use in the United States: a Retrospective Analysis of the Past 50 Years." *Current Neurology and Neuroscience Reports.*, U.S. National Library of Medicine, 1 July 2014, www.ncbi.nlm.nih.gov/pubmed/24871348.

346. Carlson, R G, et al. "Predictors of Transition to Heroin Use among Initially Non-Opioid Dependent Illicit Pharmaceutical Opioid Users: A Natural History Study." *Current Neurology and Neuroscience Reports.*, U.S. National Library of Medicine, 1 Mar. 2016, www.ncbi.nlm.nih.gov/pubmed/26785634.

347. "Morbidity and Mortality Weekly Report (MMWR)." *Centers for Disease Control and Prevention*, Centers for Disease Control and Prevention, 8 Mar. 2018, www.cdc.gov/mmwr/volumes/67/wr/mm6709e1.htm.

348. CDC. "Prescription Painkiller Overdoses ." *Centers for Disease Control and Prevention*, Centers for Disease Control and Prevention, 4 Sept. 2018, www.cdc.gov/vitalsigns/prescriptionpainkilleroverdoses/index.html.

349. Kounang, Nadia. "US Drug Overdose Deaths Reach New Record High." *CNN*, Cable News Network, 8 Aug. 2017, www.cnn.com/2017/08/08/health/drug-overdose-rates-2016-study/index.html.

350. Op Cit. www.drugabuse.gov/publications/media-guide/science-drug-use-addiction-basics

351. Whalen, Jeanne. "Overdose Deaths Drive Down U.S. Life Expectancy-Again." *The Wall Street Journal*, Dow Jones & Company, 21 Dec. 2017, www.wsj.com/articles/overdose-deaths-drive-down-u-s-life-expectancyagain-1513832460.

352. Ibid.

353. Sagon, Candy. "Medical Errors No. 3 Cause of Death in U.S." *AARP*, 4 May 2016, www.aarp.org/health/conditions-treatments/info-2016/medical-errors-leading-cause-of-death-cs.html.

354. National Center for Health Statistics. "Leading Causes of Death." *Centers for Disease Control and Prevention*, Centers for Disease Control and Prevention, 17 Mar. 2017, www.cdc.gov/nchs/fastats/leading-causes-of-death.htm.

355. McLellan, A T, et al. "Drug Dependence, a Chronic Medical Illness: Implications for Treatment, Insurance, and Outcomes Evaluation." *Current Neurology and Neuroscience Reports.*, U.S. National Library of Medicine, 4 Oct. 2000, www.ncbi.nlm.nih.gov/pubmed/11015800.

356. Op Cit. National Institute on Drug Abuse, "The Science of Drug Use and Addiction: The Basics," NIH Media Guide, July 2018

357. U.S. Department of Health and Human Services. "HHS Awards Over $1 Billion to Combat the Opioid Crisis." *HHS.gov*, US Department of Health and Human Services, 2 Oct. 2018, www.hhs.gov/about/news/2018/09/19/hhs-awards-over-1-billion-combat-opioid-crisis.html.

Chapter Twelve

358. "Key Facts about the Uninsured Population." *The Henry J. Kaiser Family Foundation*, The Henry J. Kaiser Family Foundation, 10 Dec. 2018, www.kff.org/uninsured/fact-sheet/key-facts-about-the-uninsured-population/.

359. Ibid.

360. Ibid.

361. Ibid.

362. Collins, Sara R, et al. "The Problem of Underinsurance and How Rising Deductibles Will Make It Worse." *Commonwealth Fund*, 25 May 2015, www.commonwealthfund.org/publications/issue-briefs/2015/may/problem-of-underinsurance.

363. Ibid.

364. "2018 Scorecard on State Health System Performance." *Mirror, Mirror 2017: International Comparison Reflects Flaws and Opportunities for Better U.S. Healthcare*, 2018, interactives.commonwealthfund.org/2018/state-scorecard/conclusion.

Chapter Thirteen

365. Makary, Martin A, and Michael Daniel. "Medical Error-the Third Leading Cause of Death in the US." *The BMJ*, British Medical Journal Publishing Group, 3 May 2016, www.bmj.com/content/353/bmj.i2139.

366. Wolf, Zane Robinson, and Rhonda G Hughes. "Error Reporting and Disclosure." *Current Neurology and Neuroscience Reports.*, U.S. National Library of Medicine, Apr. 2008, www.ncbi.nlm.nih.gov/books/NBK2652/.

367. "Hospital Quality Incentive (HQI) Program State Fiscal Year (SFY) 2017-2018 Q&As." *Pennsylvania Department of Human Services*, Oct. 2018, dhs.pa.gov/cs/groups/webcontent/documents/document/c_266647.pdf.

368. Putnam, Tammy. "Potential Quality Issues Overview — What and Why PQI." *The Ledger*, mazarsledger.com/article/potential-quality-issues-overview-what-and-why-pqi/.

369. "Sentinel Events (SE)." *The Joint Commission*, 1 July 2017, www.jointcommission.org/assets/1/6/CAMH_SE_0717.pdf.

POSTSCRIPT: Endnotes

370. "Serious Reportable Events." *NQF: Perinatal and Reproductive Health Project 2015-2016 - Measures*, 2011, www.qualityforum.org/topics/sres/serious_reportable_events.aspx.

371. Kohn, L T, et al. "To Err Is Human: Building a Safer Health System." *Current Neurology and Neuroscience Reports.*, U.S. National Library of Medicine, 2000, www.ncbi.nlm.nih.gov/pubmed/25077248.

372. "National Healthcare Disparities Report 2004: Data Tables." *Archive: Agency for Healthcare Research Quality*, U.S. HHS: Agency for Healthcare Research and Quality, 2004, archive.ahrq.gov/qual/nhdr04/fullreport/Data_Tables/DD_119a.htm.

373. "ADVERSE EVENTS IN HOSPITALS: NATIONAL INCIDENCE AMONG MEDICARE BENEFICIARIES." *Department of Health and Human Services OFFICE OF INSPECTOR GENERAL* , Nov. 2010, oig.hhs.gov/oei/reports/oei-06-09-00090.pdf.

374. Classen, David C, et al. "'Global Trigger Tool' Shows That Adverse Events In Hospitals May Be Ten Times Greater Than Previously Measured." *Health Affairs*, 1 Apr. 2011, www.healthaffairs.org/doi/full/10.1377/hlthaff.2011.0190.

375. "National Center for Health Statistics." *Centers for Disease Control and Prevention*, Centers for Disease Control and Prevention, 17 Mar. 2017, www.cdc.gov/nchs/fastats/leading-causes-of-death.htm.

376. Kochanek, Kenneth D, et al. "Deaths: Final Data for 2014." *National Vital Statistics Report*, 30 June 2016, www.cdc.gov/nchs/data/nvsr/nvsr65/nvsr65_04.pdf.

377. "Study Suggests Medical Errors Now Third Leading Cause of Death in the U.S. - 05/03/2016." *Is There Really Any Benefit to Multivitamins?*, 3 May 2016, www.hopkinsmedicine.org/news/media/releases/study_suggests_medical_errors_now_third_leading_cause_of_death_in_the_us.

378. Sagon, Candy. "Medical Errors No. 3 Cause of Death in U.S." *AARP*, 4 May 2016

379. American Geriatrics Society 2015 Beers Criteria Update Expert Panel. "American Geriatrics Society 2015 Updated Beers Criteria for Potentially Inappropriate Medication Use in Older Adults." *Clinical Investigations*, 2015, www.sigot.org/allegato_docs/1057_Beers-Criteria.pdf.

380. "Benzodiazepines." *UpToDate*, 2018, www.uptodate.com/contents/search?search=lorazepam.

381. "Chlorpromazine." *UpToDate*, 2018, www.uptodate.com/contents/search?search=Chlorpromazine&submit=Go.

382. "Haloperidol." *UpToDate*, 2018, www.uptodate.com/contents/search?search=haloperidol&sp=0&searchType=PLAIN_TEXT&source=USER_INPUT&searchControl=TOP_PULLDOWN&searchOffset=1&autoComplete=false&language=&max=0&index=&autoCompleteTerm=.

383. Petersen, L A, et al. "Does Housestaff Discontinuity of Care Increase the Risk for Preventable Adverse Events?" *Current Neurology and Neuroscience Reports.*, U.S. National Library of Medicine, 1 Dec. 1994, www.ncbi.nlm.nih.gov/pubmed/7978700.

384. Jena, Anupam B, et al. "Malpractice Risk According to Physician Specialty." *New England Journal of Medicine*, 8 Oct. 2011, www.nejm.org/doi/full/10.1056/NEJMsa1012370.

385. CBS News. "Malpractice 101: Which Doctors Get Sued Most?" *CBS News*, CBS Interactive, 18 Aug. 2011, www.cbsnews.com/pictures/malpractice-101-which-doctors-get-sued-most/3/.

386. "Tort." *Quizlet*, 2018, quizlet.com/144972405/legal-flash-cards/.

387. Murphy, Michael. "Medical Errors: Causes and Solutions." *ScribeAmerica.com*, 26 Aug. 2014, www.scribeamerica.com/blog/medical-errors-causes-solutions/.

Chapter Fourteen

388. "The Placebo Effect: What Is It?" *WebMD*, WebMD, 2018, www.webmd.com/pain-management/what-is-the-placebo-effect#1.

389. "Placebo Effect." *American Cancer Society*, www.cancer.org/treatment/treatments-and-side-effects/clinical-trials/placebo-effect.html.

390. Harvard Health Publishing. "Putting the Placebo Effect to Work." *Harvard Health Blog*, Harvard Health Publishing, Apr. 2012, www.health.harvard.edu/mind-and-mood/putting-the-placebo-effect-to-work.

391. "Grading Guide." *UpToDate*, 2018, www.uptodate.com/home/grading-guide.

392. "Meta-Analysis." *Merriam-Webster*, Merriam-Webster, www.merriam-webster.com/dictionary/meta-analysis.

393. Kerut, E K, et al. "Patent Foramen Ovale: a Review of Associated Conditions and the Impact of Physiological Size." *Current Neurology and Neuroscience Reports.*, U.S. National Library of Medicine, Sept. 2001, www.ncbi.nlm.nih.gov/pubmed/11527606.

394. "Patent Foramen Ovale (PFO)." *About Heart Attacks*, 2011, www.heart.org/en/health-topics/congenital-heart-defects/about-congenital-heart-defects/patent-foramen-ovale-pfo.

395. Wu, L A, et al. "Patent Foramen Ovale in Cryptogenic Stroke: Current Understanding and Management Options." *Current Neurology and Neuroscience Reports.*, U.S. National Library of Medicine, 10 May 2004, www.ncbi.nlm.nih.gov/pubmed/15136302

396. Furie, Karen L, and Haykan Ay. "Initial Evaluation and Management of Transient Ischemic Attack and Minor Ischemic Stroke." *UpToDate*, 31 May 2018, www.uptodate.com/contents/initial-evaluation-and-management-of-transient-ischemic-attack-and-minor-ischemic-stroke.

397. "Transient Ischemic Attack (TIA)." *Mayo Clinic*, Mayo Foundation for Medical Education and Research, 8 Sept. 2018, www.mayoclinic.org/diseases-conditions/transient-ischemic-attack/home/ovc-20314613?utm.

398. Caplan, Louis. "Caplan's Stroke 4th Edition- A Clinical Approach." *10th Edition*, Mosby, 21 May 2009, www.elsevier.com/books/caplans-stroke/9781416047216.

399. "Patent Foramen Ovale - Causes, Symptoms, Diagnosis & Treatment." *Health Jade*, 16 Apr. 2018, healthjade.com/patent-foramen-ovale/.

Chapter Fifteen

400. Mathews, Anna Wilde. "Cost Of Employer-Provided Health Insurance Rises Toward $19,000 a Year." *The Wall Street Journal*, Dow Jones & Company, 19 Sept. 2017, www.wsj.com/articles/cost-of-employer-provided-health-insurance-rises-toward-19-000-a-year-1505838600.

401. Miller, Stephen. "Employers Hold Down Health Plan Cost for 2019," Society For Human Resource Management, Benefits, 20 September 2018, www.shrm.org/resourcesandtools/hr-topics/benefits/pages/employers-hold-down-health-plan-costs-for-2019.aspx.

POSTSCRIPT: Endnotes

402. AHIP. "Where Does Your Healthcare Dollar Go?," 22 May 2018, www.ahip.org/health-care-dollar/.

403. Op cit. Miller, Stephen. "Employers Hold Down Health Plan Cost for 2019," Society For Human Resource Management, Benefits, 20 September 2018.

404. Evans, Melanie, et al. "The Math Behind Higher Health-Care Deductibles." *The Wall Street Journal*, Dow Jones & Company, 31 Aug. 2017, www.wsj.com/graphics/health-care-coverage/.

405. Lankford, Kimberly. "Cost of Employer Health Coverage to Rise 5% in 2019," Kiplinger, Ask Kim, 17 Aug 2018, www.kiplinger.com/article/insurance/T027-C001-S003-cost-of-employer-health-coverage-to-rise-in-2019.html.

406. Glover, Lacie. "Copay vs. Coinsurance: The Differences and Why They Matter," Nerdwallet, 16 September 2016, www.nerdwallet.com/blog/health/copay-vs-coinsurance/.

407. Ibid.

408. U.S. Department of Labor. Summary of Benefits and Coverage, https://www.dol.gov/sites/default/files/ebsa/laws-and-regulations/laws/affordable-care-act/for-employers-and-advisers/sbc-template-final.pdf.

409. Masterson, Les. "HMO vs PPO vs Other Plans: What's the Difference?" *Insurance.com*, 23 Oct. 2018, www.insurance.com/health-insurance/difference-between-ppo-hmo-hdhp-pos-epo.html.

410. "2017 Employer Health Benefits Survey." *The Henry J. Kaiser Family Foundation*, The Henry J. Kaiser Family Foundation, 31 July 2018, www.kff.org/health-costs/report/2017-employer-health-benefits-survey/.

411. SSA. "Exclusions from Coverage and Medicare as Secondary Payer." *Reports, Facts and Figures | Press Office | Social Security Administration*, Social Security Administration, 22 Feb. 2018, www.ssa.gov/OP_Home/ssact/title18/1862.htm.

412. "Summary of Benefits and Coverage and Uniform Glossary." *United States Department of Labor*, 23 Apr. 2018, www.dol.gov/agencies/ebsa/laws-and-regulations/laws/affordable-care-act/for-employers-and-advisers/summary-of-benefits.

413. Kamal, Rabah, et al. "How Much Is Health Spending Expected to Grow?" *Peterson-Kaiser Health System Tracker*, 12 Dec. 2018, www.healthsystemtracker.org/chart-collection/much-health-spending-expected-grow/.

414. Op Cit. Herman, Bob, "America's health care economy keeps ballooning," AXIOS, 21 Feb. 2019

415. "NHE-Fact-Sheet." *CMS.gov Centers for Medicare & Medicaid Services*, 6 Dec. 2018, www.cms.gov/research-statistics-data-and-systems/statistics-trends-and-reports/nationalhealthexpenddata/nhe-fact-sheet.html.

416. Teel, Prinsez. "Five Top Challenges Affecting Healthcare Leaders in the Future." *Becker's Hospital Review*, 13 Feb. 2018, www.beckershospitalreview.com/hospital-management-administration/five-top-challenges-affecting-healthcare-leaders-in-the-future.html.

417. "Summary of Benefits and Coverage." *HealthCare.gov*, 2 Jan. 2019, www.healthcare.gov/health-care-law-protections/summary-of-benefits-and-coverage/.

418. Cohen, Robin K. "MEDICAL NECESSITY DEFINITIONS IN SURROUNDING STATES." *OLR Research Report*, 11 Jan. 2010, www.cga.ct.gov/2010/rpt/2010-R-0010.htm.

419. Neumann, Peter J, and James D Chambers. "Medicare's Enduring Struggle to Define 'Reasonable and Necessary' Care | NEJM." *New England Journal of Medicine*, 8 Nov. 2012, www.nejm.org/doi/full/10.1056/NEJMp1208386.

420. "Appendix G Medical Necessity." *National Academies Press: OpenBook*, 19 Sept. 2011, www.nap.edu/read/13234/chapter/19.

421. "Home." *National Association of Insurance Commissioners* https://www.naic.org/

422. Ibid.

423. "Utilization Review Definitions." *Washington State Department of Labor and Industries*, 2 Jan. 2019, www.lni.wa.gov/ClaimsIns/Providers/AuthRef/UtilReview/definitions.asp.

Chapter Sixteen

424. Rogers, Will. "Famous Quotes & Sayings." *Quotes.*, www.quotes.net/quote/3445.

425. HHS Office Public Affairs. "Appealing Health Plan Decisions." *HHS.gov*, US Department of Health and Human Services, 31 Jan. 2017, www.hhs.gov/healthcare/about-the-law/cancellations-and-appeals/appealing-health-plan-decisions/index.html.

426. Ibid.

427. Ibid.

428. Ibid.

429. Ibid.

430. Ibid.

431. "Independent Review Organization Accreditation." *URAC*, 5 Jan. 2019, www.urac.org/programs/independent-review-organization-accreditation.

432. "Understanding the Vital Role of Independent Medical Review and Utilization Review Services." *The National Association of Independent Review Organizations*, July 2016, www.nairo.org/wp-content/uploads/2017/10/NAIRO-White-Paper-Understanding-the-Vital-Role-of-Independent-Medical-Review-and-Utilization-Review-Services.pdf.

433. *Jointcommission.org*, 2019, www.jointcommission.org/.

434. *NCQA*, 2018, www.ncqa.org/.

435. *URAC*, 2019, www.urac.org/.

436. Armour, Stephanie. "Trump Administration to Step Up Oversight of Hospital Watchdogs." *The Wall Street Journal*, Dow Jones & Company, 4 Oct. 2018, www.wsj.com/articles/trump-administration-to-step-up-oversight-of-hospital-watchdogs-1538683200.

437. Armour, Stephanie. "Psychiatric Hospitals With Safety Violations Still Get Accreditation." *The Wall Street Journal*, Dow Jones & Company, 26 Dec. 2018, www.wsj.com/articles/psychiatric-hospitals-with-safety-violations-still-get-accreditation-11545820201.

438. Ibid.

Chapter Seventeen

439. McClellan, M, et al. "A National Strategy to Put Accountable Care into Practice." *Current Neurology and Neuroscience Reports.*, U.S. National Library of Medicine, May 2010, www.ncbi.nlm.nih.gov/pubmed/20439895.

440. Fisher, E S, et al. "A Framework for Evaluating the Formation, Implementation, and Performance of Accountable Care Organizations." *Current Neurology and Neuroscience Reports.*, U.S. National Library of Medicine, Nov. 2012, www.ncbi.nlm.nih.gov/pubmed/23129666.

441. Patel, Kavita K, et al. "Accountable Care Organizations." *Circulation*, American Heart Association, Inc., 18 Aug. 2015, circ.ahajournals.org/content/132/7/603.full.

442. "Home." *CAPP*, CAPP, 30 Nov. 2018, accountablecaredoctors.org/.

443. "What Is the Patient-Centered Medical Home?" *Who We Are | Mission and Goals | Core Values | ACP*, 2019, www.acponline.org/practice-resources/business-resources/payment/models/patient-centered-medical-home/understanding-the-patient-centered-medical-home/what-is-the-patient-centered-medical-home.

444. "In The News-Shared Savings Program Final Rule." *CMS.gov Centers for Medicare & Medicaid Services*, 27 Dec. 2018, www.cms.gov/Medicare/Medicare-Fee-for-Service-Payment/sharedsavingsprogram/News-and-Updates.html.

445. Torrey, Trisha. "Capitation Refers to a Form of a Healthcare Payment System." *Verywell Health*, Verywellhealth, 26 Aug. 2018, www.verywellhealth.com/capitation-the-definition-of-capitation-2615119.

446. "Fact Sheet Medicare Accountable Care Organizations 2015 Performance Year Quality and Financial Results." *CMS.gov Centers for Medicare & Medicaid Services*, 25 Aug. 2016, www.cms.gov/newsroom/fact-sheets/medicare-accountable-care-organizations-2015-performance-year-quality-and-financial-results.

447. "Accountable Care Organizations under the Medicare Shared Savings Program." *AQ-IQ ELearning*, 24 Dec. 2018, www.aq-iq.com/accountable-care-organizations-under-the-medicare-shared-savings-program/.

448. McWilliams, J M, et al. "Changes in Postacute Care in the Medicare Shared Savings Program." *Current Neurology and Neuroscience Reports.*, U.S. National Library of Medicine, 1 Apr. 2017, www.ncbi.nlm.nih.gov/pubmed/28192556.

449. Feore, John, and Gabriel Sullivan. "Medicare Accountable Care Organizations Generate Savings." *Avalere Health*, 5 Dec. 2018, avalere.com/expertise/providers/insights/medicare-accountable-care-organizations-generate-savings-as-experience-grow.

450. Holder, Elizabeth. "Press Release May 2 2018." *National Association of ACOs*, 2 May 2018, www.naacos.com/press-release-may-2-2018.

Chapter Eighteen

451. Pifer, Rebecca. "CMMI Director Says Agency Won't Force All Providers to Assume Risk." *Healthcare Dive*, 31 Aug. 2018, www.healthcaredive.com/news/cmmi-director-says-agency-wont-force-all-providers-to-assume-risk/531333/.

452. Organization for Economic Co-operation and Development, "OECD Health Statistics 2018," OECD, Topics, Health, 8 Nov. 2018, http://www.oecd.org/health/health-data.htm

453. The National Academies of Medicine, "Shorter Lives, Poorer Health," Fig 1-9: Ranking of US mortality rates by age group among 17 peer countries, 2006-2008, 2013

454. Mercer, "Behind in Pay, Behind in Benefits," Mercer, Our Thinking, Healthcare, 17 Oct. 2014, www.mercer.us/our-thinking/healthcare/behind-in-pay-behind-in-benefits.html

455. Artiga, Samantha et al., " Key Facts on Health and Health Care by Race and Ethnicity," Henry J. Kaiser Family Foundation, Disparities Policy, 07 Jun. 2016, www.kff.org/report-section/key-facts-on-health-and-health-care-by-race-and-ethnicity-section-4-health-coverage/

456. Henry J. Kaiser Family Foundation, " Uninsured Rates for the Nonelderly by Race/Ethnicity," KFF, State Health Facts, 2016, www.kff.org/uninsured/state-indicator/rate-by-raceethnicity/?currentTimeframe=1&selectedDistributions=white--black&sortModel=%7B%22colId%22:%22 Location%22,%22sort%22:%22asc%22%7D

457. Norris, Keith et al., " Racial Differences in Mortality and End-Stage Renal Disease," Am J Kidney Dis. 2008 Aug; 52(2): 205–208., 1 Aug. 2009, www.ncbi.nlm.nih.gov/pmc/articles/PMC2601720/

458. Zarembo, Alan, " Black patients fare better than whites when both get same healthcare, study finds," Los Angeles Times, Science Now, 23 Sep. 2015, http://www.latimes.com/science/sciencenow/la-sci-sn-health-racial-disparities-va-20150922-story.html and Kovesdy, C. P. et al., "Association of Race with Mortality and Cardiovascular Events in a Large Cohort of US Veterans," Circulation. 2015 Oct 20;132(16):1538-48, 18 Sep. 2015, www.ncbi.nlm.nih.gov/pubmed/26384521

459. Thielke, Stephen M. et al., "Sex, Race, and Age Differences in Observed Years of Life, Healthy Life, and Able Life among Older Adults in The Cardiovascular Health Study," J Pers Med 2015;5(4):440-451, 25 Nov. 2015, www.ncbi.nlm.nih.gov/pmc/articles/PMC4695864/

460. Hellander, Ida, "How Much Would Single Payer Cost? A Summary of Studies," PNHP, www.pnhp.org/facts/single-payer-system-cost

461. Pollin, R., et al., "Economic Analysis of Medicare for All," Political Economic Research Institute, University of Massachusetts — Amherst, 30 Nov. 2018, www.peri.umass.edu/publication/item/1127-economic-analysis-of-medicare-for-all

462. Dusseault, Dylan, "New Report: It's Actually Easy to Pay for Medicare for All," Business Initiatives for Health Policy, 6 Feb. 2019, businessinitiative.org

463. Wasik, John F., "Are Doctors Really Ditching Medicare?" The Fiscal Times, Opinion, 4 Sep. 2013, www.thefiscaltimes.com/Columns/2013/09/04/Are-Doctors-Really-Ditching-Medicare

464. WestHealth Institute, "AMERICANS' VIEWS OF HEALTHCARE COSTS, COVERAGE, AND POLICY," NORC at the University of Chicago, 2018, www.norc.org/PDFs/WHI%20Healthcare%20Costs%20Coverage%20and%20Policy/WHI%20Healthcare%20Costs%20Coverage%20and%20Policy%20Issue%20Brief.pdf

465. Day, Himmelstein, Broder, Woolhandler — Int. J Health Serv 2014 Updated data from firms' SEC filings (Q12016)

466. 2016 Medicare Trust Fund Report, 13 Jul 2017, www.cms.gov/Research-Statistics-Data-and-Systems/Statistics-Trends-and-Reports/ReportsTrustFunds/Downloads/TR2017.pdf

467. AAFP Board of Directors Report F to the 2017 Congress of Delegates, www.ohioafp.org/wp-content/uploads/2017/11/AAFP_Board_Report_on_Single_Payer_July2017.pdf

POSTSCRIPT: Endnotes

468. Sarasohn-Kahn, Jane, "U.S. Healthcare Spending & Outcomes in Five Charts: #EpicFail in the 2017 OECD Statistics," Tincture. 13 Nov 2017, tincture.io/u-s-healthcare-spending-outcomes-in-five-charts-epicfail-in-the-2017-oecd-statistics-9d997e66249b

469. Sawyer, Bradley and Cynthia Cox, "How does health spending in the U.S. compare to other countries?" Peterson-Kaiser Health Tracking System, 7 Dec. 2018, www.healthsystemtracker.org/chart-collection/health-spending-u-s-compare-countries/#item-start

470. Op Cit. Herman, Bob, "The US spent $3.65 trillion on health care in 2018, and higher spending won't slow down," AXIOS, 21 Feb. 2019.

471. Op Cit. Sawyer, Bradley and Cynthia Cox, "How does health spending in the U.S. compare to other countries?" Peterson-Kaiser Health Tracking System, 7 Dec. 2018

472. "Health Spending," OECD Data 2017, data.oecd.org/healthres/health-spending.htm

473. Op Cit. Sawyer, Bradley and Cynthia Cox, "How does health spending in the U.S. compare to other countries?" Peterson-Kaiser Health Tracking System, 7 Dec. 2018

474. Galewitz, Phil, "Medicaid rolls fall in Missouri, Tennessee, worrying advocates for poor," Kaiser Health News, 7 Feb. 2019, www.nbcnews.com/health/health-care/medicaid-rolls-fall-missouri-tennessee-worrying-advocates-poor-n968946

475. Powers, J. "Healthcare Changes and the Affordable Care Act — A Physician Call to Action". Chapter 5. 2014.

476. Brendon, Robert J., and John M. Benson, "The Public and the Conflict over Future Medicare Spending," NEJM 369;11 nejm.org, 12 Sept. 2013, www.nejm.org/doi/pdf/10.1056/NEJMsr1307622.

477. Manchester, Julia, "Half of registered Republicans now support providing Medicare to every American," PNHP, 22 Oct. 2018, http://pnhp.org/news/half-of-registered-republicans-now-support-providing-medicare-to-every-american/

478. Finnegan, Joanne, "In major reversal, survey finds 56% of physicians now support single-payer healthcare system," FierceHealthcare, Practices, 14 Aug. 2017, www.fiercehealthcare.com/practices/major-reversal-survey-finds-56-physicians-support-single-payer-system and Merritt Hawkins, Physician Staffing Blog, www.merritthawkins.com/news-and-insights/blog/

479. Walker, Joseph, and Christopher Weaver. "The $9 Billion Upcharge: How Insurers Kept Extra Cash From Medicare." *The Wall Street Journal*, Dow Jones & Company, 4 Jan. 2019, www.wsj.com/articles/the-9-billion-upcharge-how-insurers-kept-extra-cash-from-medicare-11546617082.

480. Masterson, Les. "Court Rejects 340B Payment Cuts in Big Win for Hospitals." *Healthcare Dive*, 31 Dec. 2018, www.healthcaredive.com/news/court-rejects-340b-payment-cuts-in-big-win-for-hospitals/545028/.

Postscript

481. Armour, Stephanie and Kristina Peterson, "House Democrats Reveal Plan for Medicare for All," Wall Street Journal Politics/Health Policy, 26 Feb. 2019, www.wsj.com/articles/house-democrats-reveal-plan-for-medicare-for-all-11551219200

482. Ibid.

483. Op cit. Pollin, R., et al., "Economic Analysis of Medicare for All," Political Economic Research Institute, University of Massachusetts — Amherst, 30 Nov. 2018

484. Ibid

485. Chung, Mimi, "HEALTH CARE REFORM: LEARNING FROM OTHER MAJOR HEALTH CARE SYSTEMS," 2 Dec. 2017, Princeton Public health Review, /pphr.princeton.edu/2017/12/02/unhealthy-health-care-a-cursory-overview-of-major-health-care-systems/

486. Bump, Jesse B., "The long road to universal health coverage. A century of lessons for development strategy," PATH, 19 Oct 2010, http://brasil.campusvirtualsp.org/sites/default/files/DIM-The-Long-Road-to-UHC.pdf

487. Op cit. Chung, Mimi, "HEALTH CARE REFORM: LEARNING FROM OTHER MAJOR HEALTH CARE SYSTEMS," 2 Dec. 2017, Princeton Public health Review

488. Health.mil The official website of the Military Health System, Defense Health Agency, www.health.mil/About-MHS/OASDHA/Defense-Health-Agency

489. Ibid

490. Military Health System Communications Office , "Health leaders: Whole of military health is greater than sum of parts," Health.mil The official website of the Military Health System, Defense Health Agency, 29 Nov. 2018, www.health.mil/News/Articles/2018/11/29/Health-leaders-Whole-of-military-health-is-greater-than-sum-of-parts

491. Kendall, Brent, and Stephanie Armour. "Democratic-Led States Appeal Ruling Invalidating Affordable Care Act." *The Wall Street Journal*, Dow Jones & Company, 3 Jan. 2019, www.wsj.com/articles/democratic-led-states-appeal-ruling-invalidating-affordable-care-act-11546550585.

Made in the USA
Columbia, SC
30 March 2026